Founded
on
Freedom

Why You Should Be Proud
of the Birth of America

Daniel S. Stackhouse, Jr., Ph.D.

To all Americans.

CONTENTS

INTRODUCTION – OUR CRISIS

"These are the times that try men's souls: The summer soldier and the sunshine patriot will, in this crisis, shrink from the service of his country; but he that stands it NOW, deserves the love and thanks of man and woman. Tyranny, like hell, is not easily conquered; yet we have this consolation with us, that the harder the conflict, the more glorious the triumph. What we obtain too cheap, we esteem too lightly. – 'Tis dearness only that gives everything its value."[1]
–Thomas Paine

The American Revolution was far more than the casting off of one government and replacing it with another. Uniquely in world history, it marked the birth of a nation founded upon a set of principles. Although these principles would have been familiar to many in Europe prior to the founding of the United States, the creation of the American republic marked the first time that a country would "translate an ideology of individual liberty into a governing creed."[2] These principles are perhaps best summed up by the stirring words from the preamble to the *Declaration of Independence* of July 4, 1776:

---

[1] Thomas Paine, "The American Crisis, Number I," December 19, 1776, in *Thomas Paine – Collected Writings*, ed. Eric Foner (New York: Literary Classics of the United States, Inc., 1995), 91-99.
[2] Charles Murray, *American Exceptionalism – An Experiment in History* (Washington, D.C.: American Enterprise Institute, 2013), 2-6.

1

We hold these truths to be self-evident, that all men are created equal, that they are endowed by their Creator with certain unalienable rights, that among these are life, liberty and the pursuit of happiness. That, to secure these rights, governments are instituted among men, deriving their just powers from the consent of the governed. That whenever any form of government becomes destructive of these ends, it is the right of the people to alter or to abolish it, and to institute new government, laying its foundation on such principles, and organizing its powers in such form, as to them shall seem most likely to effect their safety and happiness.[3]

The means of applying these principles was through the United States *Constitution*, written in 1787 and ratified the following year. Its preamble explains why it was written:

We the people of the United States, in order to form a more perfect union, establish justice, ensure domestic tranquility, provide for the common defense, promote the general welfare, and secure the blessings of liberty to ourselves and our posterity, do ordain and establish this Constitution for the United States of America.[4]

One can think of these two preambles as combining to form America's "mission statement." The first part declares what we as Americans believe, while the second explains how we intend to live out those beliefs.

An organization's mission statement describes what type of an association it is as well as what it seeks to accomplish. A mission statement is not necessarily a reflection of what is: often it is aspirational, seeking to address a need or attain a goal. In America's mission statement, the Founding Fathers declared that all men are created equal in possessing "certain unalienable rights" including

[3] *Declaration of Independence* in *American Heritage – A Reader*, eds. The Hillsdale College History Faculty (Hillsdale, Michigan: Hillsdale College Press, 2011), 128-131.
[4] *Constitution* in *American Heritage – A Reader*, 146-156.

"life, liberty, and the pursuit of happiness." According to Abraham Lincoln, "This they said, and this meant." However, Lincoln explained that the founders did not claim that everyone, everywhere was currently living in a state of equality in 1776:

> They did not mean to assert the obvious untruth, that all were then actually enjoying that equality, nor yet, that they were about to confer it immediately upon them. In fact they had no power to confer such a boon. They meant simply to declare the *right*, so that the *enforcement* of it might follow as fast as circumstances should permit.

What the founders had done, said Lincoln, was "set up a standard maxim for free society," that would never be perfectly met but which would be constantly strived for to expand "the happiness and value of life to all people of all colors everywhere." Likewise, the *Constitution* was designed to create "'a more perfect union,'" not to attain perfection, an earthly impossibility.[5]

Indeed, in 1776 the world was a place where most people, both at that time and throughout human history, had not enjoyed their God-given natural rights to life, liberty, and the pursuit of happiness. Mesopotamians, Egyptians, Persians, Greeks, Romans, Huns, Arabs, Vikings, Mongols, Turks, as well as the great European empires of Spain, France, and Britain had all conquered other peoples, often with unspeakable brutality. On the other hand, this was also true of the peoples conquered in Asia, Africa, and the Americas as many of them had once been conquerors themselves. From the time that human beings had first formed into clans, tribes, nations, and empires, they viewed those outside the group as barbarians, suitable for conquering, subjugation, servitude, and even death. All of world history is replete with examples that attest to English political philosopher Thomas Hobbes's observation that life in its natural

---

[5] Abraham Lincoln, "Speech on the Dred Scott Decision at Springfield, Illinois," June 26, 1857, in *Abraham Lincoln: Speeches and Writings, 1832-1858*, ed. Don E. Fehrenbacher (New York: Literary Classics of the United States, Inc., 1989), 390-403; Harry V. Jaffa, *A New Birth of Freedom: Abraham Lincoln and the Coming of the Civil War* (Lanham, Maryland: Rowman and Littlefield Publishers, Inc., 2004.), 73-152, 103-104.

state was a state of war, which "render[ed] men apt to invade, and destroy one another" and resulted in an existence for human beings which was "solitary, poore, nasty, brutish, and short."[6]

Nevertheless, in recent years it has become fashionable to single out the United States of America as a hypocritical fraud. Critics argue that America, rather than being founded upon any kind of noble-sounding ideals, was built upon genocide against Indians and the theft of their land, the enslavement of Africans, and racism. Some even go so far as to assert that "Our founding ideals of liberty and equality were false when they were written," and therefore America's "mission statement" is a lie, and the country upon which it is based deserves contempt at best and dismantling at worst. Previously these ideas were promoted via Howard Zinn's *A People's History of the United States*. More recently, such criticisms are at the core of a philosophy known as "critical race theory," which argues that racism and oppression are our true founding principles and continue to infect our society and institutions to this day. Furthermore, the theory holds that in order to eradicate these evils "society must be fundamentally transformed though moral, economic, and political revolution." Critical race theory has filtered into national, state, and local governments, corporations, the media, the entertainment industry, and most disturbingly, our schools through means such as the *New York Times'* "The 1619 Project."[7]

Thus, our country faces a crisis, just as surely as it did during the American Revolution when pamphleteer Thomas Paine authored the words which opened this introduction. It is not a military crisis, but a philosophical, moral, and spiritual one. There is an assault on our fundamental founding principles which seeks to undermine pride in our history and confidence as a nation. If we abandon the unifying ideals of the American founding which view human beings as individuals with "certain unalienable rights," we are in danger of reverting back to a kind of "state of nature" where competing tribes

---

[6] Thomas Hobbes, *Leviathan*, ed. Richard Tuck (Cambridge, UK: Cambridge University Press, 1996), 86-90.
[7] Nikole Hannah-Jones, introduction to "The 1619 Project," *New York Times Magazine*, 18 August 2019, 14-26; Christopher Rufo, "Critical Race Theory Briefing Book," Critical Race Theory Briefing Book (christopherrufo.com), 12 June 2021.

based upon race, ethnicity, or other group identity endlessly war against one another.

This threat to our nation has arisen despite the fact that the deeply held belief in its founding principles led the new United States of America, from its very beginning, to break off from the path which most of the rest of the world had trodden throughout the ages and has continued to inspire and guide Americans ever since. Whenever threats to liberty and justice have appeared requiring the American republic to make a course correction, our founding principles have returned us to our true north.

In this book I will argue that America's founding principles are not lies, but undeniable eternal truths. I will show that the founding generation believed in and acted upon the principles that all are created by God with equal natural rights to life, liberty, and the pursuit of happiness as well as the corresponding right to form governments that secure those rights. Furthermore, I will demonstrate that it is the critics of America and its founding who are attempting to insert a lie into the American story: the Marxist notion that "The history of all hitherto existing society is the history of class struggles."[8] In its modern version, rich against poor have been replaced by competing groups based upon race, ethnicity, gender, gender identity, sexual orientation, and a myriad of other categories (e.g., white against black, male against female, etc.).

However, neither history nor human beings can be reduced to such simplistic terms. The human past has been driven by many forces beyond the mere drive to acquire material items and the power over others which accrues to those who possess and distribute them. Ideas such as faith, love, honor, duty, and yes, freedom, have also guided history. Likewise, individual human beings cannot be reduced to simply existing as members of competing groups of oppressors and oppressed. We are far more complicated than that.

In addition to this introduction, the book will be divided into three chapters and a conclusion. Chapter one will demonstrate that the first inhabitants of the land that would one day become the United States of America — called variously Indians, Native Americans, or Indigenous Peoples — were not simply docile caretakers of an idyllic paradise which was later despoiled by foreign

---

[8] Karl Marx and Friedrich Engels, *The Communist Manifesto*, ed. Joseph Katz (New York: Simon & Schuster, Inc., 1964), 57.

invaders. They were just as human as anyone else and therefore subject to the same wants, needs, and flaws. Chapter two will examine the history of slavery and place America's role in that abominable institution in its proper historical and global context. Chapter three will demonstrate that America's founding principles were understood by virtually everyone of the founding era to mean precisely what they said, despite the fact that they had not been perfectly fulfilled, and that throughout American history these principles have provided the roadmap to a more perfect union. Finally, the book will conclude that the United States of America is an exceptional nation, not only because it was founded on principles of natural rights and individual liberty, but because those principles have driven our history and continue to guide us to this day.

Americans can and should be proud of the birth of their country. America was not founded on theft and genocide. America was not founded on slavery and racism. The United States of America was founded on freedom.

1 A STATE OF NATURE

"Thus in the beginning all the World was *America.*"[1]
—John Locke

Although some today may scoff at the notion that in 1492 Columbus "discovered" America or the "New World" — the North and South American continents — the achievements of the Italian explorer, as well as numerous other Spanish, Portuguese, French, Dutch, and English adventurers thereafter, truly did result in the discovery of something new to most of the rest of the world. While the peoples of Asia, Africa, and Europe in the "Old World" had interacted with each other for thousands of years, the Americas were among the most geographically isolated and relatively sparsely populated places on the planet. Consequently, the New World never had the opportunity to participate in the global accumulation and transfer of knowledge which had marked the development of civilizations in Mesopotamia, Egypt, China, India, Greece, Rome, the Islamic Middle East, and Christian Europe.

Consider a printed book. Western writing probably began with the Phoenicians in the Middle East. Paper was invented in China. The printing press was designed in medieval Europe. When all three were brought together and combined with the Roman alphabet and Arabic numerals (by way of India) they enabled the sharing of ideas from Athens, Jerusalem, and Baghdad, which could then be spread

---

[1] John Locke, *The Second Treatise of Government*, in *Locke: Two Treatises of Government*, ed. Peter Laslett (Cambridge: Cambridge University Press, 1988), 285-302.

throughout the rest of the known world. The New World was completely deprived of this human intellectual and cultural inheritance because of its location. Particularly when one considers the spread of technological information, such isolation inevitably made the peoples of the Americas more vulnerable to conquest.

Geographical isolation also left Indians vulnerable to disease. Lack of resistance to illnesses such as smallpox devastated many New World peoples (perhaps killing 80-90%), similar to what the Bubonic plague, originating in Asia, had done to much of Europe in the 1300s. It was the microorganism, not any kind of intentional or organized genocidal scheme, which had the greatest impact on Indian populations after contact with Europeans.

Furthermore, it could be argued that much of the Americas were in a state of nature at the time of European contact. English political philosophers Thomas Hobbes and John Locke theorized that prior to the creation of governments human beings all around the globe had found themselves in such a state. For Hobbes the state of nature was a time of war when "men live without a common power to keep them all in awe."[2] Meanwhile Locke argued that the absence "of a common judge with authority, puts all men in a state of nature."[3] In "balance of power" international relations theory, the entire world is considered to be in a state of nature since there is no global government. Instead, there is "an unregulated competition of states," which "seek their own preservation," but without a "superior agent," and thus anarchy prevails.[4] As will be shown, the Americas, and particularly North America, bore many of these characteristics when Europeans first arrived.

Part of the explanation for why there was no widely-accepted sovereign or state governing a vast part of North America may be due to the fact that the lifestyles of the various cultural groups were generally not conducive to developing landed property rights. Hence, there was no need for their protection. Survival by nomadic hunting and gathering ensured that one's presence in an area was temporary. Widespread and massive agricultural production, which permitted the

---

[2] Thomas Hobbes, *Leviathan*, ed. Richard Tuck (Cambridge, UK: Cambridge University Press, 1996), 86-90.
[3] Locke, 278-282.
[4] Kenneth N. Waltz, *Theory of International Politics* (New York: McGraw-Hill, Inc., 1979), 116-122.

growth of large, settled communities in the Old World, was uncommon in North America. Even where settlement and some planting did take place, it usually only lasted for a relatively short period of time. Thereafter depletion of the soil and elimination of game animals compelled Indians to relocate to greener pastures.

Thus, North and South America did not have access to many of the ideas, inventions, and technologies from which the Old World had benefitted, the population was relatively isolated, sparse, and therefore extremely vulnerable to new diseases, and many areas were without a single, unified, sovereign power capable of maintaining order and securing rights to property. Consequently, there was a perpetual struggle for survival in many parts of the Americas, just as there had been in all parts of the world at one time or another prior to the creation of stable political societies.

The Americas Before 1607

The Americas were among the last parts of the earth to be populated, only becoming home to *homo sapiens* during the last Ice Age, approximately 10,000-14,000 years ago. As temperatures dropped, so did ocean levels while ice accumulated into huge glaciers covering much of North America. This created a land bridge – Beringia – permitting members of the Amerindian language family to cross over from Siberia in northeast Asia into the Western Hemisphere and over time populate North and South America.[5]

Evidence of the warlike nature of these first arrivals to North America, dating from long before Europeans appeared on the scene, can be found at the sites of massacres which dot the landscape. For example, in present-day central South Dakota, on what is now the Crow Creek Sioux Reservation, lie the remains of approximately 500 men, women, and children slaughtered round 1325 A.D. The victims, probably ancestors of the Arikara tribe, had their bodies mutilated, hands and feet removed, heads scalped, and remains left in the open for animals to scavenge after their village was burned. Also in South Dakota and to the north of Crow Creek is a similar site located at Whistling Elk Village dating from approximately 1300-1500 A.D.[6]

---

[5] Colin F. Taylor, *The American Indian*, (London: Salamander Books Ltd., 2004), 8-13.
[6] George Franklin Feldman, *Cannibalism, Headhunting and Human Sacrifice in North America: A History Forgotten* (Chambersburg, Pennsylvania: Alan C. Hood & Co.,

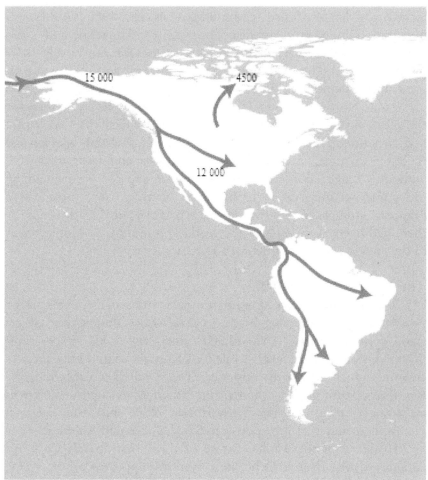

Prehistoric Amerindian settlement. Detail of image by NordNordWest. Wikimedia Commons. Public domain.

Several massacre sites have also been uncovered in California. About 20% of the remains on the Channel Islands dating from approximately 1400 B.C.-300 A.D. have skulls which were either fractured or crushed. Meanwhile, approximately 10% of the dead at the Callegas Creek site near the Santa Barbara Channel (after 500 A.D.) perished from arrows.[7]

The Four Corners region of the American Southwest where Utah, Colorado, Arizona, and New Mexico meet also testify to the

Inc., 2008), xiii-xxi.
[7] Ibid.

brutal nature of Indian inter-tribal conflict. Dozens of sites excavated in the northern San Juan River region dating from 500 B.C. to the late 1200s A.D. feature evidence of horrific deaths resulting from combat. Likewise, the prehistoric ruins of the Basket-maker culture dating from 1500 B.C.-750 A.D. show signs of an incredible number of victims, relative to the size of the population in general, who were slaughtered and scalped at the hands of perhaps 100-150 warriors.[8]

Weather and its effects were probably among the root causes of conflict. As droughts parched the land and damaged agriculture, the already fierce competition for resources only intensified. It was not unusual for groups searching for food to migrate onto lands occupied by others, and then for war to erupt. However, the degree of cruelty which apparently occurred quite frequently and led to so many atrocities probably had a cultural component. Numerous tribes developed a love of fighting for its own sake and instructed their young boys to train as warriors to win the approval of elders by way of combat. Adding to the violence were brutal practices including head-hunting, cannibalism, and human sacrifice which were simply a part of life for many tribes in North America.[9]

Initially the new arrivals from Siberia encountered large herds of Ice Age mammoths and other big game mammals upon which they depended for food and survival. The Indian population surged as a result. Nevertheless, regardless of any reverence for nature or affinity for animals they may have had, this did not prevent tribes from eventually driving mammoths to extinction.[10]

Thereafter the North American bison became a primary source of sustenance for the Indians of the Great Plains. Targeted by hunters for thousands of years, bison nevertheless survived by feeding on grasslands after the glacial ice retreated. The Indian practice of driving stampedes over cliffs is evident from at least as early as 8,500 years ago at the Olson-Chubbock site in Colorado, where the remains of 152 carcasses have been found lying at the canyon bottom. This type of mass slaughter was probably an annual event, but it was not until 500 A.D. when the bow and arrow appeared that bison hunts could truly begin in earnest.[11]

---

[8] Ibid.
[9] Ibid.
[10] Taylor.
[11] Ibid.

Herds which had been thinned out for a thousand years became even more threatened with the arrival of Europeans – but not necessarily for the reasons one might presume. Although horses had died out in North America long before, the Spanish re-introduced them in 1547. As Indians acquired these animals it added another dimension to their hunts. The depletion of bison populations accelerated further as trade with the English and French brought rifles. It was the combination of the horse and the firearm, acquired from Europeans, which created the nomadic buffalo-hunting culture of the Great Plains Indian.[12]

Indian hunting methods could contribute to overkill. Beyond driving herds off cliffs, tribesmen also dressed in buffalo skins to obtain closer shots, as well as set fire to grasslands around a herd while permitting a small opening for escape, resulting in slaughter by the dozens. Some tribes destroyed entire herds after lighting prairie fires. One division of the Sioux nation was even known as the "Sicangu," meaning "burnt thigh," in reference to the leg burns members received after starting wild blazes. Furthermore, Indians did not always use all parts of the bison, as travelers chronicled scenes of decaying carcasses with only the tail or hump removed.[13]

Indian beliefs could also lead to overhunting. Many tribes held to the idea that if one bison escaped it could warn others, and therefore the entire herd needed to be wiped out. Another assumption was that the gods provided the bison, so there was no need for concern that they might eventually become extinct. Furthermore, the Indians did not engage in herding or breeding and had no means of storing excess provisions for future use, resulting in waste.[14]

Bison nearly became extinct for numerous reasons. Opportunities for trading with Europeans was one. Long before the days of Buffalo Bill's "Wild West," various tribes of the Great Plains were only too eager to slaughter bison in order to trade for European goods, just as previously tribes in the Eastern Woodlands had

---

[12] Ibid.

[13] John J. Miller, "Buffaloed," *National Review* 9 October 2000, 28; Larry Schweikart, *48 Liberal Lies About American History (That You Probably Leaned in School)* (New York: Sentinel, 2008), 166-172.

[14] Miller.

decimated beaver and deer populations for similar reasons.[15] The Plains Indians also relied on the bison for a seemingly infinite variety of their own needs. By the 1840s they were killing approximately 600,000 per year, long before the American West was settled.[16] Other causes of the eventual near extinction of the bison were competition with horses, cattle, and sheep for food and water, the introduction of bovine diseases (anthrax, tuberculosis, and brucellosis), drought, and human settlement blocking the bison's access to water.[17]

The success of the bison hunts led to the growth of the nomadic population. However, tribes which primarily made their living via horseback still desired agricultural goods. Increased demand for these resources led to greater competition and conflict with settled populations. Over time, strong tribes such as the Sioux, Apache, and Comanche conquered, killed, or displaced weak tribes including the Hopi and the Pueblo. Therefore, when Indians later raided European settlements, they were simply continuing a practice which they had engaged in for years.[18]

Indians may have lived in a natural environment, but they were no different than other human beings in needing and using its resources to survive. This included killing animals, cutting down trees, and clearing land. They also utilized fire for a variety of purposes such as cooking seeds, driving game in one direction or another for hunting, preparing land for planting, communicating, and as a weapon for fighting enemies. Indians often managed resources like seeds, nuts, rabbits, deer, buffalo, water, and land, but could also damage resources when too many people lived in a particular area, resulting in deforestation, soil depletion, and endangerment of wildlife. Belief in reincarnation may have played some role in overhunting if it was applied to animals. Many Indians did not think in terms of waste because they assumed that as long as animals were respected, they would exist in abundance. For example, the Yupit

---

[15] Thomas Sowell, *Conquests and Cultures – An International History* (New York: Basic Books, 1998), 249-328.

[16] Miller.

[17] Dan Flores, *The Natural West – Environmental History in the Great Plains and Rocky Mountains* (Norman: University of Oklahoma Press, 2001), 65-70; Andrew C. Isenberg, *The Destruction of the Bison* (New York: Cambridge University Press, 2000), 1-12;193-198.

[18] Taylor; Dinesh D'Souza, *America: Imagine a World Without Her* (Washington, D.C.: Regnery Publishing, 2014), 89-106.

Indians of southwestern Alaska believed that the greater the amount of meat they ate and shared, the more plentiful it would be. Their primary concern was respect, not overhunting.[19]

Land ownership in the Western sense was largely unknown to the American Indians. Limited, small-scale farming as well as hunting and gathering were not conducive to the growth of large populations and discouraged long-term settlement for more than 50-100 years in any one place. The usual pattern was for land to be worked and hunted on until it became depleted of minerals and game, and then for a given population to move on to new lands with fresh soil and better hunting. Frequent movement of tribes in search of new territory led to recurring conflicts resulting in displacement and war, often with massacres and enslavement as a consequence.[20]

The English view of property would be vastly different from that of the Indians. They held to a cultural concept expressed by Locke that once you combined your labor with the land to improve it in some way – for example by planting or building something – it became yours. According to Locke's *Second Treatise of Government*, at the beginning of the world all of nature existed in common, was the property of no one, and was available to all. However, as Locke explained, "…every man has a property in his own person." In other words, a human being owns his body. From this premise several conclusions followed:

> The labor of his body, and the work of his hands, we may say, are properly his. Whatsoever then he removes out of the state that nature hath provided, … he hath mixed his labor with, and joined to it something that is his own, and thereby makes it his property. It being by him removed from the common state nature placed it in…

For Locke, America at the time of English settlement in the early 1600s was somewhat like how the world at large had been in the

---

[19] Shepard Krech III, *The Ecological Indian – Myth and History* (New York: W.W. Norton & Company, 1999), 211-213.

[20] Jeff Flynn-Paul, "The Myth of the 'Stolen Country,'" https://spectator.us/myth-stolen-country-america-new-world/, 23 September 2020.

beginning – a state of nature where everything existed in common.[21]

However, the development of personal private property was a pivotal event in the history of freedom. While sharing everything "in common" may sound harmonious, the reality of human nature is that different individuals work harder than others, and people tend to take better care of that which they own. Furthermore, the ability to support oneself provides independence from the unpredictability of the natural environment and whims of human rulers.

In the Western world of the 1600s and 1700s, the idea of property was extended beyond land and other material objects to include more abstract concepts such as life and liberty. Consequently, the notion of human rights is linked to property rights, or, as James Madison asserted, "'…as a man is said to have a right to his property, he may be equally said to have a property in his rights.'" For evidence of the inextricable link between property rights and personal freedom, one needs only to look within the Americas, where the United States has been dramatically more free and prosperous than Latin American countries, at least in part because it was founded by English settlers who believed in democracy and private property rights. Meanwhile the Spanish emphasis on dictatorship and wealth concentration left property in the hands of a relative few in many Latin American nations.[22]

The English also came from a commercial background where land was a commodity that could be bought and sold. Consequently, settlers often attempted to purchase land, not simply confiscate it. The introduction of European-style farming of rice and wheat led to the creation of large, sustainable, and permanent settlements in North America. This was aided by innovations such as the millstone to grind corn instead of by hand, the raising of livestock as beasts of burden and food and the use of their waste as fertilizer, as well as the presence of guns instead of bows and arrows for hunting and defense. As lands and forests were cleared, game was driven away, and local Indian populations were inevitably displaced.[23]

---

[21] Locke.

[22] Richard Pipes, *Property and Freedom: The Story of How Through the Centuries Private Ownership Has Promoted Liberty and the Rule of Law* (New York: Alfred A. Knopf, 2000), xi-xiv; Niall Ferguson, *Civilization: The West and the Rest* (New York: Penguin Books, 2011), 138.

[23] Flynn-Paul.

The absence of property rights may help to explain why much of North America was in a virtual state of nature. According to Locke, the reason individuals elected to join others and form a society was for "the mutual preservation of their lives, liberties, and estates," all of which he referred to as "property."[24] Without any concept of individual rights to protect, such as the right to property, there was obviously less need for a sophisticated government.

However, by the Age of Exploration, most people in the Old World had long left the state of nature, living instead in organized political units called nation-states. Some of these even qualified as empires because they had conquered other states: the Hapsburgs in Europe, the Ottomans in the Middle East, the Chinese in East Asia, the Moghuls in India, and the Mongol Empire which stretched over much of the Eurasian landmass.[25]

The Americas had empires too, such as the Aztecs of Mexico and the Incas of Peru, which possessed many of the characteristics of Old World empires including geographical size, a large population, and the conquest of other states.[26] Nevertheless, they lacked widespread writing, which only existed among a small elite in Mesoamerica, and wheels have only been found in Mexico as parts of toys.[27] These states also engaged in barbaric practices which had been abandoned long before in most societies of the Old World. For example, the Bible had outlawed human sacrifices for thousands of years.[28] In contrast, the Aztecs honored their gods by sacrificing war prisoners, slaves, and even children, who, while still alive, would be held down by priests as their hearts were cut out.[29] In 1487, five years before the arrival of Columbus, 80,000 captive human beings were slaughtered as part of a ceremony to inaugurate the Great Temple in Mexico.[30] Appeasing the sun god with blood and ensuring sufficient rain and crop fertility through the tears of children and babies were

[24] Locke, 350.
[25] Jared Diamond, *Guns, Germs, and Steel: The Fates of Human Societies* (New York: W.W. Norton & Co., 1999), 354-375.
[26] Ibid.
[27] Ibid.
[28] Dennis Prager, *The Rational Bible: Exodus – God, Slavery and Freedom*, ed. Joseph Telushkin (Washington, D.C.: Regnery Faith, 2018), 279-310.
[29] Mary Grabar, *Debunking Howard Zinn: Exposing the Fake History That Turned a Generation Against America* (Washington, D.C.: Regnery History, 2019), 63-87.
[30] Ibid.

common practices throughout the region, including by the Mayans.[31] Likewise, the sacrificial rites of the Incas in South America left their mounds and altars covered in blood.[32]

Mesoamerican human sacrifice as shown in the Codex Magliabechiano, Folio 70. Heart-extraction was viewed as a means of liberating the *Istli* and reuniting it with the Sun: the victim's transformed heart flies Sun-ward on a trail of blood. By Unknown author - Extract of Codex Magliabechiano cf. FAMSI (Foundation for the Advancement of Mesoamerican Studies, Inc.). Public domain, https://commons.wikimedia.org/w/index.php?curid=7828418.

---

[31] David S. Landes, *The Wealth and Poverty of Nations: Why Some Are So Rich and Some So Poor* (New York: W.W. Norton & Co., 1998), 103.
[32] D'Souza.

For the most part, people in the rest of the Americas lived as part of chiefdoms, tribes, or bands.[33] In North America, the Mississippi Valley settlement in what is now the southeastern United States came closest to resembling a state.[34] Political configurations without the long-term stability or security provided by nation-states often left their populations susceptible to capture by conquest and slavery, which both Indians and Europeans practiced during the early years of colonial America.[35]

One of the most impactful and long-lasting effects of the meeting of the Old and New Worlds was the transmission of diseases. After societies in Asia, Africa, and Europe developed agriculture, they then began raising livestock. Although this permitted the growth of more food to support larger and denser populations, it also exposed humans to animal viruses which later mutated and infected people. The birth of crowded cities and intercontinental trade then facilitated the spread of such diseases. Those who survived either developed an immunity to or already possessed a genetic resistance against deadly illnesses like smallpox, measles, typhus, cholera, and malaria. Survivors then passed on their genetic advantages to subsequent generations.[36]

Europeans, therefore, descended from ancestors who had been exposed to pathogens spread across Asia, Africa, and Europe for thousands of years. They also had greater numbers, genetic variation, and population density, both in their Old World lands and in their New World settlements. The lack thereof not only left Indians extremely susceptible to illnesses and made it more difficult to establish herd immunity, but probably meant that they would have succumbed in large numbers regardless of whether first contact had come from Imperial China, Mughal India, the Islamic Middle East, or sub-Saharan Africa. The unintentional transmission of diseases by individuals and groups who had no knowledge that they carried such lethality does not support a charge of genocide.[37]

---

[33] Diamond.

[34] Ibid.

[35] Thomas Sowell, "The Real History of Slavery," in *Black Rednecks and White Liberals* (San Francisco: Encounter Books, 2005), 111-169; Wilfred Riley, "Why Woke History Is Not the Answer," Why Woke History Is Not the Answer - American Greatness (amgreatness.com), 7 January 2021.

[36] Diamond., 195-214.

[37] Flynn-Paul.

Not only were most Indian deaths due to diseases, but most of those who died did so without ever encountering a European. In North America for example, Spanish explorers may have first introduced viruses to the tribes of the southeastern coast, but those diseases were then spread further by Indians to other tribes in the interior. Consequently, when Spanish explorer Hernando de Soto arrived in the Mississippi Valley during the 1540s, the devastation wrought by pathogens was already apparent in the abandoned villages he witnessed. This, of course, was still decades prior to the establishment of the first permanent English settlement at Jamestown, Virginia in 1607.[38]

Miniature by Pierart dou Tielt illustrating the Tractatus quartus by Gilles li Muisit (Tournai, c. 1353). The people of Tournai bury victims of the Black Death. 1376-1377. Wikimedia Commons. Public domain.

Furthermore, tragic decimations of populations by diseases have occurred throughout world history. Smallpox spread by trade routes connecting Europe, North Africa, and Asia killed millions in ancient Rome from A.D. 165-180.[39] The bubonic plague or "Black Death" first arrived in Europe in A.D. 542-543, later returning from 1346-1352 and killing approximately 25% of all Europeans with death rates

---

[38] Diamond, 195-214.
[39] Ibid.

in some cities reaching 70%.[40] Approximately one-third of the population of the Byzantine Empire died in 1347 alone.[41] The Black Death may have spread via trade routes running from China through Central Asia to Europe, or been brought west by the Mongols during their invasions and conquests of the 1200s.[42] However, the largest epidemic ever occurred in the twentieth century in the aftermath of World War I when the Spanish flu took the lives of 21 million human beings, including five million in India.[43] None of these tragedies is ever labelled a genocide. That charge is unfairly reserved for America alone.

In 1492 Europe had a bustling population which had recovered from the plague and experienced the rebirth of classical learning known as the Renaissance. Europeans eagerly sought prosperity by engaging in trade and other economic ventures or discovering gold and silver and striking it rich. Additionally, they desired to conquer for king and country and spread the gospel. The Mediterranean Sea and overland routes to East Asia's silks and spices were controlled by various Islamic regimes. Portugal had opted to head south and round Africa to reach India and China. Columbus, on the other hand, convinced the Spanish that he could reach the East by sailing West, something unheard of at the time and filled with great risk.

If at the time of Columbus's arrival in the New World there were roughly 100 million people residing on about 16 million square miles of land on the North and South American continents, that would result in an approximate population density of 6-7 people per square mile. Assuming that the future continental United States had 10 million souls spread out over 3 million square miles would equate to an average of three to four human beings per square mile. Consequently, the relatively sparsely populated Americas would have been uniquely situated for exploration and colonization.

Over the next century, Europeans would stake their claims in the New World. First the Spanish arrived, exploring the Caribbean and later expanding into Mexico as well as Central and South America. The Portuguese colonized Brazil. The French settled Canada.

---

[40] Ibid.

[41] J.M. Roberts *The Penguin History of the World* (New York: Penguin Books, 1992), 372.

[42] Diamond; D'Souza.

[43] Diamond; Roberts, 945.

Holland, Sweden, and even Russia (via Alaska and the Pacific Northwest) made appearances too. However, it was the English who would plant the roots of the United States of America.

The Southern Colonies

In 1607, only the subarctic region and the Sahara Desert were less populated than the Americas.[44] On May 14th of that year, three ships – the *Discovery, Godspeed,* and *Susan Constant,* – landed at a swampy, forested spot off the James River in the English territory of Virginia.[45] The fleet sailed under Captain Christopher Newport with a charter from the Virginia Company of London.[46] The colonists sought to create a stable and flourishing settlement, find gold, locate a northwest passage to China, and advance the gospel (the first structure built was a large wooden cross).[47] Jamestown would become the first permanent English settlement in America.

The Jamestown settlers did not receive a warm welcome. John Smith, later a member of the colonial council, described the scene when the English first landed:

> Anchoring in this bay twenty or thirty went ashore with the Captain, and in coming aboard, they were assaulted with certain Indians, which charged them within pistol shot: in which conflict, Captain Archer and Mathew Morton were shot: whereupon Captain Newport seconding them, made a shot at them, which the Indians little respected, but having spent their arrows retired without harm.[48]

---

[44] Flynn-Paul.

[45] James Horn, ed., *Captain John Smith: Writings with other Narratives of Roanoke, Jamestown, and the First English Settlement in America* (New York: Literary Classics of the United States, Inc., 2007), 1195-1209.

[46] Ibid.

[47] Lacey Baldwin Smith, *This Realm of England 1399 to 1688* (Boston: D.C. Heath and Company, 1966), 226-243.

[48] John Smith, "A True Relation," in *Captain John Smith: Writings with other Narratives of Roanoke, Jamestown, and the First English Settlement in America*, ed. James Horn (New York: Literary Classics of the United States, Inc., 2007), 1-36.

Eventually the colonists were able to construct a fort, but periodic raids continued.[49] These usually consisted of bow and arrow attacks as well as the theft of tools and provisions.[50] However, it was diseases like malaria as well as starvation, in part because many settlers considered themselves "gentlemen" and therefore above manual labor, which nearly wiped out the colony.[51] Only 32 of the original 104 arrivals would survive.[52] Clearly these men lacked any plan, let alone the ability, to commence with any kind of grand ethnic cleansing scheme or genocidal program against the native population.

The main Indians in the region were the Powhatans, a collection of about thirty Algonquin-speaking groups living in coastal Virginia between the James and Potomac rivers. Their supreme chief was Wahunsonacock, whom the English often referred to as Powhatan, which was also the name of his birth village. The larger region surrounding the Chesapeake Bay was also home to many other Indians, including Iroquoian and Siouan-speakers.[53]

Smith participated in or led several exploratory missions up the network of rivers in the area. Particularly as the colony's provisions became depleted, these efforts were often for the purpose of trade. Some journeys could result in friendly exchanges, with the English typically wanting corn and the Indians desiring copper items and hatchets. But on other occasions, Smith and his men were captured. After one ambush Smith and two others escaped, but a third man had his skin scraped off with mussel shells and his body burned. Later, Smith was captured again and only saved from being clubbed to death by Powhatan's daughter, Pocahontas.[54]

The Pocahontas episode may have been a Powhatan adoption ritual, whereby Smith was "killed" and "reborn" as a member of the tribe. Powhatan may have been asserting his control over the English by "adopting" Smith, their leader. (A crafty politician, Powhatan later sent an agent named Namontack to England on an apparent mission

---

[49] Horn.
[50] H.W. Crocker III, *Don't Tread on Me: A 400-Year History of America at War, from Indian Fighting to Terrorist Hunting* (New York: Crown Forum, 2006), 5-9.
[51] Steven E. Woodworth, *The Essentials of United States History: 1500 to 1789 From Colony to Republic* (Piscataway, New Jersey: Research and Education Association, 1996), 11-41.
[52] Baldwin Smith.
[53] Horn.
[54] Ibid.; Crocker.

to gather information.) Smith was told that the English could stay, provided that they trade copper, iron goods, and acknowledge Powhatan overlordship. Powhatan would later add a cannon, a grindstone, swords, and guns to his demands in exchange for providing food, particularly as he became concerned by the increasing number of newly arrived colonists. The chieftain also halted all trade when it suited him, while Smith was willing to use force to compel an exchange when he thought it was necessary.[55]

In 1608 Smith became the president of the colonial council. Bringing a military posture to his leadership, he demanded work and discipline while citing II Thessalonians 3:10: "If anyone will not work, neither shall he eat." As the colony became more desperate, he also led raids on local Indian villages for food, prompting retaliation whenever colonists ventured outside the settlement's walls.[56]

Any role race may have played in these early years was incidental. Attacks and counterattacks between rival tribes for food and other resources had been taking place in North America for thousands of years prior to the arrival of the English. Indeed, such actions have been a characteristic of human development around the world for most of history prior to the creation of capitalism, which provided a peaceful means for individuals or groups to obtain what they wanted or needed by trading something of theirs in exchange.

Neither did Smith's administration bear any apparent racial malice towards the Indians. In an effort to promote long-term peaceful relations between the English and the Powhatans, he attempted to place white males in Indian villages with the hope that intermarriages would result. His leadership also helped to bring the death rate of the colony down from about 60% during the first winter to approximately 15% the next. Nevertheless, the colonists apparently grew tired of his ways, and he was forced to return to England in 1609.[57]

Other aspects of the Jamestown story also confirm that race was a minimal, if not irrelevant factor. The Laws of Virginia (1610) enshrined the Anglican religion and a moral code based upon the Bible. The code stipulated that rape of any woman, with Indians

[55] Horn.
[56] Larry Schweikart and Michael Allen, *A Patriot's History of the United States: From Columbus's Great Discovery to the War on Terror* (New York: Sentinel, 2004), 17.
[57] Ibid.

explicitly included, was forbidden.[58]

The life of Pocahontas provides a great deal of insight into the nature of English-Indian relations during Jamestown's early years. Although captured in war by the English and held under house arrest for a time, she was later freed. During her time in Jamestown, she was exposed to the gospel by minister Alexander Whitaker. In 1613 she converted to Christianity and changed her name to Rebecca. She then married John Rolfe, one of the first successful tobacco farmers. Powhatan apparently gave his daughter away in marriage happily, even providing the young couple with an estate of thousands of acres as a wedding present. The marriage seems to have helped usher in several years of peace which may have been crucial while Jamestown was struggling to survive during its early period.[59]

The Baptism of Pocahontas (1840) by John Gadsby Chapman. Oil on canvas. Rotunda of the U.S. Capitol. Wikimedia Commons. Public domain.

---

[58] The Hillsdale College History Faculty, eds., *American Heritage – A Reader* (Hillsdale, Michigan: Hillsdale College Press, 2011), 9; *Laws of Virginia* in *American Heritage – A Reader*, eds. The Hillsdale College History Faculty (Hillsdale, Michigan: Hillsdale College Press, 2011), 9-12.

[59] Flynn-Paul; Gordon Robertson, *Pocahontas: Dove of Peace* (The Christian Broadcasting Network, 2016), DVD.

The efforts by the English in colonial America to proselytize to the Indians demonstrated that they viewed them as fellow children of God who were created in His image. Although in modern times they would be accused of "cultural imperialism," for a Christian, following Christ's "great commission" to "go and make disciples of all nations" (Matthew 28:19) is an act of obedience to God and a demonstration of love towards others. How could it be anything else for a people who genuinely believed that one's eternal soul was at stake? Consider Whitaker's sermon "Good Newes from Virginia" (1613):

> One God created us, they have reasonable souls and intellectual faculties as well as we; we all have *Adam* for our common parent: yea, by nature the condition of us both is all one, the servants of sin and slaves of the devil. Oh remember (I beseech you) what was the state of *England* before the gospel was preached in our country. How much better were we then, and concerning our souls' health than these now are? Let the word of the Lord sound out that it may be heard in these parts; and let your faith which is toward God spread itself abroad and show forth the charitable fruits of it in these barren parts of the world.[60]

First Whitaker established the essential equality of the Indians as sons of Adam with souls and intelligence. That equality extended to the need of all for redemption from sin. He also admonished his fellow countrymen that the only difference between the English and the Indians was the grace of God and the reception of the gospel. Finally, he exhorted his congregation to let their faith bear fruit by accepting the Indians into the body of Christ.

In what could be described as the first example of a diplomatic visit from America, in 1616 Mr. and Mrs. Rolfe travelled to England with their newborn son, Thomas. Pocahontas was greeted as an American princess, even meeting King James I. Unfortunately, while abroad she grew ill and passed away in 1617. She was buried in the chancel of St. George's parish church in Gravesend, Kent, England. There she is memorialized with a tablet, windows, garden, and statue

---

[60] Alexander Whitaker, *Good Newes from Virginia* (United Kingdom: Dodo Press), 33.

25

– a replica of which also honors her at Jamestown.[61]

Nothing in the life of Pocahontas appears to be any different from that which would have occurred had she been a princess from a European power. As a member of one royal family, she was given away in marriage by her father to a leading member of another nation. The marriage and child which resulted helped to bring peace between two rivals, at least for a time. She was then received abroad as a foreign dignitary, deserving of nothing less than the same respect as a princess from France or Spain.

One reason Jamestown was able to survive after its inauspicious start was old-fashioned balance-of-power politics. The various Indian tribes did not view each other as one race or one nation any more than the English viewed their European rivals as being part of the same race or nation. The English had to contend with the French in Canada to their north and the Spanish in Florida to their south just as much if not more than any particular Indian tribe. The same was true for the Powhatans, who had been warring with rival tribes such as the Doeg and the Susquehannock for many years prior to the arrival of Europeans. Thus, the English and the Powhatans could be friends when it suited them, and enemies when it did not. Such was the system of ever-shifting alliances which all groups, European and Indian, were compelled to participate in to survive in the state of nature which existed in colonial America.[62]

Consequently, it should not be too surprising that relations between the English and Powhatans eventually deteriorated. As more colonists arrived, greater pressure on resources brought renewed conflict. Opechancanough, who became chief after his brother Wahunsonacock died in 1618, was angered by increasing English settlement and influence. On Good Friday in 1622, he ordered an attack on Jamestown. The Powhatans approached the settlers under the pretense of offering game for trade. What followed was a massacre of 347 men, women, and children – about one-fourth to one-third of Virginia's settlers – possibly in retaliation for about two dozen Indian deaths at the hands of the colonists. The Virginia Company responded by declaring a "'perpetual war without peace or truce.'" Although what was termed the "First Tidewater War" ended

---

[61] "Pocahontas," Pocahontas | St George's Church Gravesend (stgeorgesgravesend.org), 7 March 2021.
[62] Schweikart and Allen, 26.

ten years later in 1632, in 1644 another 500 colonists were killed when Opechancanough ordered a second massacre, launching the "Second Tidewater War." Eventually the English proved both too many and too strong, and most of the Chesapeake Indians of Virginia and Maryland were either killed, driven further inland, or forced to make annual payments in tribute. It was immigration and warfare which defeated the Chesapeake Indians, not genocide.[63]

To the west of Virginia lay the Appalachian Mountains, forming a natural boundary to English territorial claims. The southern section of the range extended into what became the colonies of North and South Carolina as well as Georgia. Colonists in this region encountered the Cherokee Indians, an amalgam of communities associated through blood, culture, or alliances rather than a single tribe or political unit. Although the Cherokee hunted over a vastly larger region, their main area of settlement was only about 200 miles in any direction.[64]

The Cherokee were sparsely spread over what is today the southeastern United States. In 1690 they numbered about 20,000. By 1700 they were the largest group in the area, but still numbered only in the tens of thousands, while today the same land is home to tens of millions. Europe was far more densely populated at the time. By 1740 the Cherokee numbers had fallen to approximately 10,000, mostly because of diseases and war.[65]

As with many tribes, the Cherokee had obtained their territory through conquest, driving out the Shawnee, Creek, Catawba, and Tuscarora. Likewise, the Cherokees' neighbors the Iroquois to the north and Chickasaw to the west had occupied their lands through similar means.[66]

As increasing numbers of English settlers arrived and pushed west, changes came to the Cherokee. Exposure to Western languages and writing led a Cherokee named Sequoyah to create the first written language for his people. It included 85 symbols with five representing vowels, one standing for the "s" sound, and the rest referring to syllables comprised of both a consonant and a vowel.[67]

---

[63] Grabar; Crocker.
[64] Sowell, *Conquests and Cultures.*
[65] Ibid., Taylor, 15.
[66] Sowell, *Conquests and Cultures.*
[67] Taylor, 34.

The Cherokee also transitioned from relying primarily on hunting for survival to depending more on farming. Trading away an abundant resource, land, initially served to keep them well-supplied with the European goods that they desired. However, as the amount of land that they had available for exchange declined, so did their ability to hunt. Consequently, Cherokee men were compelled to become farmers, something which had traditionally been the role of women.[68]

The Northern Colonies

The Pilgrims who settled at Plymouth came to America explicitly for the purpose of creating a self-governing Christian community. As Puritan separatists from the Church of England, they not only believed that the state church was beyond saving, but that there ought not to be an official state church.[69] All Americans owe them a tremendous debt for establishing self-government and religious freedom as bedrock American principles.

As a result of their religious stance, the Pilgrims refused to recognize King James I as the leader of their faith. In the mind of James, rejecting him as a spiritual head was too close to rejecting him as a political ruler as well. Eventually his government commenced with a campaign of harassment and persecution.[70]

After an initial attempt in 1608 at making Holland their new home, the Pilgrims returned to England. In 1620 they departed once again, but this time aboard the *Mayflower* and with America as their destination. As with the Jamestown colonists, the Pilgrims possessed a charter from the Virginia Company of London. However, when storms drove them off course, the 102 passengers were forced to land outside of the Virginia territory. After two tumultuous months on the Atlantic, they had arrived off the coast of Massachusetts.[71]

Having landed outside the bounds of the Virginia territory, the lawful chain of authority from King James I to the Virginia Company to the Pilgrims had been broken. The first step to establishing a community was to re-establish the chain of authority. This was

---

[68] Sowell, *Conquests and Cultures.*
[69] The History Channel, *Desperate Crossing: The Untold Story of The Mayflower* (A & E Television Networks, 2006), DVD.
[70] Woodworth, 18-23.
[71] Ibid.

accomplished with a covenant – a type of Protestant church contract binding a congregation to each other and to its leaders, under God. Covenants in the Bible were numerous, including between God and Abraham in the Old Testament as well as between Jesus and His disciples at the Last Supper in the New Testament. When the Pilgrims signed what would come to be known as the *Mayflower Compact* on November 11, 1620, it marked the first time that such a religious instrument was applied to a political purpose.[72]

Beginning with the covenantal phrase "In the name of God, amen," the Pilgrims bound themselves "in the presence of God and one another." They agreed to "enact, constitute, and frame, such just and equal laws, ordinances, acts, constitutions and offices" as necessary "for the general good of the colony." The reasons for establishing the colony were "the glory of God," "advancement of the Christian faith," "the honor of king and country," and "our better ordering and preservation."[73]

Covenants were employed by many English settlements in colonial America. Together with the charters issued by the monarch to joint-stock companies or to individual proprietors such as William Penn, these religious instruments helped to establish written constitutionalism in America. Intended to establish order while also limiting government intrusion into individual liberty, they were a uniquely American achievement in self-government. England had and still has no written constitution. When one spoke of the English constitution, it referred to the various statutes, court rulings, and traditions which had accumulated over the centuries – not a single all-encompassing written document.

Considering the unenviable circumstances under which the Pilgrims found themselves, the notion that they came as conquerors with imperialistic designs, let alone murderous intent, is as laughable as it is improbable. They were humble religious people, driven from their homeland, seeking to worship in peace. Lost and anchored off the windswept New England coast, they had been compelled to draft, to the best of their ability, some kind of statement to provide a sense

---

[72] Charles Kesler, Government 169 lecture notes, Claremont McKenna College, fall 2006.
[73] "The Mayflower Compact," November 11, 1620, in *American Heritage – A Reader*, eds. The Hillsdale College History Faculty (Hillsdale, Michigan: Hillsdale College Press, 2011), 13-14.

of legitimacy and reconnect them to their homeland.

They were also up to their necks in debt. In exchange for funding from a group known as the Merchant Adventurers, the Pilgrims had committed themselves to indentured servitude – thereby requiring them to work for years simply to repay the cost of their passage across the ocean.[74]

As the Indians had no writing, the only records available detailing the experiences of the Pilgrims and the various tribal peoples of New England are those of the English. One of the most comprehensive accounts is *Of Plymouth Plantation* by William Bradford, the longtime governor of the colony. Bradford reported that on November 15th, 1620, the colonists first disembarked onto the beach off Cape Cod. While there, a Pilgrim exploratory party uncovered several large baskets of corn and later some beans. However, as Bradford explained, "the people had run away and could not be seen." He conceded that the party took the food and "thus got seed to plant corn the next year, or they might have starved." He added that they fully intended to provide the rightful owners with "full satisfaction when they should meet with any of them." Sometime shortly thereafter, the Pilgrims were attacked by a group of Indians at an area along the beach that the English dubbed "First Encounter." About six months later, they discovered that some of those who had attacked them on the beach were the Nausets, the rightful owners of the purloined corn. True to their word, the Pilgrims provided restitution when the Nausets turned over a young man in their possession named John Billington, who had wandered off and became lost in the woods.[75]

The only reason this incident is part of the historical record is because Bradford and other Pilgrims were honest enough to report it. Their willingness to include unflattering information about themselves lends credibility to their overall accounts. Meanwhile, the fact that the Pilgrims did give the Nausets "full satisfaction" reflects positively on their character and intentions.

After departing from Cape Cod on December 16th, the Pilgrims landed at their final destination, Plymouth.[76] At that time there were

---

[74] Flynn-Paul.

[75] William Bradford, *Of Plymouth Plantation* (San Antonio: Vision Forum, 2008), 67-74, 84-95.

[76] Ibid., 67-74.

more than four square miles of land for every Indian man, woman, and child in New England.[77] Unsurprisingly then, the immediate area which the Pilgrims surveyed appeared to be unoccupied. That had not always been so. Although most had succumbed to disease, the Patuxet Indians had once dwelt where Plymouth Plantation was established.[78] However, it was not the Pilgrims who were the vectors but independent fishermen who had brought disease years before.[79]

After several weeks, the Pilgrims encountered the people with whom their fate would be tied for the next half century – the Wampanoag Indians. For the initial encounter the Wampanoag sent Samoset, who was not a member of the tribe but had picked up some English from fishermen and traders in Maine. The Pilgrims noted that he was a striking man, tall with long black hair and wearing nothing more than a leather strap around his waist. They did not refer to the color of his skin. Samoset explained that the chief or sachem of the Wampanoag, Massasoit, lived about forty miles away at a place called Pokanoket. The tall stranger added that there was another at Pokanoket who spoke even better English than he did, Tisquantum or Squanto. As the English would later discover, Squanto was one of the last survivors of the Patuxet tribe. He later became the Pilgrims' interpreter.[80]

Massasoit had been studying the Pilgrims at a distance for some time. He received reports regarding their building projects as well as secret burials, which were intended to hide just how deadly the first winter of 1620-1621 had been for the Plymouth community. The Pilgrims were unlike the other Europeans that the Indians of New England had seen. They had come as men, women, and children – as families. Furthermore, unlike the European fishermen and traders that the Indians had met previously, these newcomers were mostly content to keep to themselves and build their settlement. After consulting with Squanto, Massasoit decided that these strangers could be important allies against the rival Narragansett tribe, which at that time was too strong for the Wampanoag to overcome alone.[81]

---

[77] Alden T. Vaughan, *New England Frontier – Puritans and Indians, 1620-1675* (Norman: University of Oklahoma Press, 1995), 309-338.
[78] Flynn-Paul.
[79] Ibid.
[80] Nathaniel Philbrick, *Mayflower: A Story of Courage, Community, and War* (New York: Viking, 2006), 93-103.
[81] Ibid.

Massasoit first presented himself to the English with about sixty warriors. They were much taller than the Pilgrims and in far greater numbers, as the English probably only had about twenty healthy, able-bodied men available at the time. After an initially tense period of acclimation, both sides eventually overcame their suspicions of one another and established peaceful relations.[82]

On April 1, 1621, Massasoit and Governor John Carver of Plymouth agreed to a six-point treaty of friendship:

1. That neither he nor any of his, should injure or harm any of their people.

2. That if any of his did any harm to any of theirs, he should send the offender, that they might punish him.

3. That if anything were taken away from any of theirs, he should cause it to be restored; and they should do the like to his.

4. If any made unjust war against him, they would aid him; if any made war against them, he should aid them.

5. He should send to his neighboring confederates, to certify them of this, that they might not wrong them, but might be likewise comprised in the conditions of peace.

6. That when their men came to them, they should leave their bows and arrows behind them.[83]

It was the beginning of 54 years of peace between the Pilgrims and Wampanoag. By September, nine other chiefs had also signed onto various agreements with the Plymouth settlers.[84] The early diplomatic successes of the Pilgrims testify to their true intentions as well as to the possibility of achieving real peace in colonial America.

Besides the formal bond between the Pilgrims and the Wampanoag, individual Englishmen and Indians established personal relationships. As with the example of Pocahontas, such stories reveal

---

[82] Ibid.
[83] Bradford, 75-83.
[84] Philbrick, 104-120.

that the English did not simply view Indians as mere savages or sub-humans worthy of nothing more than conquest and exploitation. For example, when the Pilgrims got word that their friend, Massasoit, was deathly ill, Governor Bradford sent Edward Winslow to visit him. Winslow provided the Wampanoag chieftain with medicine and helped nurse him back to health, after which Massasoit reportedly said: "Now I see the English are my friends and love me; and whilst I live, I will never forget this kindness they have showed me."[85]

Even more remarkable is the story of Squanto. After being kidnapped by pirates several years earlier, taken to Spain, and sold into slavery, he escaped to England where he was taken in by a London merchant and learned English. Eventually he made it back to Newfoundland and finally to New England just before the Pilgrims landed. Bradford called Squanto "a special instrument sent of God for their good, beyond expectation," and credited him as their translator and guide to the local vegetation and best places to hunt and fish.[86]

Just as Squanto shared knowledge with the Pilgrims, so too did the English have much to offer the Indians. For example, Bradford noted that initially the Wampanoag did not possess a great deal of corn. It was only after they had been introduced to tools such as hoes and witnessed the example of English labor that they were able to make greater use of the available land.[87]

When abundant harvests arrived in the fall, the Pilgrims honored God with a feast that has come to be known as the first Thanksgiving. Massasoit and about 100 other Indians brought five fresh deer. Turkey, ducks, and fish were also part of the celebration. The recently harvested barley crop permitted the English to finally brew beer, undoubtedly adding to the joy of the occasion as well.[88]

Future governor Edward Winslow described the events of the day which would become the most American of all holidays:

[85] Edward Winslow, *Good Newes from New England: A True Relation of Things Very Remarkable at the Plantation of Plimoth in New England*, (Bedford, Massachusetts: Applewood Books), 31-39.
[86] Bradford.
[87] Ibid., 84-95.
[88] Philbrick.

Our harvest being gotten in, our governor sent four men on fowling, that so we might after a special manner rejoice together after we had gathered the fruit of our labors. They four in one day killed as much fowl as, with a little help beside, served the company almost a week. At which time, amongst other recreations, we exercised our arms, many of the Indians coming amongst us, and among the rest their greatest king Massasoit, with some ninety men, whom for three days we entertained and feasted, and they went out and killed five deer, which they brought to the plantation and bestowed on our governor, and upon the captain and others.[89]

The First Thanksgiving (1914) by Jennie Augusta Brownscombe (1850-1936). Oil on canvas. Pilgrim Hall Museum, Plymouth, Massachusetts. Wikimedia Commons. Public domain.

The Pilgrims had endured their own "starving time," with only 44 of the 102 *Mayflower* passengers surviving the first winter of 1620-

---

[89] Edward Winslow, "A Letter sent from New England to a Friend in these parts, setting forth a brief and true declaration of the worth of that plantation; as also certain useful directions for such as intend a voyage into those parts," in *Mourt's Relation: A Journal of the Pilgrims at Plymouth*, ed. Dwight B. Heath (Bedford, Massachusetts: Applewood Books, 1963), 81-87.

1621. Nevertheless, adhering to their faith, they labored, overcame the natural elements, cultivated friends and allies, and built a successful colony. Eventually they were able to repay their financial backers and gain more local control while continuing to operate without an official charter. Meanwhile another group – the Puritans – established their own much larger colony nearby. In 1691 the approximately 7,000 members of Plymouth Plantation merged with the neighboring colony of Massachusetts Bay.[90]

As with their Pilgrim Separatist cousins, the Puritans were driven from England in search of a new home where they could practice their faith freely. However, the Puritans did not seek to separate from the Church of England, but to "purify" it. King James I had not acted against them as they gained power in Parliament. Nevertheless, his son, Charles I, dismissed the legislature in 1629, engaged in a "personal" rule, and instructed Archbishop of Canterbury William Laud to persecute the Puritan sect. This led to a great Puritan exodus in the next decade, far more numerous than that of the Pilgrims, totaling about 75,000 and including approximately 20,000 who arrived in New England.[91]

The Massachusetts Bay Company had been chartered to raise money for a Puritan passage to America. In order to minimize royal involvement, the Puritans based the joint-stock company's headquarters in Massachusetts rather than in England. In 1630 a grand total of 17 ships and 1,100 passengers traversed the Atlantic and established the Massachusetts Bay Colony. Its leader was John Winthrop, an attorney and manor lord in England, who had walked away from much to lead the new religious experiment.[92]

As with Plymouth, Massachusetts Bay was also founded with a covenant. Winthrop, possibly while still on board the ship *Arbella*, outlined the covenant's terms in a sermon entitled "A Model of Christian Charity":

> Thus stands the cause between God and us. We are entered into covenant with Him for this work. We have taken out a commission, the Lord has given us leave to draw our own articles…Now if the Lord shall

---

[90] Woodworth.
[91] Ibid.
[92] The Hillsdale College History Faculty, 15-16.

please to hear us, and bring us in peace to the place we desire, then has He ratified this covenant and sealed our commission, [and] will expect a strict performance of the articles contained in it; but if we shall neglect the observation of these articles which are the ends we have propounded, and, dissembling without God, shall fall to embrace this present world and prosecute our carnal intentions, seeking great things for ourselves and our posterity, the Lord will surely break out in wrath against us; be revenged of such a perjured people, and make us to know the price of the breach of such a covenant..[93]

The Puritans believed that England was on the verge of becoming a failed state. As proof of a decaying society, they could point to such acts of corruption as Henry VIII confiscating Catholic Church lands and awarding them to "placemen" in Parliament – those who were loyal to him – as well as the dismissal of Parliament by Charles I. The Puritans were committed to creating a new kind of community built upon the spirit of loving one's neighbor. If they upheld the covenant, God would make them "a praise and glory that men shall say of succeeding plantations, 'the Lord make it like that of NEW ENGLAND.'" But if they failed, they would "open the mouths of enemies to speak evil of the ways of God, and all professors for God's sake." For people who took their religion very seriously, the stakes could not have been higher.[94]

Neither ignorant nor bigoted, the Puritans were knowledgeable about the Bible and committed to living out their faith. Hence, they sought to treat the Indians in a way which upheld their covenant with God. As a result, race was much less of a factor in their behavior than considerations like spreading the gospel, politics, trade, and the administration of justice.[95]

---

[93] John Winthrop, "A Model of Christian Charity," in *American Heritage – A Reader*, eds. The Hillsdale College History Faculty (Hillsdale, Michigan: Hillsdale College Press, 2011), 16-28.

[94] Kesler; Winthrop.

[95] Vaughn.

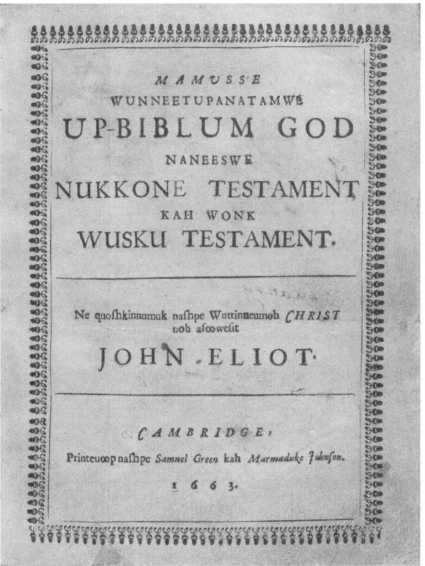

Title page of John Eliot's Indian Bible written in Massachusett. AC6 Eℓ452 663m, Houghton Library, Harvard University. Wikimedia Commons. Public domain.

Taking Christ's "great commission" to "go and make disciples of all nations" to heart, Puritans like Reverend John Eliot converted many Indians to Christianity. By 1650 there were approximately 1,000 people living in "praying villages" – communities of Christian Indians who in adopting a new inner faith had also adopted a new outer lifestyle, including literacy, monogamy, and more modest clothing. With the assistance of an Indian convert named Job Nesutan, Eliot translated the Bible into Massachusett, an Algonquin language. In 1663 it became the first Bible printed in the New World and exposed the Indians of the region to both Christianity and written language, as they had not developed a writing system of their own.[96]

The simple act of settlement by Europeans was not necessarily perceived as a threat by tribal peoples, provided that they came as friends. Evidence of this is seen in both the relationships of the Pilgrims with the Wampanoag as well as in interactions between the Puritans and many of the tribes surrounding Boston Harbor. If there was a dispute regarding the rightful possessors of a piece of land, the Puritans usually ended up trading for it or purchasing it. Typically, a deed was drawn up, translated (usually by an Indian), signed, and recorded by colonial officials. Land deeds also gave Indians continued access to hunting and fishing. The Puritans generally continued the English practice of permitting hunting and fishing on any unfenced land as well.[97]

The two peoples also engaged in mutually beneficially trade, not exploitation and theft. The Puritans did not cheat Indians by simply trading alcohol or worthless items for land. Many tribes desired the manufactured goods which English merchants sold, including time-saving tools such as hoes and hatchets, as well as woolen clothing which proved to be more comfortable than animal skins.[98]

One of the primary items which the New England tribes had to trade was land, which they did not value particularly highly. Land was of minimal importance because most tribes only engaged in basic farming, relying more on hunting and gathering for their sustenance. And due to sparse population patterns, it was available in abundance. The notion that the Indians thought all of it belonged to them is a modern conception projected back into history.[99]

The other commodity which Indians had in abundance was fur. It is the fur trade which illustrates how English settlers, rather than being exploiters of Indians, actually served as middlemen in a growing intercontinental trading market. Although it may not have

---

[96] Ibid.
[97] Ibid.
[98] Ibid.
[99] Ibid.

been as highly valued by the tribes of New England, fur was in great demand during the cold winters in Europe. As Indians traded furs and skins to settlers in exchange for woolen cloth, cloth garments, guns, and ammunition, the settlers then proceeded to trade the fur and skins which they had obtained from the Indians to Europe for more manufactured goods.[100]

The Puritan courts also demonstrated the sincere desire of the English to recognize the common humanity of the Indians of New England. The punishment for murder was execution, period. The Plymouth authorities, determined to demonstrate a commitment to the terms of their peace agreement with the Wampanoag, hunted down Englishmen accused of crimes committed against Indians and hung those convicted of murder. Likewise, in the summer of 1676 four Puritan men were charged in a Massachusetts Bay court with the murders of three Indian women and three Indian children – all four were found guilty with two being executed. Other harsh punishments meted out, regardless of race, included stocks, whipping, imprisonment, and servitude for defaulting on debts.[101]

When conflicts arose, they were almost never of the simple Indian vs. English variety. In what was a common experience for many different groups of settlers throughout the colonial era, both Pilgrims and Puritans participated in a system of balance-of-power politics and shifting alliances to survive. For example, when the Pilgrims entered into their alliance with the Wampanoag, Massasoit had more in mind than simply befriending the English strangers – he was seeking also to offset the power of the rival Narragansett tribe. Likewise, the Puritans often benefitted from alliances with friendly tribes including the Mohegans, Massachusetts, and the Nausets who warned the settlers of potential attacks from less friendly Indian rivals.[102]

The Pequot War of 1637 provides a fitting example. Although it is sometimes described as if it was a Puritan war against all Indians, the reality is that this conflict was triggered by competition for the fur trade amongst the Pequot, the Narragansetts, the Mohegans, the Dutch, and the English. An endless series of attacks and counterattacks included a Pequot siege of Fort Saybrook, an English

---

[100] Sowell, *Conquests and Cultures.*
[101] Vaughn, Flynn-Paul.
[102] Ibid.

trading post. The Pequot inflicted hideous tortures on English captives including burnings, stripping off skin, and cutting off fingers and toes before killing them. This was followed by numerous raids on several Connecticut towns where thirty settlers were murdered, a large portion of the Puritan population. In May, several of the towns along the Connecticut River formed a small army totaling about 100 men. The Puritans were joined by over 200 Narragansett, Mohegan, and Niantic Indians in a pre-dawn retaliatory raid on a Pequot village along the Mystic River. The outnumbered settler army set the village on fire and prevented any escape, resulting in hundreds of Pequot deaths. It was a brutal massacre, but it was not unprovoked, and it certainly was not an attempt to perpetrate genocide against all Indians.[103]

As the decades passed following the founding of Plymouth and Massachusetts Bay, other Puritan settlements took root in New England which would grow into the colonies of Rhode Island, Connecticut, and New Hampshire. An increase in Puritan numbers led to a greater demand for natural resources – including land – which led to higher prices. The Indians continued to sell and the Puritans continued to pay, but nevertheless tension grew between the English and such tribes as one-time friends the Wampanoag. Meanwhile, missionary efforts had led to Christian converts known as "praying Indians" living in "praying villages" where they adopted many of the Puritan ways and became trustworthy English allies.[104]

By 1675 the increased presence and cultural influence of the English had triggered resentment on the part of some Indians. Illustrating the tenuousness of alliances in the virtual state of nature which existed in colonial America, Metacomet (known as King Philip to the Puritans), son of the now-deceased Wampanoag chief Massasoit, formed new alliances with several other tribes including the Narragansetts – the very group with which his father had been so concerned years before. On the other hand, Christian tribes including the Mohegans, Massachusetts, and Nausets, as well as former enemies the Pequots, allied with the Puritans.[105]

Consequently, although Metacomet may have considered his

---

[103] Michael Medved, *The 10 Big Lies About America: Combating Destructive Distortions About Our Nation* (New York: Crown Forum, 2008), 11-45.
[104] Vaughn.
[105] Ibid.

campaign to be "a war of extermination against the English," King Phillip's War (1675-1676) cannot truly be described as a race war, but rather, as with most colonial era conflicts, between interest and interest and alliance and alliance. Metacomet and his allies raided and burned towns and frontier villages while putting Puritans to death via the tomahawk. They also devastated colonial armies by way of ambush. Thousands of Indians were killed by the Puritans and their Indian partners as well. The injury and death toll for Puritan colonists surpassed that of any later American conflict. Those killed in battle surpassed 10%. Metacomet was killed by another Indian, and his wife and son were sold into slavery. Captured males suspected of aiding Metacomet faced execution or enslavement, something not uncommon for that time. Ultimately the Wampanoag were defeated and dispersed from their traditional lands. Finally, it must be noted that Christian Indians were among the most loyal to the English, were viewed with suspicion and hatred by other tribes, and probably made the difference in turning the tide for Puritan New England. Their contributions were recorded in **Daniel Gookin's** *Historical Account of the Doing and Sufferings of the Christian Indians of New England* (1677).[106]

Neither the Pilgrims nor the Puritans committed genocide against anyone. There were, however, conflicts such as the Pequot War in 1637 and later King Phillip's War brought on by the arrival of new settlers, increased competition for natural resources, and shifts in balances of power and influence. In both conflicts, Indians fought with and against the English. Nevertheless, the total amount of Indians killed in such fighting accounted for only a fraction of the decline in the overall New England Indian population, perhaps 15-20%. The rest came as a result of disease and displacement by a people more numerous and technologically advanced and with greater degrees of organization, discipline, and unity.[107]

The Middle Colonies

In the midst of England's burgeoning New World empire lay New Netherland and its capital, New Amsterdam. The Dutch West Indies Company had established the colony in 1623 along the Hudson River for trade, particularly beaver skins for hats. The

---

[106] Ibid.
[107] Ibid.

supposed 1626 "swindle" of Manhattan's 22,000 acres from the local Indians for a mere $24 worth of goods was probably not the deal of the century for the Dutch. The value accorded to Manhattan real estate and the rest of what would become New York City in the years and centuries thereafter came as a result of what was built on the land by settlers and its role as a center of international commerce – not by any kind of inherent worth in the soil itself.[108]

After a brief threat of competition from the New Sweden colony (1638-1655) formed along the nearby Delaware River, the true challenge to New Netherland appeared in the form of the English. With Virginia to the south and New England to the north, King Charles II was determined to rid himself of the Dutch intrusion. Consequently, he promised the territory to his younger brother, James, Duke of York (the future King James II), if he could conquer it. Accordingly, in 1664 the English successfully wrested control of New Netherland, renaming it New York. By the early 1700s, the English had also added the colonies of Pennsylvania, New Jersey, and Delaware, thereby securing nearly complete control of the Atlantic coastline of the future United States of America.[109]

The colonies of Pennsylvania, New Jersey, and Delaware all met in the Delaware Valley. Beginning with the establishment of Pennsylvania in 1682, this region became the prime place of settlement for the English religious dissenters known as the Quakers. Although they referred to themselves as the Religious Society of Friends or just "the Friends," they had earned the appellation "Quakers" because they were known to quake when religiously inspired. Amongst their controversial beliefs was the notion that everyone possessed an "inner light" which allowed them to speak to God directly, thus rendering unnecessary the Bible, churches, or ministers. They also rejected titles in favor of complete human equality under Christ. Their refusal to accept the official church as well as their radical social views made them targets of persecution in England and brought trouble in America as well.[110]

The Friends' leader in Pennsylvania was William Penn, a member of an esteemed family, who had been drawn to Quakerism at a young age. In 1681 he received a land grant from King Charles II

[108] D'Souza.
[109] Woodworth, 25-37.
[110] Ibid.

in payment for a debt owed to his father. The following year he established his "Holy Experiment" – a haven for the Quakers in America where he could test his theories about government. Naming it Pennsylvania ("Penn's Woods") after his father, he also personally planned out the city of Philadelphia (Greek for "city of brotherly love") between the Delaware and Schuylkill Rivers.[111]

As with other colonies founded with an expressed religious purpose in mind, Penn and the Quakers were sincere and genuinely sought to live out their faith in a meaningful way. While at the time of Pennsylvania's founding there were only about 2,000 Europeans living along the Delaware River (and not too many more Indians), Penn wanted to build a society where all people, of all faiths, could live in peace. He made a *Great Treaty of Friendship* with the Lenni Lenape or Delaware Indians upon his arrival in 1682 and over the following two years paid about 1,000 pounds for lands in Philadelphia, Chester, and Bucks Counties. This was in spite of the fact that the Delaware Indians had no conception of private land ownership and may have thought they were simply acknowledging the right of the Quakers to share the land.[112]

Quaker policies helped to contribute both to seventy years of peace with the Delaware Indians and the long-term survival of Pennsylvania.[113] The Friends encouraged open immigration, offered generous land grants, and promoted religious toleration.[114] They also expressed disapproval of slavery and continued to seek peaceful relations with the Indians.[115] Rather than seeing them as a threat, the Quakers bestowed gifts and made treaties with the tribes that they encountered.[116] They even resisted the establishment of a militia or defensive fortifications out of a belief that peaceful relations would preclude the need for either.[117] The Friends also consistently sought

[111] Ibid.

[112] Mary Maples Dunn and Richard S. Dunn, "The Founding, 1681-1701," in *Philadelphia: A 300-Year History*, ed. Russell F. Weigley (New York: W.W. Norton & Company, 1982), 1-32.

[113] Margaret H. Bacon, *The Quiet Rebels: The Story of the Quakers in America* (New York: Basic Books, Inc., 1969), 46-48.

[114] Woodworth.

[115] Ibid.

[116] Sowell, *Conquests and Cultures.*

[117] Gary B. Nash, *Quakers and Politics: Pennsylvania, 1681-1726* (Princeton, New Jersey: Princeton University Press, 1968), 82-83.

to purchase land, with Penn himself known to sometimes pay twice for the same piece of real estate if the Indians could not agree amongst themselves as to the rightful owner.[118] The right to trial by jury, with jurors comprised of both settlers and Indians, as well as the opportunity to submit grievances to arbitration were among other examples of the Quakers' benign treatment of Indians.[119]

Penn's Treaty with the Indians (1771-1772) by Benjamin West. Oil on canvas. State Museum of Pennsylvania. Wikimedia Commons. Public domain.

However, there was a wide variety of experiences in settler-Indian relations in Pennsylvania – probably more so than in any other American colony.[120] Although Quakers of English and Welsh extraction dominated the northern counties, their friendly Indian policies caused conflict with Pennsylvanians in the southern counties, where Swedes and former Marylanders were the majority.[121] The Quakers maintained an almost pacifistic stance, while the southern county residents wanted both river forts and armed citizens to

---

[118] Bacon, 58-59.
[119] Ibid., 46-48.
[120] Sowell, *Conquests and Cultures.*
[121] Nash.

protect against pirates and French raiders.[122] Likewise, neighboring colonies Delaware, New Jersey, and New York all desired some means of common defense against French and Indian attacks.[123]

The Quakers also faced opposition from Scots-Irish settlers along Pennsylvania's western frontier who resented what they viewed as soft Indian policies.[124] Originating from the border region of lowland Scotland and northern England, these Scottish Presbyterians were dispatched by the English to colonize Catholic Ireland in the 1600s.[125] High rents and other economic maladies later drove them from Ulster in northern Ireland to the backwoods of colonial America in the 1700s.[126] Bringing their democratic style of church government and a reputation as fierce fighters, they typically settled along the frontier where land was still available.[127] This often placed them in the Allegheny foothill region, part of the larger Appalachian Mountain range stretching from New York in the north to Georgia in the south. Here fighting was both frequent and fierce, and the Scots-Irish proved to be worthy adversaries as some of the first Indian fighters.[128] A naturally rebellious people had settled in a wild frontier region representing the point of the spear in a clash of cultures.

One case where the Quakers did not live up to their ideals regarding the treatment of Indians was the "Walking Purchase," but even in this instance the story is complicated. In 1686 Penn had reached an agreement with Indians in Bucks County to purchase land as far as a man could walk in a day and a half – a distance understood to equal about thirty miles. In 1737, about twenty years after William Penn's death, his son Thomas conspired and contrived to stretch a walk for sixty miles through various means of subterfuge. However, the Minisink Indians refused to sell, and the state legislature, under Quaker control, refused to release the funds for the purchase.[129]

Nevertheless, the Quaker policy of peace towards the Indians eventually came to an end as new settlers began to dominate the

[122] Ibid.
[123] Ibid., 134-135.
[124] Bacon, 69.
[125] Woodworth, 38-46.
[126] Ibid.
[127] Ibid.
[128] Gordon Morris Bakken, History 393 lecture notes, California State University, Fullerton, spring 1992.
[129] Bacon, 65-66.

colony. In 1742 an anti-Quaker faction conspired with the powerful Iroquois Confederacy to coerce the vassal Minisink and other Delaware Indians into selling their land. Eventually the anti-Quakers, including some of Penn's sons, acquired a stranglehold on the government. In 1754 they purchased most of the rest of the land in western Pennsylvania from the Iroquois. Ultimately the change in government policy helped drive many of the Indians towards the French and end decades of peaceful Indian-settler relations in Pennsylvania.[130]

The Iroquois Confederation was one of the most dominant Indian presences in the region. Comprised of first five and then six Algonquin-speaking tribes (Mohawks, Senecas, Cayugas, Oneidas, Onondagas, and Tuscaroras), they were primarily located in New York, Canada, and northern Pennsylvania. As with other Indian populations, they were relatively small in number, perhaps totaling merely 16,000 individuals in the late 1600s.[131]

The need to create such a confederation is further evidence of the insecurity present in the state of nature which existed in pre-settlement and colonial America. Formed in about 1570, the Iroquois Confederation was intended specifically to end the constant warfare amongst its member tribes as well as provide security from outsiders. Whereas other political arrangements – such as those of the Aztecs and Incas for example – featured autocratic rule, the confederation required agreement from member tribes to initiate actions. Despite membership, individual tribes could engage in war with outsiders and occasionally did so amongst each other as well.[132]

Some have argued that the Iroquois Confederation and its constitution were the inspiration for the US *Constitution* of 1787. This probably stems from a comment made by Benjamin Franklin while he was attempting to forge a mutual defense pact among the thirteen English colonies during the French and Indian War of 1754-1763. In crafting and promoting his Albany Plan of Union, Franklin noted that if the Iroquois could create such an alliance, then the English colonists ought to be able to do so as well. However, the Iroquois constitution was unwritten, and so its laws and regulations were

---

[130] Ibid.
[131] Sowell, *Conquests and Cultures*; Taylor, 226.
[132] Taylor, 229; Sowell, *Conquests and Cultures*.

passed down orally,[133] probably making it largely inaccessible to the English. Furthermore, the US *Constitution* is rightly seen as a product of both Christian covenantal theology and Enlightenment social contract theory, whereby a community forms a compact amongst its members and with its leaders, being accountable to one another and, in the case of a covenant, to God.

The Iroquois lifestyle did not lend itself to long-term settlement, large-scale agriculture, or lasting economic development. They possessed no writing system with which to keep records, no wheels for transport, and no large draft animals needed to farm anything beyond the "three sisters" of maize, squash, and beans. Without manure for fertilizer, the soil quickly became depleted of minerals, requiring the Iroquois to relocate regularly every few years.[134]

Hunting was primarily for obtaining deerskins for clothing. Consequently, a large amount of land was required to ensure access to enough deer to clothe a small number of individuals. The Mohawks, for example, numbered only about 8,000, but controlled a hunting territory with approximately 75,000 deer. Perhaps 25,000 could be killed annually without endangering the species.[135]

When it came to brutality in warfare, the Iroquois were second to none. The capture of an enemy warrior was the ultimate prize. Males were taken back to the village to be humiliated and tortured in ritualistic fashion – sometimes for days. This could be followed by enslavement, death, and even cannibalism. However, adoption into the tribe could instead be a captive's fate, especially to replace a fallen member. Meanwhile, captured women and children could either be killed on the spot or blended into the conquering tribe. Such treatment of other tribes was later extended to European missionaries, settlers, and soldiers.[136]

For example, in the early 1640s French Jesuit Isaac Jogues was leading his companions on a journey up the St. Lawrence River to re-supply a mission serving the Huron Indians. Historian Francis Parkman in *The Jesuits in North America in the Seventeenth Century* described the scene after the missionary fleet of twelve canoes was ambushed by the Iroquois, its passengers brutally beaten, and the

---

[133] Taylor, 229.
[134] Sowell, *Conquests and Cultures.*
[135] Ibid.
[136] Ibid.

captives forced to march to a Mohawk town:

> They [the Mohawks] ranged themselves in a double
> line, reaching upward to the entrance of the town;
> and through this 'narrow road of paradise,' As Jogues
> calls it, the captives were led in single file, Couture in
> front, after him a half-score of Hurons, then Goupil,
> then the remaining Hurons, and at last Jogues. As
> they passed, they were saluted with yells, screeches,
> and a tempest of blows. One, heavier than the others,
> knocked Jogues's breath from his body, and stretched
> him on the ground; but it was death to lie there, and,
> regaining his feet, he staggered on with the rest.

Parkman added that Jogues and Goupil later each had a thumb cut off. A clam shell was used to heighten the pain. At night, the captives were placed in a house and forced to lie on their backs with their limbs stretched out on the ground and their wrists and ankles secured to stakes. Children then placed hot coals and ashes on their naked bodies. Several of the Hurons were burned to death as well. Such treatment continued for days as the captives were marched to various Mohawk towns for continuing mockery, humiliation, and torture. Couture was eventually adopted into a family, but both Jogues and Goupil were killed by the Mohawks.[137]

In *La Salle and the Discovery of the Great West*, Parkman chronicled the experiences of a party of French explorers in the late 1670s. Once while staying with the Senecas in western New York, the Frenchmen witnessed the shocking treatment of an enemy captive who was tied to a stake, tortured for six hours, and ultimately cut up and eaten. On another occasion near Niagara, they witnessed an Indian prisoner being burned, apparently as entertainment for forty-two Seneca chiefs. As the explorers continued on to Illinois, they came upon the aftermath of an Iroquois battle:

> As they drew near the mouth of the stream, they saw
> a meadow on their right, and, on its farthest verge,

---

[137] Francis Parkman, "The Jesuits in North America in the Seventeenth Century," in *France and England In North America, vol. I*, ed. David Levin (New York: Literary Classics of the United States, Inc., 1983), 550-557; 611.

several human figures, erect, yet motionless. They landed, and cautiously examined the place. The long grass was trampled down, and all around were strewn the relics of the hideous orgies which formed the ordinary sequel of an Iroquois victory. The figures they had seen were the half-consumed bodies of women, still bound to the stakes where they had been tortured. Other sights there were, too revolting for record. All the remains were those of women and children. The men, it seemed, had fled, and left them to their fate.[138]

Parkman characterized the Iroquois as "incorrigible warriors" who "pushed their murderous raids to Hudson's Bay, Lake Superior, the Mississippi, and the Tennessee." They were "the tyrants of all the intervening wilderness."[139]

The French and Indian War (1754-1763) and Pontiac's Rebellion (1763)

As opportunities developed to trade for European manufactured goods, many Indian tribes increased their deer, beaver, and bison hunting. Meanwhile, European settlers continued to serve essentially as middlemen, trading European goods for Indian skins and pelts. Many tribes gladly replaced deerskins with comfortable woven clothing and exchanged earthenware pots for copper bowls and cups. They also adopted iron and steel tools, utensils, and arrowheads.[140]

In addition to trade, many tribes sought alliances with various European nations for the advantages that these could provide over their Indian rivals. For example, when the Iroquois traded fur for firearms, it enabled them to overwhelm opposing tribes, drive them out, and take their territory. Such alliances often were the deciding factor in tipping tribal balance-of-power relations one way or the other. Nevertheless, many Indians viewed these agreements as transitory, permitting them to play the Europeans against one

---

[138] Francis Parkman, "La Salle and the Discovery of the Great West," in *France and England In North America, vol. I*, ed. David Levin (New York: Literary Classics of the United States, Inc., 1983), 736-737; 814-815, 863.

[139] Parkman, "The Jesuits in North America in the Seventeenth Century," 710.

[140] Sowell. *Conquests and Cultures.*

another as necessary. In fact, it is not an exaggeration to suggest that as long as the English and French were battling each other for control of North America, many tribes were able to thrive amidst the competition taking place around them.[141]

This would change, however, with the French and Indian War (1754-1763), which brought the nearly 75-year Anglo-French struggle for control of North America to an end. The last of four major conflicts between England and France dating back to 1689, the contest was known as the Seven Years War (1756-1763) in Europe, but had started a couple of years earlier in America. The area of immediate competition was the Ohio River Valley and western Pennsylvania, but with the concluding *Treaty of Paris* (1763), virtually the entire French Empire in North America was wiped off the map. Besides Canada, the victorious English also secured control of America all the way to the Mississippi River.[142]

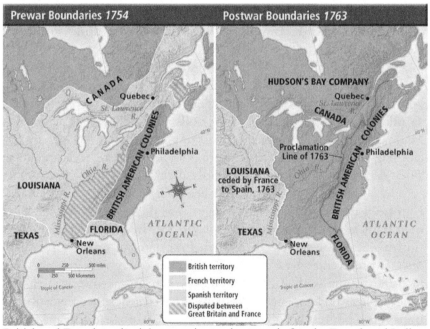

British and French territorial possessions prior to and after the French and Indian War (1754-1763). http://creativecommons.org/licenses/by-sa/3.0/

---

[141] Ibid.
[142] Woodworth, 39-41, 44-46.

For years the French had actively courted many Indian tribes, including even Quaker friends such as the Delaware, as allies against both the English army and American colonists. Indians serving the French terrorized soldiers and settlers along the western frontier of America for decades, including perpetrating a massacre at Fort William Henry in what is now upstate New York. It was there in August, 1757, after the English had surrendered, that France's Indian allies murdered the wounded and attacked a column of prisoners being escorted away from the camp. Angered at the lack of rum and other war booty which they had been promised by the French, the Indians descended on the prisoners, robbing and tomahawking the officers and men, while seizing or murdering the women and children. Abenaki Indians then proceeded to kill or abduct about eighty New Hampshire men who formed the rear of the column.[143]

However, after the French and Indian War many tribes were left without their French patrons, leaving them enraged. This new political dynamic led to a pan-Indian effort to eliminate the English from America. The plan was to attack all frontier forts on the same day. The settlers would be left defenseless so that "the English should all be driven into the sea."[144]

Commencing in the spring of 1763, Pontiac, Chief of the Ottawa, led a coalition of tribes to war in the Ohio River Valley and Great Lakes region.[145] A former ally of the French, Pontiac later sought to engage the English when it appeared that they had gotten the upper hand.[146] Indeed, the mass of Indians involved in the rebellion included not only former allies of the recently defeated French, but also Britain's ex-partners who resented no longer receiving the gifts which had been part of a now unneeded alliance.[147]

---

[143] Francis Parkman, "The Conspiracy of Pontiac and the Indian War after the Conquest of Canada," in *The Oregon Trail/The Conspiracy of Pontiac*, ed. William R. Taylor (New York: Literary Classics of the United States, Inc., 1991), 475-488; Francis Parkman, "Montcalm and Wolfe," in *France and England In North America, vol. II*, ed. David Levin (New York: Literary Classics of the United States, Inc., 1983), 1166-1194.

[144] Francis Parkman, "The Conspiracy of Pontiac and the Indian War after the Conquest of Canada."

[145] Woodworth, 47-61.

[146] Parkman, "The Conspiracy of Pontiac and the Indian War after the Conquest of Canada."

[147] Medved; Robert J. Allison, "Pontiac's Revolt Against the British," *Before 1776: Life in the American Colonies* (Chantilly, Virginia: The Teaching Company/The Great

These included virtually all of the Algonquins, the Wyandots, the Senecas (the only nation of the Iroquois Confederacy to join), and various tribes from the lower Mississippi River region.[148] However, the entire Indian fighting population of the area above the Ohio River to the Great Lakes was perhaps only 10,000 at the time.[149]

On May 1, Pontiac reportedly stated, "'It is important for us, my brothers, that we exterminate from our lands this nation which seeks only to destroy us.'" Over the following several months Pontiac's warriors engaged in bloody, murderous attacks against British forts and settlements along the frontier. Eventually eight forts were destroyed and hundreds of the English were murdered, with civilians, including women and children, among the butchered dead. Fates endured by victims included torture, scalping, burning at the stake, dismemberment, and even cannibalization.[150]

The savagery with which the English Army had to contend is illustrated by the fate of a detachment under Lieutenant Cuyler. Leaving Fort Niagara on May 13th, 1763, Cuyler and his men were en route to resupply the garrison at Fort Detroit. While moving up the northern shore of Lake Erie, they decided to land and set up camp on the 28th. While onshore, they were suddenly attacked by Wyandot Indians emerging from the forest. Hurriedly pouring back into their boats, the English attempted to escape. Three of the vessels were captured. After being forced to strip naked, the men were beaten, shot through with arrows, cut up, cooked, and eaten. Other victims had their hands and feet cut off and bled to death. About sixty of Cuyler's ninety-six men were captured, tortured, and killed. A few who survived were made slaves.[151]

It was in the context of this brutal life and death struggle that one of the most pernicious and evil lies about America was born – the charge that Indians were given blankets infected with smallpox as a form of primitive biological warfare. Besides being highly improbable, the allegation defies reason. Why would anyone want or

---

Courses, 2009), CD.

[148] Parkman, "The Conspiracy of Pontiac and the Indian War after the Conquest of Canada."

[149] Ibid., 459.

[150] Medved; Allison.

[151] Parkman, "The Conspiracy of Pontiac and the Indian War after the Conquest of Canada," 539-557.

need to handle blankets with a potentially deadly disease and then proceed to distribute them to a people who had already been decimated by that very illness through natural transmission?

Furthermore, the only significant evidence for the smallpox charge is a series of letters between the high commander of the British military in America, Lord Jeffrey Amherst, and his subordinate, Colonel Henry Bouquet of Philadelphia. On June 22, 1763, Indians began a siege of Fort Pitt, which was then providing refuge to about 550 farmers and townspeople, including over 200 women and children. In correspondence written over the following several weeks, Amherst and Bouquet discussed how to rescue the fort, which was probably the most important British military garrison on the frontier. Several of the letters included postscripts mentioning whether the distribution of infected blankets to the enemy might be employed as a desperate means of ending the siege. In his letters, Amherst described the need to "extirpate" the Indians, particularly when expressing outrage and utter disgust at some of their tactics including scalping live victims, branding, piercing bodies with dozens of arrows, and even cutting out and eating hearts.[152]

It was not just the English army which was under assault. American settlers along the frontier were also threatened by the ongoing conspiracy of Pontiac. In western Pennsylvania, whenever an alarm sounded signaling that an attack was imminent, families would desert their farms and flee to the nearest frontier fort for protection until the danger had passed. When Bouquet reached Fort Carlisle in late June on his way to Fort Pitt, he found that every building was filled with families seeking protection from Pontiac's men. On July 13, 1763, he wrote to Amherst:

'The desolation of so many families, reduced to the last extremity of want and misery; the despair of those who have lost their parents, relations, and friends, with the cries of distracted women and children, who fill the streets, -form a scene painful to humanity, and impossible to describe.'[153]

---

[152] Medved.
[153] Parkman, "The Conspiracy of Pontiac and the Indian War after the Conquest of Canada," 640-658.

However, settlers who had been unable to take refuge in one of the frontier forts were even less fortunate. As Parkman explained:

> The people of Virginia betook themselves to their forts for refuge. Those of Pennsylvania, ill supplied with such asylums, fled by thousands, and crowded in upon the older settlements. The ranging parties who visited the scene of devastation beheld, among ruined farms and plantations, sights of unspeakable horror; and discovered, in the depths of the forest, the half-consumed bodies of men and women, still bound fast to the trees, where they had perished in the fiery torture.[154]

Thus, it was only the relentless ferocity of Pontiac's Rebellion and the desperation of the English Army to protect soldiers and civilians on the frontier that led to the draconian proposal to use smallpox-infected blankets on the Indians – not some kind of casual racist or genocidal impulse.

Most importantly, there is no proof that Amherst ever actually ordered such an action or that Bouquet ever attempted it. Bouquet did, however, defeat the Indians besieging Fort Pitt by leading 500 men to victory at the Battle of Bushy Run on August 20. David Dixon, the author of a history of Pontiac's Rebellion entitled *Never Come to Peace Again*, concluded that smallpox-infected blankets were not one of the means by which Indians contracted the disease.[155]

Nevertheless, just prior to the Amherst-Bouquet correspondence, a couple of traders at Fort Pitt reportedly did pass along blankets and a handkerchief from the fort hospital. Nevertheless, this did not lead to an outbreak amongst the attacking Indians, who continued to besiege the fort for another six weeks. In fact, Elizabeth Feen, author of *Pox Americana: The Great Smallpox Epidemic of 1775-82*, answered "no" when asked whether there was any evidence that germ warfare had been a major cause of Indian casualties and deaths.[156]

Finally, it is important to remember that this entire episode took

---

[154] Ibid., 677-694.
[155] Medved.
[156] Ibid.

place while the American colonies were still under the sovereignty of the British Empire. It would be another thirteen years before the *Declaration of Independence* gave birth to the United States of America.

As was so often the case in human history, violence led to more violence. A group of Scots-Irish on the Pennsylvania frontier known as the Paxton Boys, seeking revenge, attacked a Christian Indian village. When the survivors fled to Lancaster, the sheriff attempted to ensure their safety, but they were nonetheless killed. Moving on to attack the Moravian Indians in Philadelphia, the Paxton Boys were not stopped until a militia led by Benjamin Franklin brought the madness to an end.[157]

Pontiac's Rebellion helped to initiate a long series of British policies that would ultimately culminate in the American Revolution. In October of 1763, newly installed Prime Minister George Grenville ordered that no colonists were to settle beyond the Appalachian Mountains into the Ohio Valley. This was intended not only to avoid further provoking Indians on the frontier, but also as a means of saving on the costs of administering an expanded empire after victory in the French and Indian War. The anti-American Grenville also desired to keep the colonists under his control, which left many feeling betrayed after they had contributed to the French defeat. Furthermore, Grenville felt compelled to address Britain's enormous national debt incurred from the recent war. Subsequent measures to raise revenue by taxing the colonists would be among the immediate causes of the American War for Independence (1775-1783).[158]

Although relations were by no means always peaceful, in general the settlers in the Southern, Northern, and Middle colonies did not simply view Indians as objects to be exploited and disposed of. This was demonstrated in legal codes, treaties, and court records. It was also shown through sincere efforts at spreading the Christian gospel of love for one's neighbor and with a degree of religious toleration virtually unknown in Europe.

Indeed, the historical record shows that the clash of civilizations which took place when Europeans arrived in the New World was no worse, and in many cases markedly better, than similar collisions throughout world history. For example, it is estimated that the

---

[157] Allison.

[158] David Van Deventer, History 471 lecture notes, California State University Fullerton, fall 1994.

Muslim conquest of India resulted in the brutal slaughter of tens of millions of Hindus over the course of about 500 years. However, in the European conquest of the Western Hemisphere, people unknowingly carried diseases to which the Indians had no resistance, while the settlement of the American colonies led to the ultimate displacement of the tribes of the Eastern Woodlands through immigration and war.

Neither of these is without historical precedent and neither has anything to do with race or ethnicity. Numerous outbreaks of diseases and pandemics spurred by the movement of people and goods have occurred throughout world history. Likewise, massive displacements of populations due to migration occurred in the Middle Ages when central Asian nomadic tribes, including the dreaded Huns, reached the periphery of the Roman Empire. This resulted in subsequent waves of Germanic and Slavic migrations, helping to collapse the empire in 476 A.D. and transforming Europe forever.[159]

A similar process took place in Britain, where Germanic Angles, Saxons, and Jutes arrived from continental Europe between 450-600 A.D. after Rome had withdrawn its legions. Romanized Celts were then pushed to the island's western region, now known as Wales. Similarly, beginning in the 1100s Anglo-Norman settlement in Ireland pushed the native Irish into the rural west, "beyond the pale."

America was neither stolen from nor did Americans commit genocide against the Indians. The transformation of the North American continent resulted from new diseases, a numerically dominant new culture, more advanced technology, alcohol and alcoholism, railroads, and the almost complete decimation of the bison.[160] It was a complex process that cannot be boiled down to a single cause or interpreted exclusively through an ideological lens which views everything as a power struggle between races, classes, and genders.

---

[159] Sowell, *Conquests and Cultures*.
[160] Ibid.; Thomas A. Bailey and David M. Kennedy, *The American Pageant*, vol. 2, *Since 1877,* tenth ed., (Lexington, Massachusetts: D.C. Heath and Co., 1994), 597-614.

2 OF HUMAN BONDAGE

"He who kidnaps a man and sells him, or if he is found in his hand,
shall surely be put to death."[1]
– Exodus 21:16 (NKJV)

"There is neither Jew nor Greek, there is neither slave nor free, there
is neither male nor female; for you are all one in Christ Jesus."[2]
–Galatians 3:28 (NKJV)

No race, ethnic group, culture, nation, or civilization in world history has been exempted from the chains of human bondage. One needs only to look to the Holy Bible for proof of slavery's existence since ancient times. Slavery is a violation of both divine law and natural law, which is the basis of the natural rights philosophy of the American founding. This philosophy asserts that all are endowed by their Creator with rights to life, liberty, and the pursuit of happiness simply by virtue of their nature as human beings. Furthermore, these rights are inalienable, meaning that they are nether granted nor revokable by any government, ruler, or law.

Although slavery's immorality is obvious today, it was only relatively recently in world history that some began to question it. Beginning in the Western world in the 1600s and 1700s, particularly the English-speaking part of it, Christian dissenters challenged the

---

[1] Exodus 21:16 (NKJV).
[2] Galatians 3:28 (NKJV).

authority of established churches and governments, as well as the morality of certain practices and traditions.[3] Unlike Islamic law, the Judeo-Christian scriptures of the Bible expressly prohibited what might be termed "man-stealing" for the purpose of enslavement.[4] Any apparent endorsement of other forms of slavery in the Bible could always be countered by the fact that Jesus did not own slaves.[5] However, Muhammad did, and this undoubtedly would have made it difficult if not impossible for human bondage to be condemned on the grounds of Muslim theology.[6] Meanwhile, increasing literacy and the invention of the printing press permitted the free flow of ideas, including opposition to slavery, in books and pamphlets across Europe and North America.[7] No leading moralists outside of the Western world spoke against slavery prior to this era.[8]

Americans also contended with slavery. Opposition came first from Christian religious dissenters like the Quakers and the Puritans. Religiously-based opposition to slavery later combined with colonial resistance to British policies in the 1760s and 1770s (which many Americans likened to slavery) to create a founding ideology that not only led to the birth of the United States, but would ultimately put slavery on the path to extinction.

Slavery Around the World

Slavery arose as human beings transitioned from living as nomadic hunters and gatherers or in primitive tribes into more advanced societies including chiefdoms and states. For most of human history, securing enough food was a more or less individual responsibility. However, the development of large-scale agriculture about 10,000 years ago permitted some people to remain in one location and produce a sufficient food supply to feed a growing

---

[3] Larry Elder, "Slavery: What They Didn't Teach in My High School," Townhall.com, 12 July 2018; Thomas Sowell, "The Real History of Slavery," in *Black Rednecks and White Liberals* (San Francisco: Encounter Books, 2005), 111-169.

[4] Dennis Prager, *The Rational Bible: Exodus – God, Slavery and Freedom*, ed. Joseph Telushkin (Washington, D.C.: Regnery Faith, 2018), 279-310.

[5] Rodney Stark, *The Victory of Reason – How Christianity Led to Freedom, Capitalism, and Western Success* (New York: Random House, 2005), 26-32.

[6] Ibid.

[7] Hugh Thomas, *The Slave Trade – The Story of the Atlantic Slave Trade: 1440-1870* (New York: Simon & Schuster Paperbacks, 1997), 791-798.

[8] Sowell, "The Real History of Slavery."

population. This in turn permitted the division of labor into those possessing specialized skills and others who occupied themselves with more laborious tasks.[9]

This "agricultural revolution" had other effects as well. These included harnessing the power of large animals known as "beasts of burden" such as cattle and horses to assist with farming and the domestication of sheep, goats, pigs, and chickens as a source of food. Around the same time some societies realized that they could use war captives to perform some of the more tedious, arduous, and lowly tasks of daily life as well.[10]

Any individual or group that was vulnerable to invasion, conquest, and kidnapping could become enslaved. Therefore, it was not race that mattered but whether or not people could protect themselves from outsiders. Slavery declined in modern times in part because of the development of large, organized nation-states that could defend their citizens. However, people living in regions that were not under the sovereignty of a strong government remained vulnerable. Thus, capture by conquest is as old as humanity itself but was only outlawed by the Revised Geneva Convention in 1954.[11]

Slavery was common in the ancient world. Whether it came as a result of capture in war, punishment for a crime, or as a means of repaying a debt, the existence of a servile class was an accepted part of ancient societies. Nearly 3,000 years before Christ, ancient Egyptians began enslaving fellow Africans to the south and slavery remained a part of their civilization thereafter. Mesopotamian city-states such as Ur and later powerful empires like those of the Akkadians and Assyrians claimed human beings as part of the fruits of victory over their enemies. Sargon of Akkad had thousands of slaves circa 2300 B.C., and the first written body of laws in world history, the Babylonian Code of Hammurabi (c. 1750 B.C.), included laws regarding slaves as property.[12]

---

[9] Jared Diamond, *Guns, Germs, and Steel: The Fates of Human Societies* (New York: W.W. Norton & Co., 1999), 265-273.

[10] Michael Medved, *The 10 Big Lies About America: Combating Destructive Distortions About Our Nation* (New York: Crown Forum, 2008), 46-71.

[11] Sowell, "The Real History of Slavery"; Wilfred Riley, "Why Woke History Is Not the Answer," Why Woke History Is Not the Answer - American Greatness (amgreatness.com), 7 January 2021.

[12] J.M. Roberts *The Penguin History of the World* (New York: Penguin Books, 1992), 60-61; Medved.

The great classical civilizations of Greece and Rome had slavery as well. One estimate contends that when ancient Athens reached the zenith of its development, a quarter of the population was in bondage.[13] The Greek philosopher Plato (427 B.C.-347 B.C.) believed that foreigners and other barbarians were suited only to serve as slaves in his vision of the ideal republic.[14] Another philosopher, Aristotle (384-322 B.C.), argued that without slavery, more intelligent men would not have the time to study and contemplate in order to attain wisdom and virtue.[15] Both men believed that some were by their nature slaves, and ruminated only on how to properly treat them, not whether slavery itself was right or wrong.[16] Later in Rome, a slave revolt during the last years of the republic in 73 B.C. required three years to suppress and resulted in 6,000 crucifixions.[17] Then during the first century A.D., the Roman Empire developed extensive plantations on country estates worked by slaves.[18] As Rome reached its summit of power and influence, slaves counted as anywhere from twenty-five to forty percent of the population.[19]

When the Roman Empire finally collapsed in 476 A.D., medieval Europe inherited Roman-style slavery.[20] In fact, the word "slave" derived from the Slavs, people inhabiting Eastern Europe who were regularly used as slaves during the Middle Ages, both in Europe and the Middle East.[21] Germanic tribes ruling Europe in the wake of Rome's fall had legal codes in which slaves were equated with animal property.[22] However, by the 1300s Italian merchants were selling Germans and others from central Europe as slaves to Arabs in Africa and the Levant.[23] In the medieval period, both Slavs captured from port cities on the Black Sea as well as Muslim prisoners-of-war worked Mediterranean sugar plantations on the islands of Cypress,

[13] Roberts, 170-171.
[14] Stark.
[15] Ibid.
[16] Ibid., Riley.
[17] Roberts, 245.
[18] Ibid., 247.
[19] Medved.
[20] Dinesh D'Souza, *America: Imagine a World Without Her* (Washington, D.C.: Regnery Publishing, 2014), 121-135.
[21] Sowell, "The Real History of Slavery."
[22] Stark.
[23] Roberts, 497.

Crete, and Sicily.[24] These plantations later served as models for the sugar plantations established by the Portuguese in the Western Hemisphere[25] and emulated by the Spanish, Dutch, French, and British in the Caribbean.

However, in addition to slavery, Europe also inherited Christianity from Rome. Over five hundred years from roughly 500-1000 A.D., human bondage virtually disappeared from Western Europe. The decision of the Roman Catholic Church to permit all, even slaves, to partake in the holy sacraments was probably a key event in changing attitudes towards bondage. Including everyone in the rituals surrounding Christian worship and salvation undoubtedly made it increasingly difficult to justify keeping any of God's children in a state of subjugation. Eventually the Church in Europe imposed a general ban on slavery of both Christians and Jews.[26]

Although slavery was replaced by serfdom, serfs had freedoms which slaves did not. Serfs were tied to the land on which they worked, but they owned themselves and this entitled them to such rights as making contracts and marrying. Ironically, this drastic change from slavery to serfdom took place in the supposed "Dark Ages" of Europe between the end of the Classical Era and before the "rebirth" of learning known as the Renaissance.[27]

Russia, spanning from Eastern Europe to Asia, had millions of slaves during the reign of the czars. One estimate holds that as late as 1837 up to thirty-five million of Russia's sixty million people may have been enslaved.[28]

Many nations in Asia have practiced slavery as well. At one time Imperial China was one of the largest slave markets in the world. At least as early as the Han Dynasty (220 B.C.-220 A.D.) slavery was practiced in the Far East, only being interrupted for a short interval during the Hsin Dynasty (8 A.D.-25 A.D.) under Emperor Wang Mang. When the emperor attempted to ban private slavery as part of a land collectivization program, he was murdered, and the Han

---

[24] James Oliver Horton and Lois E. Horton, *Hard Road to Freedom – The Story of African America*, vol. 1, *From African Roots Through the Civil War* (New Brunswick, New Jersey, Rutgers University Press, 2001), 6-25.

[25] Ibid.

[26] D'Souza; Stark.

[27] D'Souza.

[28] Medved.

Dynasty and slavery were restored.[29]

Also in East Asia, Korea's Yi Dynasty (established in 1392) practiced human bondage. The lowest level of society was made up of the ch'onmin ("base people"), which included both private and government slaves. In 1484 there were approximately 350,000 government slaves alone, nearly equal to the entire total of Africans who were brought to the United States from 1619-1808.[30]

As recently as World War II, Japan used slaves to mine coal. Previously, such work had been done by ethnic Japanese known as the *burakumin* – a class of people at the bottom rung of society, somewhat similar to the Dalits or "untouchables" of India's ancient caste system. However, whenever enough Japanese laborers could not be found, such as during wartime, captive Koreans and Chinese were condemned to the mines as modern-day slaves.[31]

South Asia too has had a long history with slavery. At one time the total number of slaves in India was estimated to surpass that of the entire Western Hemisphere. Additionally, the English word "thug" comes from "Thugs," organized bands of criminals who attacked, robbed, and murdered travelers as well as kidnapped children for enslavement. In Southeast Asia slaves used to make up the majority of the population in some cities.[32]

In the New World, centuries before Columbus and the arrival of Europeans, Indians enslaved other Indians. For example, the Iroquois of the Eastern Woodlands of what is today the United States often tortured and enslaved war captives. Meanwhile the Maya in modern-day Mexico occasionally used their slaves as human sacrifices.[33]

The Muslim world has engaged in slavery since the birth of Islam in the 600s. Muhammad held slaves and often enticed warriors into battle with the promise of human war booty – particularly women. In the 1300s and 1400s as the Ottoman Turks expanded into Southeastern Europe and conquered Greece and the Balkans, they

---

[29] Sowell, "The Real History of Slavery"; John K. Fairbank, Edwin O. Reischauer, and Albert M. Craig, *East Asia – Tradition and Transformation* (Boston: Houghton Mifflin Company, 1989), 75.

[30] Fairbank, Reischauer, and Craig, 308, 319.

[31] David S. Landes, *The Wealth and Poverty of Nations: Why Some Are So Rich and Some So Poor* (New York: W.W. Norton & Co., 1998), 390.

[32] Sowell, "The Real History of Slavery."

[33] Ibid.

compelled Christian families to pay a "devsirme" (child-levy or child-tax). Young boys would be taken from their families, converted to Islam, and trained to serve in the Ottoman government or military.[34]

In North Africa, Muslim and black pirates of the Barbary states enslaved anywhere from one to two million Europeans between 1500-1800, far surpassing the number of African slaves brought to America during the same time period. Sailors, mariners, and other Europeans were typically used as galley slaves. Later such impressment or kidnapping of American sailors led to the entry of the United States into the Barbary War of 1801-1805. The words "to the shores of Tripoli" (modern-day Libya) in the US Marine Corps Hymn is a reference to American rescue missions of the time. In 1865 European slaves were still being sold in Egypt after black slaves had been freed in the U.S. In fact, the Anglo-Egyptian Treaty of 1877 prohibited the import and export of Sudanese and Abyssinian black slaves but did not prohibit the sale of white slaves until 1885.[35]

The African Slave Trade in Africa

Slavery of Africans by Africans has been practiced for millennia. The enslaved were typically prisoners of war who probably would have been killed otherwise.[36] As individuals were transported further from home, their value rose since escape or rescue became less likely.[37] For example, at least as early as 2900 B.C. during the age of the pharaohs ancient Egyptians were enslaving Ethiopian blacks and transporting them north.[38] Cleopatra, the Ptolemaic (Greek) Queen of Egypt (b. 69 B.C.), reportedly tested her poisons by giving them to slaves. Later, Africans sold other Africans to Arabs and Europeans, but always kept most slaves for themselves.[39]

One of the reasons for the widespread use of slavery in sub-Saharan Africa was the tropical climate where the tsetse fly flourished. This blood-sucking insect feasted on mammals, spreading the deadly trypanosomiasis disease (also known as Sleeping Sickness), and generally making life for humans and livestock miserable if not

---

[34] Ibid.
[35] Ibid.
[36] Horton and Horton, *Hard Road to Freedom*.
[37] Ibid.
[38] Thomas.
[39] Elder; Thomas Sowell, *Conquests and Cultures – An International History* (New York: Basic Books, 1998), 99-173.

impossible. Without any other means of transport, slaves were relied upon to carry items long distances.[40]

The fact that slavery lasted for so long in the region, even into modern times, is attributable in part to the fact that sub-Saharan Africa remained one of the last places in the world to be governed by nation-states.[41] Thus, invasion, capture, and enslavement were a constant threat.

In West Africa, the kingdom of Ghana came to prominence in the 700s. Serving as middlemen, the Ghanaians regulated trade from central Africa to Europe via the Sahara, as well as from West Africa to the Arabs in the Middle East. By charging tariffs on slaves transported from the central African grasslands, Ghana prospered mightily. However, in 1076 the capital was conquered by Muslims who killed all who refused to convert to Islam. Such losses led to the kingdom's decline by the late 1100s.[42]

Arising in the 1200s, Mali became the next kingdom to dominate West Africa. Its greatest leader was Mansu Musa, a devout Muslim. In 1324 when he made the traditional Islamic pilgrimage to Mecca, he reportedly arrived with 500 slaves and thousands of servants as part of his entourage.[43]

By 1500, the kingdom of Benin emerged as a prime trading partner for Europeans exploring the West African coast. Benin typically obtained copper, coral beads, and guns in exchange for slaves who had been captured in war. The Portuguese were first, primarily interested in trading for slaves to work in southern Portugal, the West African coastal islands of Madeira, Sao Tome, and Cape Verde, and eventually in Brazil across the Atlantic. Slaves worked sugar plantations, tended animals, and functioned as various kinds of servants. In the 1700s Benin was succeeded by the Yoruba Empire of Oyo which continued providing slaves to the Portuguese.[44]

---

[40] Landes, 9.
[41] Sowell, "The Real History of Slavery."
[42] Horton and Horton, *Hard Road to Freedom*.
[43] Ibid.
[44] Ibid.

Mansu Musa (1280-1337). Attributed to Abraham Cresques - This file comes from Gallica Digital Library and is available under the digital ID btv1b55002481n. Wikimedia Commons. Public domain.

Most slaves who were brought to the Americas came from West Africa. As trade with Europeans increased and the Spanish, French, Dutch, and English joined the Portuguese, African coastal tribes gained access to goods like guns, making them both powerful and wealthy. Tribes such as the Ashanti of Ghana engaged in raids against weaker inland groups including the Igbo of Nigeria, capturing, enslaving, and transporting them to the coast to be sold at ports.[45]

The African slave trade in Africa was not limited to any one region of the continent. In general Africans did not see each other as part of a larger African or black identity. Tribal affiliations ruled over all else. Consequently, in East Africa the Masai enslaved the Kikuyu and the Kamba, while the Kamba enslaved the Ndorobo. In Ankole the Nyoro and Hima enslaved women and children of the Toro people. And in Rwanda, the Tutsis enslaved the Hutus.[46]

---

[45] Sowell, *Conquests and Cultures.*
[46] Sowell, "The Real History of Slavery."

The Islamic Slave Trade in Africa and the Middle East

Muslims have been involved in the African slave trade for almost as long as Africans. Following the death of the Islamic prophet Muhammad in 632 A.D., Arabs conquered lands to the east and the west of the Arabian Peninsula from Persia to Spain. In addition to the slaves that Arabs acquired through conquest, they also secured access to human chattel through tribute agreements with vassal states who made annual payments of human beings in return for maintaining a nominal degree of independence. Perhaps the first of these was reached in 652 A.D. when the black African kingdom of Nubia agreed to contribute hundreds of slaves annually to the burgeoning Arabic Empire.[47]

Hundreds of years before Europeans first started their exploratory journeys along the west coast of Africa, Arabs had already initiated explorations along the eastern shores. Starting from trading centers on the island of Zanzibar off the coast of Tanzania, Muslims eventually conquered significant parts of the coast and dominated the slave trade in East Africa for over a thousand years. Arab involvement in trade with East Africa led to the development of Swahili, a language of commerce based upon the Bantu African tongue with many foreign word borrowings. Both "Swahili" (Arabic for "coast") and "Zanj," (Persian for "black," i.e., a black slave) are examples. The language was originally written in the Arabic script as well.[48]

At least as early as the Abbasid Caliphate which ruled the Arabic Empire from 750-1258, Zanj slaves were used as soldiers and laborers in Iraq. Their work included clearing the salt flats in the south to prepare the ground for planting, probably sugar. In 869 A.D. they revolted and overthrew their Arab masters, ruling southern Iraq until 883.[49]

In the later Middle Ages, Arabs shipped African goods throughout the eastern world. Chief among these were ivory and slaves. From the 1100s to the 1400s, China and India were both destinations for shipments of ivory, while in India and Iraq slaves

---

[47] Bernard Lewis, *Race and Slavery in the Middle East: An Historical Inquiry* (New York: Oxford University Press, 1990), 3-15.

[48] Sowell, *Conquests and Cultures*; Elder.

[49] Dr. Jack Crabbs, History 466A lecture notes, California State University, Fullerton, fall, 1993; Lewis, 54-61.

were continually in high demand.[50]

Unlike European slave traders who purchased slaves from Africans along the west coast, Arabs journeyed far inland to capture and kidnap their own bond servants.[51] Typical routes included from Morocco and Tunisia in the North via the Sahara desert into West Africa, from Libya across the desert to Chad, from Egypt along the Nile River to Sudan and Ethiopia, and from Arabia and the Persian Gulf across the Indian Ocean and the Red Sea to East Africa.[52] The slaves' forced march north across the Sahara Desert has been likened to the "Middle Passage" when slaves were inhumanly crammed into ships as part of the Trans-Atlantic slave trade. Indeed, more slaves probably died during the forced journey through the arid Sahara than even those who perished in the holds of ships heading to the Americas.[53] Even if slaves survived the trek through the desert, they usually lasted only about five years when working in the Sahara salt mines of the Ottoman Turks.[54] Also in contrast to the Trans-Atlantic slave trade, Arabs and other Muslims took more women than men to have them serve as sex slaves in harems throughout the Middle East.[55] Meanwhile, enslaved men were often castrated in order to serve as eunuchs or attendants for those harems.[56] Such procedures often took place in desert conditions without regard to safety and hygiene, resulting in slaves being mutilated and left to bleed to death in the sand.[57]

The Muslim slave trade in Africa reached its height in the 1800s. Arabs from Oman, located at the southeastern end of the Arabian Peninsula, had engaged in slavery along the East African coast for many hundreds of years. However, by the early 1800s one estimate suggested that the entirety of the Omani government's income was derived from import taxes on slaves. Scores of captives were imported annually, with at least two thousand remaining and many others being sold along the nearby Makran coast bordering India and

[50] Ronald Segal, *Islam's Black Slaves: The Other Black Diaspora* (New York: Farrar, Straus and Giroux, 2001), 89-102.
[51] Sowell, *Conquests and Cultures.*
[52] Lewis, 3-15.
[53] Elder.
[54] Ibid.
[55] Sowell, *Conquests and Cultures.*
[56] Sowell, "The Real History of Slavery."
[57] Ibid.

Iran. An 1840 estimate put Oman's African population at one-third. Omanis transported an additional 13,000-15,000 slaves annually from the African mainland to work on clove plantations at Zanzibar.[58]

Indian bankers and merchants in East Africa provided much of the financial backing for expeditions into the African interior to obtain slaves. Typically, bankers would lend money and offer goods on credit to the slave traders. Obviously, these financiers anticipated receiving significant returns on their investments.[59]

Christian missionaries serving in Africa during the 1800s testified to witnessing caravans of slaves marched north to markets in Cairo or east to Zanzibar and other locations along the coast. Any captive unable to maintain the pace was either shot or left to starve. The slavers' paths could be tracked by following a trail of skeletons.[60]

In 1858 while exploring the Zambesi River in southeastern Africa, missionary David Livingstone observed the following:

> ...A long line of manacled men, women and children, came winding their way round the hill and into the valley, on the side of which the village stood. The black drivers, armed with muskets and bedecked with various articles of finery, marched jauntily in the front, middle, and rear of the line; some of them blowing exultant notes out of long horns.[61]

Upon seeing the missionaries, the guards fled and Livingstone and his companions attempted to free the captives:

> Knives were soon busy at work cutting the women and children loose. It was more difficult to cut the men adrift, as each had his neck in the fork of a stout stick, six or seven feet long, and kept in by an iron rod which was riveted at both ends across the throat.[62]

---

[58] Segal, 145-176.
[59] Ibid.
[60] Ibid.
[61] Anne Farrow, "Chapter Seven: The Last Slaves," Chapter Seven: The Last Slaves - Hartford Courant, 29 September 2002.
[62] Ibid.

Livingstone reported that 19,000 slaves from Nyasaland alone were transported to Zanzibar in 1860.[63]

By the 1880s, years after slavery had been abolished in the United States, Tippu Tip (Hamad bin Muhammad bin Juma bin Rajab el Murjebi) had established himself as the leading Afro-Arab slave trader in East Africa. While journeying to Lake Tanganyika, Alfred J. Swann, another missionary, witnessed Tip's ivory caravan including slaves who had travelled 1,000 miles from the Upper Congo. The captives were marched in long lines while chained to one another by the neck, some connected with forked sticks as well, while the women could be seen carrying babies on their backs. Swann noted that the victims were in a pitiful condition and bore signs of whipping:

> ...Feet and shoulders were a mass of open sores, made more painful by the swarms of flies which followed the march and lived on the flowing blood. They presented a moving picture of utter misery, ...

They still had another 250 miles to go, including a journey across Lake Tanganyika while stuffed into canoes.[64]

Egypt had previously relied mainly on white slaves from Circassia and Georgia. However, by the early 1800s this supply had begun to dry up, prompting Egyptians to focus greater attention on black slaves to the south. Captives would be marched to the Es Siout market, approximately 250 miles south of Cairo. Anywhere from 5,000-6,000 mostly female slaves arrived annually in Egypt at this time. The number rose to 10,000-12,000 per year by 1838, with men mainly used for military service and women assigned to domestic work. The journey to Egypt was often the most grueling aspect of the slave trade, with an estimated fifty slaves dying for every ten that made it to Cairo. In 1869 Egypt's ruling family had a purported two thousand slaves in its household alone, with hundreds more working on sugar plantations in Upper Egypt.[65]

---

[63] Sowell, "The Real History of Slavery."
[64] Segal; Farrow.
[65] Segal.

Tippu Tip (Hamad bin Muhammad bin Juma bin Rajab el Murjebi) (1832-1905) by Coutinho brothers. Wikimedia Commons. Public domain.

The Ottoman Turks were also heavily involved in the African slave trade. Previously they had relied primarily on white slaves from Eastern Europe, Ukraine, and other neighboring lands which they purchased from the Tatars or Mongols. However, after Russia conquered Crimea in 1783, the Caucasus from 1801-1828, and began asserting its control in Eastern Europe, the supply of white slaves to the Ottoman Empire dwindled to a trickle. This resulted in the

Ottomans turning their attention to Africa, which in the 1800s became the primary source of slaves throughout the Muslim world from Morocco to Asia. With many of the most significant Red Sea ports under Ottoman control, by the 1860s Ottoman ships transported as many at 15,000 slaves annually during the pilgrimage season when Muslims from around the world journeyed to Mecca. In 1878 London's *Anti-Slavery Reporter* estimated that 25,000 slaves per year were traded or sold in the Islamic holy cities of Mecca and Medina. Here slaves could be obtained and dispersed throughout the Muslim world as their new masters returned to their respective homelands.[66]

The Trans-Atlantic Slave Trade

In contrast to the Muslim slave trade in East Africa, the Trans-Atlantic slave trade focused primarily on West Africa, was shorter in duration, and involved fewer slaves. Lasting for about 350 years from 1525-1866, approximately 12 million human beings were shipped to the New World from trading posts in West Africa, with about 10.7 million surviving the brutal and inhuman "Middle Passage" – the hellish journey across the Atlantic in which people were packed into the holds of ships with little regard for comfort, hygiene, or even life. However, for the great majority of these slaves the final destination was not the American colonies but the sugar plantations of the Caribbean and South America. For example, Brazil alone was the recipient of about 4.86 million slaves. Meanwhile, Cuba received approximately 787,000. Both figures far surpassed the number which were ever brought to the United States.[67]

The slaves who were sent to the Western Hemisphere were sold by Africans to Europeans at slave markets along the West African coast.[68] Europeans had neither the knowledge nor the ability to travel deep into the interior of Africa to track down and capture slaves.[69] Not only had the trade long been controlled by wealthy coastal tribes, but most Europeans in Africa found that they lacked resistance to

---

[66] Lewis, 3-15, 72-77; Segal.

[67] Elder; Larry Schweikart and Michael Allen, *A Patriot's History of the United States: From Columbus's Great Discovery to the War on Terror* (New York: Sentinel, 2004), 256-261.

[68] Sowell, *Conquests and Cultures*.

[69] Ibid.

diseases like malaria and rarely survived for more than a year on the continent.[70] Instead, they established 50 forts spanning 300 miles of West African coastline from the Senegal River in the northwest to Angola in central Africa.[71]

Numerous African nations, tribes, chieftains, kings, nobles, and businessmen participated in the Trans-Atlantic slave trade, just as they had engaged in slavery within Africa and with the Muslim world for centuries before. Among the items that they received in exchange for slaves were guns, clothing, alcohol – including brandy and rum – cowrie shells, beads, and horses. Whether they were from Benin, the Congo, Dahomey, Loango, or Nigeria, very few Africans objected to selling other Africans to Europeans because their primary identity was tribal, not racial.[72]

African chiefs were elevated to kingly status due to the wealth and power generated by the slave trade. They could hire gangs or even virtual armies to raid weaker inland tribes, capture men, women, and children, and march them hundreds of miles west to the coasts. Millions of people were enslaved in this manner and millions were killed in the process. It was truly a Hobbesian nightmare of the powerful against the weak, as seemingly anyone, regardless of familial, tribal, linguistic, or political affiliation, without the ability to protect themselves could be next.[73]

Among Europeans, Portugal led the way in Africa. Even before the discovery of the Americas, black slaves were being sold in Lisbon as early as 1444.[74] In the second half of the 1400s, the Portuguese began exploring for alternate routes to the Far East to trade for Indian spices and Chinese silks. They were also searching for gold.[75] Finding little to none, they began trading for slaves, which were initially taken to Portugal or Spain.[76] Around 1481-1482, the Portuguese built one of the first forts or castles along the Gold Coast of West Africa at Elmina.[77] Intended to facilitate slave trading, the

---

[70] Sowell, "The Real History of Slavery."

[71] Horton and Horton, *Hard Road to Freedom.*

[72] Thomas, 9-15; 791-798.

[73] Ira Berlin, *Many Thousands Gone – The First Two Centuries of Slavery in North America,* (Cambridge, Massachusetts: Belknap, 1998), 95-108.

[74] Roberts, 538.

[75] Thomas, 9-15.

[76] Ibid.

[77] Horton and Horton, *Hard Road to Freedom.*

Castle Sao Jorge da Mina and the town which grew up around it became a meeting place for Europeans and Africans interested in trading a myriad of goods.[78] Elmina eventually developed into the leading Portuguese center for trade until it was taken over by the Dutch.[79] Later more of these "feitorias" or trading factories would spring up along the West African coast.[80] Portugal's King John (1502-1557) was one of the first European monarchs to permit African slaves to be sent to the Americas; however, private businessmen called "lancados" also competed against the Portuguese government for access to African rulers and the slaves which they could deliver.[81]

Slave trading centers such as Elmina were both more numerous and larger than anything comparable in the American colonies. In 1776 Charles Town, South Carolina was the largest example in the United States, but even it was smaller than Elmina in West Africa.[82]

After King John of Portugal, Spain's King Ferdinand (1452-1516) likewise approved shipping African slaves to the New World. In fact, despite the claim of "The 1619 Project" to the contrary, the first slaves to come to America did not arrive in 1619 at the English colony of Jamestown, but in 1526 when a Spanish settlement was established in what is now the southeastern United States. Nevertheless, the African captives later rebelled, and the colony had to be abandoned the next year.[83]

In 1532 the first slave ships travelled directly from Africa to the Americas. Early on, most of these ships were Spanish and headed to the West Indies. By the mid-1500s the Portuguese emerged as the prime buyers of slaves, ultimately transporting millions of human beings, mostly men, to work on sugar plantations in Brazil.[84]

Numerous other European nations followed in the footsteps of Portugal in establishing trading outposts on Africa's western shores.

---

[78] Ibid., Berlin, 17-28.
[79] Berlin.
[80] Ibid.
[81] Thomas, 791-798; Berlin.
[82] Berlin.
[83] Thomas, 791-798; Michael Guasco, "The Misguided Focus on 1619 as the Beginning of Slavery in the U.S. Damages Our Understanding of American History," The Misguided Focus on 1619 as the Beginning of Slavery in the U.S. Damages Our Understanding of American History | History | Smithsonian Magazine, 13 September 2017.
[84] Horton and Horton, *Hard Road to Freedom*.

Under Louis XIV, the French established Saint Louis. The Dutch founded Fort Nassaw and later took Elmina from Portugal in 1637. By 1682 the population of the former Portuguese-run enclave had reached 15,000-20,000.[85]

In 1672, England's King Charles II placed his younger brother James (the future King James II) in charge of the Royal African Company to oversee Great Britain's slave trade. The British went on to establish Fort Kormantsee and seize New Amsterdam from the Dutch, both in West Africa.[86]

Despite its association with the antebellum American South, the plantation system originated long before and far away during the 1100s in the eastern Mediterranean. Then and there, large gangs of laborers were first assembled by planters seeking to capitalize on the sugar trade. Other cash crops grown via similar means included coffee, hemp, rice, tobacco, and cotton.[87]

However, more than anything else it was probably the addictive sweetness of sugar that encouraged the development of plantations and the expansion of slave labor. Arabs had discovered sugar in India and introduced it to the Middle East. From there they transported it to the Mediterranean where it was grown on the islands of Cypress and Crete as well as in North Africa. Crusaders returning from the Middle East then brought sugar back to Europe where it became highly desired. As Europeans conquered Mediterranean islands, they discovered that Arab sugar had been grown by slaves, mostly East African.[88]

Over the following several centuries the organization and techniques of the sugar plantation spread across the Mediterranean Sea to Greece, Sicily, Spain, and Portugal. It then made its way onto the Atlantic islands of the Azores, Canaries, and Cape Verde, finally rounding the coast of West Africa to Sao Tome, Fernando Po, and Principe in the Gulf of Guinea. By the late 1500s the Portuguese had established plantations across the Atlantic and onto the Brazilian coast. From there the plantation system gradually spread north into the Caribbean and finally to the southern American colonies.[89]

---

[85] Berlin.
[86] Thomas, 9-15; Berlin.
[87] Berlin, 95-108.
[88] Landes, 68-72.
[89] Berlin.

Throughout the centuries of its development, plantations utilized any labor they could find without regard to race, color, or creed. In the Mediterranean whites from Southern and Eastern Europe and blacks from Africa toiled. Off the African coast blacks and deported European Jews toiled. Then in the Americas, Indians, Europeans, and Africans toiled.[90]

The American Colonies

In the context of the global history of slavery, the United States played a relatively minor role. Even if one focuses exclusively on the Trans-Atlantic slave trade, America's part must be considered with some sense of perspective. According to the Trans-Atlantic and Intra-American Slave Trade Database compiled by the Emory University Center for Digital Scholarship, the University of California at Irvine, the University of California at Santa Cruz, the Hutchins Center at Harvard University, and the National Endowment for the Humanities, 10,702,654 Africans were brought to the New World from 1525-1866. Of these, 388,747 arrived on the North American mainland – essentially what is now the United States – a mere 3.6% of the total slaves transported across the Atlantic. When the approximate total of 17,000,000 slaves abducted from sub-Saharan Africa during the thousand-year Muslim slave trade is factored in, the share of the 27.7 million slaves taken from Africa who came to the United States of America falls to less than 2%.[91]

Furthermore, it was only due to certain social, economic, and even epidemiological factors that race-based lifetime chattel slavery developed in America. There was never any plan or program by the early settlers of the American colonies, much less by the Founding Fathers of the United States of America, to create a society based upon people of one race ruling over and exploiting another.

On the contrary, virtually the entire founding generation recognized slavery as inconsistent with everything for which they had been fighting. The inherent conflict between a belief in natural rights

---

[90] Ibid.
[91] John Hinderaker, "Slavery? We Were a Footnote," https://www.powerlineblog.com/archives/2019/11/slavery-we-were-a-footnote.php?utm_source=facebook&utm_medium=sw&utm_campaign=sw&fbcl id=IwAR0MTGEL1bHDCZ2Xoaz_j5vxqlPgSdK4Lg-eswwdzd5gZcd13tJufOYBJII, 29 November 2019.

and maintaining human bondage was just too obvious to ignore. Justifications for slavery based upon race only developed *after* the American Revolution as slavery's opponents increasingly confronted slavery's supporters with the words of the *Declaration of Independence* that "all men are created equal." It was only then that slaveholders began concocting twisted theories of racial inferiority to justify the unjustifiable in order to protect their economic interests.

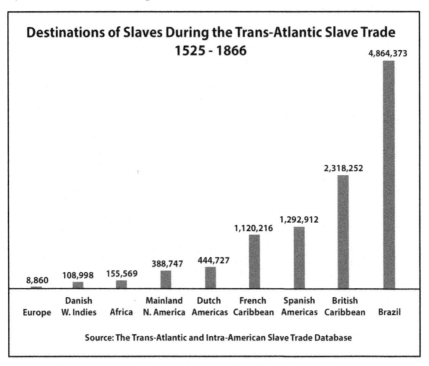

Graph by Christine Jeanbart Stackhouse

It is difficult to overstate how marginal the American colonies were as a marketplace for the Trans-Atlantic slave trade relative to the rest of the Western Hemisphere. Not only did virtually all African slaves prior to 1619 end up either in the Caribbean or South America, it was not until around 1700 that African slavery emerged as the primary form of unfree labor in the future United States.[92] Europeans desired sugar far more than any other cash crop, making it the most lucrative for planters to grow. However, growing sugar was also extremely labor-intensive. That meant workers were most

---

[92] Berlin, 17-28.

needed in the tropical middle latitudes of the West Indies where sugar crops could flourish, not in North America. For example, from 1643-1660 the black population of the island of Barbados grew from 6,000 to more than 50,000.[93] Even when Africans were brought to the American colonies in the 1600s, it was usually on ships which had travelled north from the West Indies, not directly from the African continent.[94] Not until the middle 1700s were slaves regularly transported directly from Africa to the eastern seaboard of what is now the United States.[95]

It took many years for settlers in colonial Maryland, Virginia, and South Carolina to develop reliable and exportable crops such as tobacco, rice, and indigo. Eventually small farmers were driven away as the plantation system took root in the American South. This created a hierarchical society with a few extremely wealthy plantation owners at the top. Initially, virtually all unfree labor was performed by white indentured servants who resided at the bottom of society's ranks.[96]

Any suggestion that Jamestown, Virginia, let alone the entire United States of America, was established on the basis of racism and slavery demonstrates either a complete ignorance or misunderstanding of English society in the 1600s. As textiles, woven cloth and clothing, developed into a lucrative industry in Europe, the increased demand for wool incentivized landowners in England to enclose significant portions of their property in order to focus on raising sheep. When the land ceased to be available for growing crops, tenant farmers who rented the land and itinerant peasants who worked it were evicted and left without a source of income. Having moved to cities like London, many of these recently impoverished caused overcrowding and some became sources of crime and other forms of general societal disruption. Consequently, England viewed Virginia as a place to dispense with its urban poor, and indentured servitude was designed to entice them to leave.[97]

Such individuals were often told that they would receive a

[93] Roberts, 624.
[94] Horton and Horton, *Hard Road to Freedom.*
[95] Ibid.
[96] Berlin, 64-76.
[97] Horton and Horton, *Hard Road to* Freedom, 27-51; Steven E. Woodworth, *The Essentials of United States History: 1500 to 1789 From Colony to Republic* (Piscataway, New Jersey: Research and Education Association, 1996), 11-41.

chance to start over, acquire their own land, and prosper.[98] Unable to afford the cost of a ticket to America, many signed indentures – contracts whereby the Virginia Company or a private colonist would pay the costs of a laborer's passage in exchange for a commitment to work a term usually ranging from five to seven years.[99] However, workers could be mistreated, have their term extended,[100] and find themselves unable to acquire good farmland. Approximately 300,000 men, women, and children were shipped from Great Britain and Ireland to America and the Caribbean from 1607-1776 as indentured servants,[101] not always willingly.

Contrary to the *New York Times's* "The 1619 Project," the true founding of America did not occur in 1619 when the first African slaves arrived at Jamestown, Virginia. Literally every part of that publication's central thesis is untrue. The first Africans to arrive at Jamestown in August of 1619 were not slaves because Virginia did not yet have slavery. They were not even the first Africans to reach America's shores. It was the Spanish, founders in 1526 of the short-lived colony of San Miguel de Gualdape on the coast of Georgia, who first brought African slaves to the North American mainland. It is true that twenty to thirty Africans arrived at Jamestown in 1619 aboard a Dutch ship named *The White Lion* that had been seized by English pirates. However, because slavery was not part of English common law and no slave statutes had been enacted in the colonies at that time, the captives were probably treated as indentured servants. Many of them worked alongside English and Irish laborers under John Rolfe and were eventually released. One of them may have been Anthony Johnson, who later married, started a family, purchased land, and became a slave owner himself.[102]

Maryland, founded in 1634 as a refuge for persecuted Catholics, had an early development which was similar to that of Virginia. As with its Chesapeake neighbor, tobacco soon became an important

---

[98] Horton and Horton, *Hard Road to* Freedom.

[99] Woodworth; Ibid.

[100] Woodworth.

[101] Edmund S. Morgan, *American Slavery, American Freedom* (New York: W.W. Norton & Company, 1975), 295-315; Don Jordan and Michael Walsh, *White Cargo – The Forgotten History of Britain's White Slaves in America* (New York: New York University Press, 2008), 11-19.

[102] Peter W. Wood, *1620: A Critical Response to the 1619 Project* (New York: Encounter Books, 2020), 18, 34-50.

cash crop and there was no slavery initially. Indentured servants who had volunteered were first, but later British convicts were sent to meet chronic labor shortages. Indentured servitude lasted much longer than in Virginia, and for many years blacks and whites lived, worked, and escaped alongside one another.[103]

Only in South Carolina can it be said that slavery was a major reason for the colony's founding. However, even in this case, when it began as simply "Carolina" in 1670, it was primarily to support Britain's much more lucrative sugar plantations in the West Indies. Sugar required extensive planting and intensive labor, leaving little room or time to grow much else. Consequently, Carolina was originally conceived as a place to raise food crops for West Indian plantations like Barbados. Among the other products grown in Carolina were wine, silk, olive oil, rice, and indigo.[104]

From 1640-1690 more than 250,000 slaves were brought to the Caribbean to meet labor demands. By 1700 blacks in the West Indies outnumbered whites approximately 4:1. Under these circumstances, in 1661 the white minority drafted extremely harsh slave codes to control the black majority. Smaller landholders, pushed out by the larger plantation owners, moved to the mainland while bringing their slaves and slave codes to Carolina. Initially slaves included both Indians and Africans.[105]

Rice grown by West African slaves became Carolina's main export crop. The Gambia region from which many of the slaves originated had a sub-tropical humid climate, similar to that of tidewater South Carolina, and many West Africans had grown rice for centuries back home. This enabled them to teach their white masters in America how it was done. Weather and diseases such as malaria drove many whites further inland, leaving blacks as the majority in the tidewater region. South Carolina as a whole would eventually have a slave majority outnumbering free people 2:1 and be home to the largest plantations in North America. This led both to the growth of Charles Town (Charleston) into the South's main seaport and to the imposition of South Carolina's own set of harsh slave codes (1696).[106]

---

[103] Woodworth; Horton and Horton, *Hard Road to Freedom.*
[104] Woodworth.
[105] Ibid.
[106] Woodworth; Horton and Horton, *Hard Road to Freedom.*

The northern part of Carolina was settled by small farmers fleeing Virginia's aristocratic environment. There they focused primarily on planting tobacco. In 1712 it broke away to form the colony of North Carolina. Due to its founding by smaller landholders, neither plantations nor slavery were present early on.[107]

As with Virginia, Maryland, and North Carolina, slavery was not a major part of the early founding of Georgia. Established in 1733 by the British primarily to provide a buffer against encroachment by the Spanish in Florida and the French in Louisiana, Georgia's settlement was driven by philanthropy, not slavery. In 1732 General James Oglethorpe led a group in obtaining a charter expressly for creating a refuge for debt prisoners and poor people. Methodism's founder, John Wesley, served as a missionary both to the poor and the Indians of the region.[108]

As a colony founded for philanthropic purposes and comprised mainly of small farmers, slavery was unwanted, unneeded, and even restricted. When some colonists began demanding the right to import slaves, the Georgia Trustees resisted, suggesting that a colony of loosely spread-out plantations would be difficult to administer and defend. Eventually the trustees looked the other way as slaves began to arrive. By 1750 there were approximately 350 in Georgia and within twenty years the slave population would almost equal the free population.[109]

The Chesapeake in the 1600s

In the 1600s, most unfree labor in colonial America was performed by indentured servants, white and black. Although many of the white servants had sold themselves for a period of five to seven years in exchange for passage across the Atlantic, others were abducted and sold for as long as fourteen years. Those who had been "barbadosed," kidnapped by gangs from city streets or the rural countryside, had no choice in being sentenced to a life of virtual enslavement for years. Typically they were sent to labor on sugar

---

[107] Woodworth.

[108] Ibid.

[109] Robert J. Allison, "Georgia – Dreams and Realities," *Before 1776: Life in the American Colonies* (Chantilly, Virginia: The Teaching Company/The Great Courses, 2009), CD; Woodworth.

plantations in Barbados and elsewhere in the West Indies or to work the tobacco fields of Virginia and Maryland. Most were promised freedom, but in the early years of colonial settlement about half died from malnutrition, disease, or exhaustion. Millions of white Americans are descended from those who survived.[110]

Indentured servants came from three main groups. Children could end up indentured if their parents sold them due to poverty or because they genuinely believed that their offspring would have a better life overseas. Other indentured children included lost, abandoned, or homeless urchins – even toddlers – picked up from London or other city streets. The next group included 50,000-70,000 of society's undesirables, whether they were criminals, vagrants, religious dissenters, or other societal outcasts such as prostitutes, beggars, or Quakers. The Irish were a common source of indentured servants as well. However, their terms of indenture could range from seven to as long as twenty years.[111]

More than half of all immigrants to America from 1607-1776 came as indentured servants, willingly or not.[112] Although most in this category were white, at least until 1660-1661 Africans arriving on the shores of Virginia were generally considered indentured servants as well.[113] Black servants could eventually be freed, although some were compelled to serve longer terms than their white counterparts.[114] Most served in similar roles as white laborers.[115]

Life as an indentured servant in the early Chesapeake bore many of the hallmarks of slavery: long hours at hard labor in tobacco fields, punishments, including whippings, improper attention to basic needs (food, clothing, shelter), and the potential to be bought, sold, or traded like any other farm tool, product, or animal.[116] Although they could marry, it was only with permission, and there was never any guarantee that they would not be separated from their families.[117]

---

[110] Morgan; Jordan and Walsh.
[111] Ibid.; Kathleen Brush, *Racism and anti-Racism in the World: before and after 1945* (Kathleen Brush, 2020), 55.
[112] Howard Zinn, *A People's History of the United States* (New York: Harper Perennial, 2005), 39-58.
[113] Horton and Horton, *Hard Road to Freedom.*
[114] Ibid.
[115] Woodworth, 28-37.
[116] Morgan; Jordan and Walsh.
[117] Zinn.

However, since planters primarily wanted males, there were probably few opportunities to find a mate and procreate anyway.[118]

Many indentured servants never experienced a better life in America. Perhaps only 40% ever lived long enough to serve out their contracts. They faced lives of drudgery, with little chance of ever improving their economic conditions or acquiring land. Women also experienced sexual exploitation. Some acquired "freedom dues" upon release which could include food and clothing, guns, as well as land.[119]

Race was not the dominant factor in Chesapeake society for much of the 1600s. Being poor, having a criminal background, or coming from a questionable family were greater detriments than race in determining one's social status. Furthermore, both indentured servitude and slavery developed around tobacco plantations. Indentured servants, slaves, masters, women, and even children could all be found working alongside one another in the fields. Black and white laborers were generally treated equally, and discipline was typically meted out by the courts, not by a master or overseer. Blacks and whites were commonly permitted to own some land of their own and had personal time to work and raise enough money to potentially purchase their freedom as well.[120]

Early Chesapeake society was highly class based, but also somewhat fluid. Slavery as a permanent, lifetime condition did not yet exist, and slaves could purchase their freedom and even become slaveowners themselves. Many blacks and whites, slaves and servants, free and unfree, desired to enter the slaveholding class because of the social prestige it brought.[121]

A case in point is that of Anthony Johnson. In 1621 or 1622, Johnson arrived in Virginia from Angola. Although black, he lived as an indentured servant and eventually obtained his freedom. He later became a farmer and by the 1650s was one of the first slaveowners.[122]

After sponsoring servants to Virginia, Johnson earned a 250-acre headright in 1651. As an independent farmer he was entitled to the fruits of his labor as well as the labor of his servants and slaves. One

---

[118] Woodworth.
[119] Brush.
[120] Berlin, 1-14, 29-46.
[121] Ibid., 1-14.
[122] Horton and Horton, *Hard Road to Freedom.*

of these, a black man named John Casar, declared that he was free and escaped. Johnson had been feuding with his white neighbors, Robert and George Parker. When the Parkers sheltered Casar, Johnson took them to court and won. Casar became a slave for life and Johnson was awarded damages from the Parkers.[123]

Further evidence of the limited importance of race and labor status in early Chesapeake society was the ability to access the court system. Not only could a servant or slave get a case heard against a master, but all free blacks and whites could have their property and debts recorded, marriages recognized, and children baptized. Black slaves and white servants sometimes intermarried and were known to associate with one another socially as well.[124]

Overall, in the early 1600s there were very few Africans in America. Even by mid-century, only about 100 had arrived on the North American mainland.[125] However, that total grew rapidly by the end of the century and into the next. From 1675-1695 approximately 3,000 Africans arrived in the Chesapeake, with an even larger number being imported in just the five years after that.[126] By 1700 about 1 in 3 tobacco laborers were slaves, and about 80% of all unfree laborers in the Chesapeake were black.[127]

Gradually slavery began to replace indentured servitude as the primary form of unfree labor. In 1660 Virginia passed the first law making slavery a lifetime condition. Two years later a law was passed in Virginia undoing the common law tradition that a child born to a free father and a slave mother was free. The following year in 1663 Maryland made black slavery perpetual and hereditary. The year after that Maryland began requiring a white woman who married a black slave to serve the slave's owner for as long as her husband was alive. In 1669 Virginia decided that slaveowners would not be held liable for corporal punishment of a slave that resulted in death, supposedly because it was assumed that no one would intentionally destroy their own "property." In 1700 Maryland determined that interracial marriage needed to be discouraged through the imposition of heavy penalties. Such policies illustrated what would become a common

[123] Berlin, 29-46.
[124] Ibid.
[125] Hinderaker.
[126] Berlin, 109-141.
[127] Ibid., Horton and Horton, *Hard Road to Freedom.*

occurrence: wherever reliance on slavery grew, so did the severity of the restrictions and punishments against slaves.[128]

The Carolinas in the 1600s

Societal development in the Carolinas was like that of the Chesapeake, with a few important distinctions. Northern Carolina had more small farmers, while large plantation owners dominated in the southern part of the colony. The tendency to form hierarchical and even aristocratic societies held true throughout much of the South.[129]

The Carolinas were highly dependent on various forms of unfree labor. Whether it was for growing tobacco in the northern region or raising rice and indigo crops in the southern tidewater region, indentured servants and slaves were vital to the economies of the Carolinas. In southern Carolina, initially the majority of the unfree population were European servants. By the end of the 1600s two-thirds of the overall population was still European, with Indians and small groups of slaves making up the rest. However, by the early 1700s, blacks would outnumber whites as slavery replaced indentured servitude as the primary form of unfree labor.[130]

Nevertheless, in the 1670s and 80s, the Carolinas were not yet highly segregated societies where free and unfree and white and black lived in different worlds. As in the Chesapeake, landowners worked alongside their laborers, which included black slaves, white indentured servants, Indians, and some European wage earners. Slaves in Carolina could be tasked with defending the colony from Indians to the west and the Spanish to the south. If a slave killed an invader, he could receive his freedom. The fact that slaveowners would permit slaves to be armed, something unthinkable in the next century when slaves became the majority, indicates both the genuine level of danger from outsiders which existed in the colony's early years as well as a surprising degree of trust between masters and slaves relative to later periods. Nevertheless, some slaves did escape and form colonies of maroons in the lowland swamps or in the wild backcountry.[131]

---

128 Horton and Horton, *Hard Road to Freedom.*
129 Woodworth.
130 Woodworth.; Berlin, 64-76.
131 Berlin, 64-76.

As in the Chesapeake, slaves were permitted a certain amount of free time to earn money and participate in the growing economies of the Carolinas. The fact that not until the 1680s was a law passed prohibiting trading between slaves and servants suggests that previously such interactions had been commonplace. Not until 1691 were slave codes enacted limiting slave movements, punishing whites who traded with slaves, and even prohibiting slaveowners from giving their slaves Saturday afternoons off. A 1714 law preventing slaves from having hogs, cattle, or horses had little effect but illustrates the level of slave involvement in the economy. As in the Chesapeake, these restrictive measures indicate that as the slave population grew, so did the desire of those in power to exercise greater authority and control.[132]

Bacon's Rebellion (1676)

What caused Southern planters to transition from relying primarily on indentured servants to depending on slaves for their labor needs? How did what Ira Berlin calls "societies with slaves" become "slave societies"?[133] It certainly was not part of any pre-ordained plan.

One of the reasons why slavery took years to take hold as the dominant form of unfree labor in the South was its economic impracticality. Since laborers often died after a few years, it did not make sense to pay the higher price for a lifetime worker. Slaves were much more expensive than indentured servants, black and white, and since most laborers did not last long due to the intensity of the work in the disease-ridden and swampy climate, it was wiser to make a short-term investment rather than a longer one.[134]

However, there were also problems with the system of indentured servitude. Every year, the contracts of indenture were ending for one servant or another. This led to an ever-growing population of unattached, landless men with few prospects in the aristocratic societies developing in the South. Controlling this potentially insurrectionary class was always a concern for the elite families of colonial Virginia. One technique was to arbitrarily extend a servant's term. Since this could only continue for so long, other

---

[132] Ibid.
[133] Ibid., 8.
[134] Morgan; Jordan and Walsh.

methods included making life as a freeman virtually impossible by limiting access to land and even imposing penalties for killing animals such as hogs for food. If a freeman was able to earn some kind of living, inevitably he was then subjected to a seemingly endless array of taxes, fees, and rents. This was an untenable situation causing rebellion to always be in the air. Eventually it would come and change Southern society forever.[135]

If there was one event which more than any other led to slavery replacing indentured servitude and the creation of slave-based economies in the American South, it was Bacon's Rebellion. This class-based, multi-racial uprising so shook Southern society that the planter aristocrats at the top became determined to re-establish control in a way that would make it impossible for any such catastrophe to ever occur again.

After the English Civil War and the restoration of the monarchy in 1660, King Charles II was determined to assert his authority in the colonies. Charles and his advisors began strictly regulating trade to America so as to maximize the benefits England received from its empire. Virginians were then forced to sell their crops exclusively to English merchants, limiting competition and causing prices to fall. At the same time, Virginia Governor Sir William Berkeley was enacting high taxes and implementing policies favorable to his powerful friends. Meanwhile, the elites who ran the colony and lived along the coastal region seemed either uninterested or unwilling to provide any kind of assistance for the small farmers on the frontier who typically bore the brunt of Indian attacks.[136]

Into this unstable environment stepped Nathaniel Bacon in 1674. A nobleman, yet lacking any wealth and bringing with him a questionable past, Bacon sought but failed to join Governor Berkeley's inner circle. Upon being excluded from the upper echelon of society, he began opposing the governor, thereby becoming the unofficial leader of a myriad of unhappy Virginians including impoverished freemen, indentured servants, and slaves.[137]

Bacon drew the ire of colonial officials after he led a multi-racial army of frontiersmen against the Indians. His army then turned against the colony's ruling class, leading the governor to declare them

---

[135] Ibid.
[136] Woodworth.
[137] Ibid.

outlaws. Ultimately, the rebellion was defeated after Berkeley assembled a colonial army to crush the insurrection.[138]

The largest rebellion in the American colonies prior to the revolution had consisted of a mob of small landholders, slaves, and servants and awakened Virginia's elite to the colony's underlying social instability.[139] In the closing decades of the 1600s, dramatic changes would come to Virginia, the Chesapeake region, and ultimately much of the American South.

First, the British crown attempted to increase its control of Virginia. This included sending ships, troops, and a commission to investigate what had happened. Although Governor Berkeley hanged 23 rebels, he was nevertheless deposed. London made it clear to his successors that Virginia was an English colony, and it would be administered in a way that benefitted England first and foremost.[140]

Second, Virginia's large landholders united as a class. Although Bacon's Rebellion had divided them, increased royal control compelled them to protect their common interests against government dictates. As large plantation owners solidified their dominance over life in the Chesapeake, smaller farmers were left with few alternatives but to move to the frontier.[141]

Third, around this same time economic conditions in England had started to improve due to declining birthrates, increased job opportunities, and rising wages. Consequently, fewer impoverished Englishmen were willing to sell themselves and leave home for a chance at starting a new life in America.[142]

Fourth, as colonists became acclimated to life on Virginia's swampy plantations, mortality rates fell. Thus, buying slaves became a better investment than purchasing indentured servants for merely five to seven years. Although the number of slaves imported to work on the sugar plantations of Barbados, Jamaica, and the Leeward Islands in the West Indies continued to surpass the total which came to America, because work on tobacco plantations was relatively less onerous the slave population in the Southern colonies grew [143]

---

[138] Horton and Horton, *Hard Road to Freedom*.
[139] Morgan; Berlin, 109-141.
[140] Woodworth.
[141] Woodworth; Berlin.
[142] Morgan; Horton and Horton, *Hard Road to Freedom*.
[143] Morgan.

Finally, slavery began to replace indentured servitude as the dominant form of unfree labor in the American South. Along with the growth of plantations came an increased demand for field workers. Indentured servants had proven to be long-term liabilities because once freed, they joined a growing class of unattached, landless men with few economic options and who stewed with animosity towards their former masters and society in general. Slavery as a lifetime condition then became a more viable option to address a seemingly endless need for labor.[144]

By 1700 slavery had replaced indentured servitude as the main source of unfree labor in North America.[145] For example, in Virginia, 45,000 slaves were imported between 1700-1750 and the black population increased by a factor of ten to reach 100,000.[146] Rather than being a fundamental part of colonial society since 1619, slavery only became commonplace in Virginia when planters began importing greater numbers of slaves after Bacon's Rebellion.[147] Virginia did not even have a fully developed legal code regarding slavery until 1705.[148]

This period is essential to understanding how, over time, slavery became racialized as it developed as an institution. After Bacon's Rebellion, it became imperative for the planter aristocrats to divide poor whites, blacks, and Indians so as to prevent them from uniting as a class. By consolidating their hold on land and power, Virginia's elite compelled less well-off whites to seek land on the frontier, provoking conflict with Indians. Meanwhile, the replacement of indentured servitude with race-based slavery separated poor whites from blacks.[149]

---

[144] Woodworth.

[145] Robert J. Allison, "The Atlantic Slave Trade and South Carolina," *Before 1776: Life in the American Colonies* (Chantilly, Virginia: The Teaching Company/The Great Courses, 2009), CD.

[146] Morgan

[147] Ibid.

[148] Mary Grabar, *Debunking the 1619 Project: Exposing the Plan to Divide America* (Washington, D.C.: Regnery History, 2021), 65-77.

[149] Zinn.

"The Burning of Jamestown" (1905) by Howard Pyle. Wikimedia Commons. Public domain.

Racism, therefore, became a tool utilized by Virginia's ruling elite to maintain control over the lower classes through a strategy of divide and conquer.[150] Not only were poor whites and blacks kept apart, but racism would later serve as a means of justifying the obvious contradiction between slavery on the one hand and the natural rights philosophy of the American founding on the other.[151] Racism began to formally manifest itself in laws segregating poor whites from blacks including but not limited to prohibiting interracial marriage.[152] Meanwhile, slave codes expressly designated people of African ancestry for slavery and made it both a lifetime and hereditary condition.[153] Slaves gradually came to be seen as a uniquely inferior class meriting less freedom and more control.[154]

By the mid-1700s, slavery had become firmly entrenched in the Southern colonies. In South Carolina, Virginia, and Maryland, the percentage of the population that was enslaved was respectively 61%, 46%, and 31%. Human bondage was much less prevalent outside of the South, with only New York and Rhode Island having slave populations reaching percentages in double digits.[155]

However, there were also substantial numbers of free black people in the American colonies. Free blacks were most numerous south of Maryland and Virginia, but in the Middle and New England colonies the percentage of the black population that was free was higher. Religion could be a tremendous factor in fostering anti-slavery sentiment. Thus, the Quakers of the Middle colonies and the Puritans of New England were influential in limiting the growth of slavery outside of the South.[156]

Early Colonial Anti-Slavery Efforts (1619-1763)

Almost from the very beginning, the presence of slavery in the American colonies was accompanied by forces opposed to it. Far from being societies founded on slavery, many of the American colonies attempted to restrict slavery and deny it legitimacy early on. The "Massachusetts Body of Liberties" enacted by Puritans in 1641

[150] Ibid.
[151] Sowell, "The Real History of Slavery."
[152] Horton and Horton, *Hard Road to Freedom.*
[153] Berlin.
[154] Ibid.
[155] Horton and Horton, *Hard Road to Freedom.*
[156] Ibid.

was based in part on the Bible's Mosaic code. Echoing Exodus 21:16, the tenth capital crime listed in the "Body of Liberties" stated: "If any man stealeth a man or mankinde, he shall surely be put to death." In New England this was interpreted as referring to slave trading and was later expanded to include all other aspects of slavery.[157]

A few years later in 1648 Rhode Island took steps to prevent lifetime servitude. Instead, those who were held in bondage had to be freed after ten years, as was the custom with servants in England.[158]

The Quakers were among the leading opponents of slavery throughout the colonial period. From the time that they had first settled in the Delaware Valley in the 1670s and 1680s, the Friends maintained their beliefs that all were children of God and that slavery was therefore a sin – both against the slave and against God.[159] Genuinely committed to equality, the Quakers helped to establish abolitionism in America and gradually anti-slavery thinking began to take root in the North.[160] As early as 1688, the Quakers of Germantown, Pennsylvania issued perhaps the first formal anti-slavery declaration in the history of the world:

> There is a saying, that we shall do to all men, like as we will be done our selves: making no difference of what generation, descent, or Colour they are. And those who steal or rob men, and those who buy or purchase them, are they not all alike? Here is liberty of Conscience, which is right & reasonable, here ought to be likewise liberty of ye body, except of evildoers, which is an other case. But to bring men hither, or to rob and sell them against their will, we stand against.[161]

---

[157] "The Massachusetts Body of Liberties," in *Puritan Political Ideas 1558-1794*, ed. Edmund S. Morgan (Indianapolis: Hackett Publishing Company, Inc., 2003), 177-203; Wallbuilders, "America's Exceptional History of Anti-Slavery," America's Exceptional History of Anti-Slavery - WallBuilders, 6 April 2020.

[158] Medved.

[159] Charles Kesler, Claremont McKenna College, Government 169 lecture notes, fall 2006.

[160] Schweikart and Allen, 227-228.

[161] "Resolution of Germantown Mennonites," in *American Antislavery Writings*, ed. James G. Basker (New York: Literary Classics of the United States, 2012), 1-3. (Some spelling has been modernized for clarity.)

In 1700 Boston Puritan Samuel Sewall published the first antislavery tract in New England, "The Selling of Joseph: A Memorial." As with the Quakers, Sewall based his opposition to slavery on Christian doctrines concerning equality, citing both the Old and New Testaments:

> It is most certain that all Men, as they are the Sons of Adam, are Co-heirs, and have equal Right unto Liberty, and all other outward Comforts of Life. GOD hath given the Earth [with all its Commodities] unto the Sons of Adam, Psalms 115-16. And hath of One Blood, all Nations of Men, for to dwell on all the face of the Earth; and hath determined the Times before appointed, and the bounds of their habitation: That they should seek the Lord. Forasmuch them as we are the Offspring of God...Acts 17.26, 27, 29.[162]

During the 1700s, one of the typical means employed by opponents of slavery was to pressure colonial legislatures to charge import taxes on slaves, with the intention of discouraging the slave trade by making it less profitable. In 1700 a group of Massachusetts citizens petitioned the state legislature to pass a 40-shilling duty on the import of slaves. The following year they attempted to limit the length of time anyone could be a slave to five years. In 1703 Rhode Island began charging a tax of three pounds on imported slaves. Massachusetts finally enacted a four-pound import duty on slaves in 1705. Although other colonies including New York and Pennsylvania also sought to pass laws restricting slavery, they were repeatedly thwarted by the Crown on the grounds that the slave trade was too lucrative for England.[163]

Quakers continued to trailblaze against slavery throughout the 1700s. In Pennsylvania, the Friends in the colonial legislature pushed through a law in 1700 to end the importation of slaves into the

---

[162] James G. Basker, ed., *American Antislavery Writings* (New York: Literary Classics of the United States, 2012), 9; Samuel Sewall, "The Selling of Joseph: A Memorial," in *American Antislavery Writings*, ed. James G. Basker (New York: Literary Classics of the United States, 2012), 9-14. (Some spelling has been modernized for clarity.)
[163] Wallbuilders.

colony, but it was rejected by the Crown.[164] Undaunted, in 1701 they attempted to enact a twenty-pound duty per slave, but it too was vetoed by the monarch.[165] Several decades later in 1727 the Quakers formally denounced the slave trade.[166] In 1737 Benjamin Lay, an English Quaker and immigrant to Philadelphia, condemned his slave-owning co-religionists as hypocrites fated for "the hottest place in Hell."[167] Eventually Philadelphia Quakers banned their members from owning slaves in 1758.[168] Thereafter, other Quaker groups began encouraging their members to free their slaves as well.[169] Then in 1759 another Philadelphia Quaker, Anthony Benezet, proclaimed to all who would listen that there was a great and ongoing evil in their midst:

> ...allow me, gentle Reader! to recommend to thy serious Consideration, a Practice that prevails among several Nations who call themselves Christians, and I am sorry to say it, in which we as a Nation are deeply engaged, & which is of such a Nature, as that nothing can be more inconsistent with the Doctrines and Practice of our meek Lord and Master, nor stained with a deeper Dye or Injustice, Cruelty and Oppression, I mean the SLAVE TRADE...[170]

Perhaps the most significant social development in the colonies prior to the American Revolution and which also contributed to the growth of anti-slavery sentiment was a religious revival known as "The Great Awakening." Taking place throughout America from the

---

[164] Margaret H. Bacon, *The Quiet Rebels: The Story of the Quakers in America* (New York: Basic Books, Inc., 1969), 94-121.
[165] Ibid.
[166] Robert J. Allison, "Benjamin Franklin and Slavery in America," *The Age of Benjamin Franklin* (Chantilly, Virginia: The Teaching Company/The Great Courses, 2018). CD.
[167] Basker, 23; Benjamin Lay, "All Slave-Keepers the Keep the Innocent in Bondage," in *American Antislavery Writings*, ed. James G. Basker (New York: Literary Classics of the United States, 2012), 23-24.
[168] Sowell, "The Real History of Slavery."
[169] Bacon, 76.
[170] Anthony Benezet, "Observations on the Inslaving, Importing and Purchasing of Negroes," in *American Antislavery Writings*, ed. James G. Basker (New York: Literary Classics of the United States, 2012), 28-33.

1720s-1740s, this resurgence of religious commitment and fervor not only changed the way Americans viewed their relationship with God, but promoted a spirit of democracy and egalitarianism.[171] This helped to prepare the ground for the American Revolution and change the way many Americans viewed slavery. The awakening was driven by several factors, including greater choices in churches after the arrival of recent immigrants such as German Lutherans and Scottish Presbyterians, a fear of declining spirituality, and a general desire to improve society.[172]

At the heart of the revival was the belief in the necessity and the pure joy of experiencing a true conversion experience. This encouraged an emotional style of preaching and worship, disdain for the formality and rigid hierarchical structures of the older, traditional churches, and the idea that all, white and black, had the ability to commune with God individually.[173]

One of the leading preachers of the Great Awakening was Massachusetts minister Jonathan Edwards. In numerous writings, Edwards described how the revival had resulted in many conversions, both in his Northampton congregation as well as in the surrounding communities. His 1736 essay "A Faithful Narrative of the Surprising Work of God," specified that the newly saved had come from the ranks of the young and old, black and white. Such clear evidence of God's saving grace being available to all undoubtedly contributed to a greater awareness of the inherent equality of all of God's children.[174]

In "History of the Work of Redemption," a 1739 sermon, Edwards declared that God's plan for history was to redeem mankind and society. He believed that the general morals of people had improved as a result of the revivals in Northampton from 1734-1735.

[171] Horton and Horton, *Hard Road to Freedom*, 53-75.
[172] Robert J. Allison, "The Great Awakening," *Before 1776: Life in the American Colonies* (Chantilly, Virginia: The Teaching Company/The Great Courses, 2009), CD; Alan Heimert, introduction to *The Great Awakening*, ed. Alan Heimert and Perry Miller (Indianapolis: Bobbs-Merrill Educational Publishing, 1967), xiii-lxi.
[173] Horton and Horton, *Hard Road to Freedom*.
[174] Jonathan Edwards, "A Faithful Narrative of the Surprising Work of God in the Conversion of Many Hundred Souls in Northampton, and the Neighbouring Towns and Villages of the County of Hampshire, in the Province of the Massachusetts-Bay in New-England," in *Jonathan Edwards: Writings From the Great Awakening*, ed. Phillip F. Gura, (New York: Literary Classics of the United States, 2013), 1-83.

Such observations helped lead to the notion that a broader revival of the spirit could improve society at large and usher in God's Kingdom. From this came various reform movements, including the drive to end the slave trade and abolish slavery.[175]

The informal meetings which were hallmarks of the Great Awakening encouraged interracial gatherings of believers. Almost anyone, including free blacks and slaves, who felt inspired by the Holy Spirit could preach and lead worshippers. Inevitably, this encouraged opposition to slavery, with evangelical ministers, both in the North and the South, taking stands against human bondage. Although societal elites viewed evangelicalism as destabilizing, regular people of varied backgrounds were drawn to the liberating message of personal salvation. Spiritual equality before the Almighty brought black people and white people together, helping to encourage physical equality, opposition to slavery, and eventually, the abolitionist movement.[176]

Even with its heavy dependency on slave labor, the South was not immune to the anti-slavery implications of the Great Awakening. In the Chesapeake, white preachers welcomed all, white and black, to repent. Many slaves were attracted to the evangelical preachers who opposed the aristocratic pretensions and ostentatiousness of the planter elites. The message of all being created in the image of God as well as the need of all for salvation implied equality between everyone – even master and slave. Spiritual equality created hope in earthly equality and found a receptive audience among those occupying the lowest rungs of society. Slaves also related to the suffering of the Hebrew slaves in ancient Egypt and Christ's suffering on the cross. By the time of the American Revolution, black preachers and black churches appeared, adding their voices to calls for liberation from despotism and sin.[177]

In the Carolinas and Georgia, the revival was led by preachers including Englishman George Whitefield and his American converts, planters Hugh and Jonathan Bryan. Inspiring slaves with promises of salvation and equality in God's eyes, they drew large crowds to the Charleston and Savannah rice ports. Meanwhile in the more rural inland regions, spiritual freedom became connected to earthly

---

[175] Heimert.

[176] Horton and Horton, *Hard Road to Freedom*.

[177] Berlin, 109-141.

freedom as black preachers taught plantation slaves the story of the enslaved Israelites in ancient Egypt who were eventually liberated by God. When tensions with Britain began to mount, it would not take too much imagination to liken King George III to Pharaoh, and the Americans, black and white, slave and free, to the ancient Hebrews.[178]

The American Revolution and Anti-Slavery (1763-1776)

In the years leading up to the American Revolution, colonial resistance to British policies merged with religiously-based opposition to human bondage to create a vigorous anti-slavery movement in America. Although there had been prior colonial efforts to limit slavery, these had always been thwarted by Britain. Thus, in contrast to the charge of the *New York Times'* "The 1619 Project" that "one of the primary reasons the colonists decided to declare their independence from Britain was because they wanted to protect the institution of slavery," the quest for independence was inextricably linked first to *restricting* and then *eliminating* slavery. This occurred initially in the Northern and Middle colonies, and then continued as abolitionists cited the language of the *Declaration of Independence* that "all men are created equal" in opposing human bondage during the years leading to the Civil War.[179]

In the Western world, the 1600s was the age of scientific revolutions, but the 1700s was the age of philosophical and political revolutions. This period, roughly encompassing 1689-1789, is known as "The Enlightenment," a European intellectual movement. Just as Isaac Newton (1643-1727) and others had employed the scientific method to ascertain the physical laws governing the universe, Enlightenment philosophers attempted to use reason to discover the natural laws governing human beings and societies. The Enlightenment's two core principles were rationalism and deism. The first argued that human reason was the best way to understand the world, while the second asserted a belief in a creator, but a distant

---

[178] Ibid., 142-176.
[179] Thomas Sowell, *Ethnic America – A History* (New York: Basic Books, Inc., 1981), 183-224; Nikole Hannah-Jones, introduction to "The 1619 Project," *New York Times Magazine*, 18 August 2019, 14-26.

one who did not interfere in human affairs or respond to prayer.[180]

The Enlightenment philosopher who probably had the greatest influence on the American founders was Englishman John Locke (1632-1704). Locke's *Second Treatise of Government* (1689) was written in part to justify England's 1688 "Glorious Revolution" when King James II, a Catholic, was overthrown by Parliament and replaced with William and Mary, both Protestants. Locke theorized that people possessed certain "natural rights" which could be derived from their natures as human beings. Upon observation, it was clear that all people were born with life, liberty, and the ability to mix one's labor with the natural environment and create something that was theirs – property. Governments, according to Locke, were established by a "social contract" among people who had agreed to form a community and then chose rulers to protect their individual rights, all of which he put in the category of "property." Although the people gave up a portion of their freedom to the government in exchange for that protection, they maintained the right to change or overthrow their government. This amounted to the right of revolution.[181]

Despite the secular nature of the Enlightenment in Europe, for many in overwhelmingly Christian America, Locke's natural laws were understood to be part of the laws of God. Indeed, the Apostle Paul (d. 65 A.D.) had described a natural law that was written in the human heart, something like conscience. This included Gentiles – those who had never been exposed to the Bible:

> ...for when Gentiles, who do not have the law, by nature do the things in the law, these, although not having the law, are a law to themselves, who show the work of the law written in their hearts...[182]

Likewise, Locke's concept of a "social contract" resembled a covenant, a religious instrument whereby individual believers agreed to form a congregation and then chose a leader, all under God. When the Pilgrims signed *The Mayflower Compact* in 1620, it marked the first time such a religious covenant had been extended to include a political purpose. The only difference in Locke's conception of the

---

[180] Woodworth, 38-46.
[181] Ibid.
[182] Ibid.; Romans 2:14-15 (NKJV).

social contract was that he omitted God from the equation. Nevertheless, he did identify God as the author of the laws of nature.[183]

The conflict between Britain and America centered on who held the power to pass legislation for the colonies, Parliament or the colonial legislatures. While the Americans acknowledged parliamentary jurisdiction over external matters concerning the empire such as regulating trade through import duties, the colonists argued that the elected representatives of the people in the legislatures had the exclusive right to pass legislation concerning the internal affairs of the colonies, including taxation.

As this issue was analyzed, debated, and expounded upon in books, newspapers, pamphlets, and sermons throughout the 1760s and 1770s, Americans began describing British policies as an encroachment on their historic rights as Englishmen and even as a form of slavery.[184] For example, Rhode Island governor Stephen Hopkins reacted to the *Sugar Act* (1764), Parliament's first attempt to raise a revenue in the colonies, by arguing that those "whose property may be taken from them by taxes, or otherwise, without their own consent, and against their will are in the miserable condition of slaves."[185] Jonathan Mayhew, a minister from Boston's West Church, described the *Stamp Act* of 1765, which required all paper products to be affixed with a stamp to indicate that a tax had been paid, as an attempt by Parliament "to reduce us to a state of slavery" and celebrated the act's repeal in 1766.[186] Then in 1768 Philadelphia attorney John Dickinson responded to the *Townshend Acts*, which was perceived as an attempt to raise revenue through import duties on such items as glass, lead, paint, and tea, with the following syllogism:

---

[183] Edmund S. Morgan, ed., *Puritan Political Ideas 1558-1794* (Indianapolis: Hackett Publishing Company, Inc., 2003), xli.

[184] Bernard Bailyn, *The Ideological Origins of the American Revolution* (Cambridge, Massachusetts: The Belknap Press of Harvard University Press, 1992), 232-246.

[185] Gordon S. Wood, ed., *The American Revolution: Writings from the Pamphlet Debate 1764-1772* (New York: Literary Classics of the United States, Inc., 2015), 121; Stephen Hopkins, "The Rights of the Colonies Examined," in *The American Revolution: Writings from the Pamphlet Debate 1764-1772*, ed. Gordon S. Wood (New York: Literary Classics of the United States, Inc., 2015), 121-142.

[186] Ellis Sandoz, ed., *Political Sermons of the American Founding Era, 1730-1805*, vol. 1, 2nd ed. (Indianapolis: Liberty Fund, 1998), 232; Jonathan Mayhew, "The Snare Broken," in *Political Sermons of the American Founding Era, 1730-1805*, ed. Ellis Sandoz, vol. 1, 2nd ed. (Indianapolis: Liberty Fund, 1998), 233-264.

> Those who are taxed without their own consent, expressed by themselves or their representatives, are slaves. We are taxed without our own consent, expressed by ourselves or our representatives. We are therefore – SLAVES.[187]

As the colonists increasingly resorted to such language in their various protests against British policies, the contradiction between their demands for freedom and the presence of slavery in their midst became increasingly impossible to deny. Thus, especially for many in the Northern and Middle colonies, the fight against imperial control and the fight against slavery became intertwined.[188]

As early as 1764, Massachusetts pamphlet writer James Otis wrote: "The Colonists are by the law of nature free born, as indeed all men are, white and black," and called the slave trade "the most shocking violation of the law of nature." In 1773, doctor and future signer of the *Declaration of Independence* Benjamin Rush authored a pamphlet entitled "'On Slave Keeping'" in which he pleaded with his fellow Americans to "'espouse the cause of humanity and general liberty'" while adding "'The plant of liberty is of so tender a nature that it cannot thrive long in the neighborhood of slavery.'"[189]

Adding to the anti-slavery literature of the period was Phillis Wheatley, a Boston slave who became the first black published author in America with *Poems on Various Subjects, Religious and Moral* (1773). Moved by the evangelical message of the Great Awakening, Wheatley also became an ardent believer in the American cause.[190]

In Wheatley's poem to the Earl of Dartmouth, the king's principal secretary of state for North America, she dreamed of the day when both America and the slaves would be free:

> No more, America, in mournful strain
> Of wrongs, and grievance unredress'd complain,

---

[187] John Dickinson, "Letters From a Farmer in Pennsylvania," in *Colonies to Nation, 1763-1789: A Documentary History of the American Revolution*, ed. Jack P. Greene (New York: W.W. Norton & Company, 1975), 122-133.
[188] Bailyn.
[189] James Otis, "The Rights of the British Colonies Asserted and Proved," in *The American Revolution: Writings from the Pamphlet Debate 1764-1772*, ed. Gordon S. Wood (New York: Literary Classics of the United States, Inc., 2015), 41-119; Bailyn.
[190] Horton and Horton, *Hard Road to Freedom*.

No longer shall thou dread the iron chain,
Which wanton Tyranny with lawless hand
Had made, and with it meant t' enslave the land.

Should you, my lord, while you peruse my song,
Wonder from whence my love of Freedom sprung,
Whence flow these wishes for the common good,
By feeling hearts alone best understood,
I, young in life, by seeming cruel fate
Was snatch'd from Afric's fancy'd happy seat:

Wheatly gained her freedom shortly thereafter.[191]

Another poem which Wheatley dedicated to General George Washington so affected the future president that he invited her to meet him at his headquarters. On February 28, 1776, Washington wrote:

I thank you most sincerely for your polite notice of me, in the elegant Lines you enclosed; and however undeserving I may be of such encomium and panegyrick, the style and manner exhibit a striking proof of your great poetical Talents…If you should ever come to Cambridge, or near Head Quarters, I shall be happy to see a person so favoured by the Muses, and to whom nature has been so liberal and beneficent in her dispensations.

The eloquence with which Wheatley expressed her desire to see freedom for both America and the slaves may have influenced Washington in his own moral struggle between human bondage on the one hand and the fight to establish a new nation based upon individual natural rights on the other. What is certain is that the father of our country later freed his slaves.[192]

---

[191] Phillis Wheatley, "To the Right Honourable William, Earl of Dartmouth, His Majesty's Principal Secretary of State for North-America, & c." in *American Antislavery Writings*, ed. James G. Basker (New York: Literary Classics of the United States, 2012), 54-55; Basker, 54.
[192] George Washington, "To Phyllis Wheatley," February 28th 1776, in *George Washington: Writings*, ed. John Rhodehamel (New York: Literary Classics of the United States, 1997), 216; Horton and Horton, *Hard Road to Freedom.*

Phillis Wheatley (1773) by Scipio Moorhead. Frontispiece to Phillis Wheatley's *Poems of Various Subjects, Religious and Moral* (1773). Wikimedia Commons. Public domain.

In 1774 another future president, Thomas Jefferson, tied the cause of resisting British tyranny to that of abolishing the slave trade in "A Summary View of the Rights of British America." The tract became Virginia's response to the hated *Boston Port Act*, passed by Parliament in retaliation for the December, 1773 Boston Tea Party. The *Port Act* completely shut down commerce in and out of Boston Harbor. In a foreshadowing of what was to appear in the original draft of the *Declaration of Independence* two years later, Jefferson listed a series of charges against the king including the use of the royal veto to prevent the colonies from restricting the slave trade:

> The abolition of domestic slavery is the great object of desire in those colonies, where it was unhappily introduced in their infant state. But previous to the enfranchisement of the slaves we have, it is necessary to exclude all further importations from Africa; yet our repeated attempts to effect this by prohibitions, and by imposing duties which might amount to a prohibition, have been hitherto defeated by his majesty's negative.[193]

When Jefferson referred to "repeated attempts" at prohibiting the slave trade, he was not exaggerating. According to historian Benjamin Brawley, by 1772 Virginia alone had passed more than thirty laws to either restrict or end the importation of slaves outright. Each was vetoed by the British government.[194]

Colonial ministers were among those most boldly calling out the hypocrisy of demanding liberty for oneself while remaining silent as it was denied to others. Preachers expounded a "covenantal theology" arguing that Americans had broken their "covenant" or "contract" with God through their sins – and slavery was a sin. Consequently, English tyranny was part of God's divine punishment, and He would not hear the cries of the Americans if they did not repent. Thus, the outcome of the revolutionary struggle with Britain became directly

---

[193] Merrill Jensen, ed., *Tracts of the American Revolution* (Indianapolis: Hackett Publishing Company, Inc., 2003), 256-257; Thomas Jefferson, "A Summary View of the Rights of British America," in *Tracts of the American Revolution*, ed. Merrill Jensen (Indianapolis: Hackett Publishing Company, Inc., 2003), 256-276.
[194] Grabar *Debunking the 1619 Project: Exposing the Plan to Divide America.*

dependent on whether the people reformed themselves, and for many, ending slavery was part of that reformation.[195]

For example, in 1770 Samuel Cooke delivered an election day sermon where he declared that God was "'no respecter of persons,'" and urged Massachusetts' leaders to battle slavery as they fought for their own freedoms. In 1774 Congregationalist minister Levi Hart proclaimed that Christ was "'the giver and supporter of original, perfect freedom'" and argued that a society withholding liberty from innocent people was committing tyranny and oppression: "'When, O when shall the happy day come, that Americans shall be *consistently* engaged in the cause of liberty?'" exclaimed Hart.[196]

Also in 1774, Congregationalist minister Ebeneezer Baldwin of Danbury, Connecticut reviewed all that had befallen the colonies over the previous decade and sought to determine the source of America's troubles: "The present alarming situation of things…calls upon us to examine what sins in particular have provoked heaven thus to come out in judgment against us." Baldwin concluded that besides worldliness, covetousness, selfishness, and dishonesty, first and foremost was the sin of enslaving human beings:

> Are not the colonies guilty of forcibly depriving them
> of their natural rights?…And is it not easy, to see there
> is something retributive in the present judgments of
> heaven? We keep our fellow men in slavery – heaven
> is suffering others to enslave us.

For Baldwin, the chief cause of America's ongoing struggle against British tyranny was clear: the colonies had permitted the enslavement of others, so God was permitting Britain to enslave them.[197]

Another Congregationalist minister, Samuel Hopkins, cried

---

[195] Bailyn; Gordon Wood, *The Creation of the American Republic 1776-1787* (New York: W.W. Norton & Co., Inc., 1993), 114-118.

[196] Bailyn.

[197] Gordon S. Wood, ed., *The American Revolution: Writings from the Pamphlet Debate 1773-1776* (New York: Literary Classics of the United States, Inc., 2015), 343; Ebeneezer Baldwin, "An Appendix, Stating the Heavy Grievances of the Colonies Labour under from Several Late Acts of the British Parliament, and Shewing What We Have Just Reason to Expect the Consequences of These Measures Will Be," in *The American Revolution: Writings from the Pamphlet Debate 1773-1776*, ed. Gordon S. Wood (New York: Literary Classics of the United States, Inc., 2015), 343-378.

"'Oh, the shocking, the intolerable inconsistence!'" when describing the irony of the colonies struggling for liberty while Africans were being held in bondage. His sermon, "'A Dialogue Concerning the Slavery of Africans; Shewing It To Be the Duty and Interest of the American Colonies To Emancipate All the African Slaves...'" (1776) linked the religious and secular arguments for emancipation with the plight of the American colonies.[198]

Hopkins specifically addressed his sermon to "'the Honorable Members of the Continental Congress,'" then meeting in Philadelphia, to urge them to act against slavery. Like Baldwin, he suggested that the ongoing struggle with Britain was part of God's punishment upon the Americans for permitting human bondage:

> ...if it be a sin...which is most particularly pointed out by the public calamities which have come upon us, from which we have no reason to expect deliverance till we put away the evil of our doings, this reformation [of slavery] cannot be urged with too much zeal, nor attempted too soon, whatever difficulties are in the way.[199]

Even in the slave-holding South, one could find colonial ministers speaking out against the injustice of slavery in the years leading up to the American Revolution. In 1774 in Fairfax County, Virginia, itinerant preacher Elhanan Winchester condemned human bondage by citing both the Christian scriptures as well as the natural law doctrine which was to be at the heart of the American founding:

> ...if the thing itself is a crime, as may be proved from our Saviour's words, 'Therefore all things, whatsoever ye would that men should do to you, do ye even so unto them; for this is the law and the prophets,' Matt. vii. 12. Luke vi. 31. what have not those to expect who break the law of nature, the law of God, who

---

[198] Bailyn.

[199] Basker, 69; Samuel Hopkins, "A Dialogue Concerning the Slavery of the Africans, Shewing It To Be the Duty and Interest of the American Colonies To Emancipate All the African Slaves...," in *American Antislavery Writings*, ed. James G. Basker (New York: Literary Classics of the United States, 2012), 69-74.

transgress against the instruction of the prophets, and violate the commands of Christ and his apostles?[200]

Black people, slave and free, were not simply onlookers to the evolving imperial crisis between England and America. They experienced the effects of British encroachment on individual liberties that all Americans did. Furthermore, they were participants in some of the most noteworthy events leading up to the *Declaration of Independence*. The outcome of the struggle mattered to them too.

Perhaps as much or more than any other issue, impressment – the kidnapping and forcing of men into the British navy – most angered regular Americans, black and white. "Press gangs" scoured the colonies, searching both rural areas and towns for new "recruits" to His Majesty's Navy. Taverns where common folk passed the time were a prime source of victims of all races. Consequently, the reactions were also multi-racial, with riots breaking out in Boston during the 1740s and then becoming more frequent in the 1760s with tensions mounting between the mother country and her colonies. Maine, Rhode Island, New York, Maryland, and Virginia all witnessed violent outbreaks against impressment in the years leading up to the American Revolution.[201]

When the British Parliament issued the *Stamp Act* in 1765, the first attempt to directly tax the colonies by requiring a paid stamp to be affixed to various printed items, the reaction was swift and violent across class and racial lines. In New York City in particular, leaders opposing the new legislation met at Queen's Head Tavern to plan their strategy. The proprietor of the tavern was "Black Sam" Frances, a mulatto man from the West Indies.[202]

Five years later on March 5, 1770, Crispus Attucks, a former slave of both African and Nantucket Indian ancestry, was at the center of a melee in Boston between American colonists and British troops. Amidst ongoing imperial-colonial tensions, Attucks led a group of patriots from Dock Square to King Street and the customs

---

[200] Basker, 57; Elhanan Winchester, "The Reigning Abominations, Especially the Slave Trade, Considered as Causes of Lamentation," in *American Antislavery Writings*, ed. James G. Basker (New York: Literary Classics of the United States, 2012), 57-60.
[201] Horton and Horton, *Hard Road to Freedom*.
[202] Ibid.

house where import taxes were collected. The mob advanced towards the guard standing watch, attacking him with ice, snowballs, and anything else they could find. When British soldiers arrived on the scene, the crowd proceeded to attack them with snowballs and clubs. Apparently one solider fired before being given an actual command to do so. When the rest of Britain's redcoats fired into the crowd, Attucks was one of five Americans killed. He is believed to be the first American killed during the revolution. All of the fallen were later honored as martyrs and patriots in what came to be known as "the Boston Massacre." News of the event spread up and down the colonies, further turning American opinion against Britain. Six years later on the anniversary of the event, General Washington is reported to have said: "'Remember, it is the 5th of March, and avenge the death of your brethren!'"[203]

The Boston Massacre (c. 1856). Lithograph by John Buford. National Archives at College Park. Wikimedia Commons. Public domain.

---

[203] William Cooper Nell, *The Colored Patriots of the American Revolution* (Robert F. Wallcut, 2017), 11-14.

By the eve of the American *Declaration of Independence* on July 4, 1776, the colonies had already made great efforts to either halt or at least limit the slave trade – the importation of slaves. Massachusetts attempted to stop the slave trade in 1767. Then in 1771 and again in 1774 the colonial legislature passed legislation to abolish it, only to have the crown-appointed royal governor veto it on both occasions. However, when the Continental Congress representing the colonies convened in Philadelphia in 1774, it agreed to halt the slave trade everywhere as part of a general boycott of British commerce. Rhode Island and Connecticut declared that any slave setting foot within their respective boundaries would instantly be considered free. Delaware banned the importation of slaves and Pennsylvania taxed slavery out of existence.[204]

Although they had been among the leaders of the opposition to slavery throughout much of the colonial period, the Quakers re-doubled their efforts during the Revolutionary Era. By now the Friends' patience was growing thin, and numerous yearly meetings that had previously encouraged their members to free their slaves began disowning those who would not. The New England Yearly Meeting was first in 1773, followed in 1776 by the Philadelphia, New York, and North Carolina Quakers. In 1778 Baltimore Friends did the same as did those in Virginia in 1784.[205]

In 1775 Philadelphia Quakers helped to establish "The Pennsylvania Society for Promoting the Abolition of Slavery, the Relief of Free Negroes Unlawfully Held in Bondage, and for Improving the Conditions of the African Race," possibly the first abolitionist organization in the world. Seeking to end slavery in Pennsylvania and the nation, this group influenced the rise of other abolitionist groups. Such organizations formed the foundation for the larger abolitionist movement during the Revolutionary Era and into the early years of the American republic. In 1780 the society's efforts contributed to the abolition of slavery in Pennsylvania.[206]

There were positive steps in the plantation-dominated South as well. The Southern colonies agreed to include slaves in the Continental Congress's non-importation agreements as part of the general boycott of British trade. In 1774 the Virginia House of

---

[204] Bailyn.
[205] Bacon, 76.
[206] Ibid., 94-121.

Burgesses, the colony's legislature, approved the Fairfax Revolves abolishing the slave trade. Nevertheless, as had happened on so many prior occasions, it was vetoed by King George III.[207]

As Phillip W. Magness and Peter W. Wood each point out, there were two events in the 1770s which, if not properly understood, could be used to support the claim of "The 1619 Project" that a primary reason that the American colonies declared independence was to protect slavery. The first was a 1772 case in Great Britain known as *Somerset v. Stewart*, involving a slave named James Somerset who had been bought in Boston by a British customs officer and brought back to England. After Somerset fled, he was apprehended, jailed, and threatened with being sent to work on one of the brutal sugar plantations in Jamaica. Somerset's Christian godparents then intervened, and together with abolitionist Granville Sharp, he won his freedom in court. The judge ruled that slavery was not protected by the English common law, but the decision only applied to England, not its colonies. At the time of the *Declaration of Independence* in 1776, the abolition of the slave trade and slavery in the British Empire was not even on the horizon. This helps to explain why Britain's West Indian sugar plantations, where slavery was far more common and of much greater economic consequence than in America, did not appear to be the least bit concerned by the *Somerset* decision or the possibility of abolition. Indeed, British colonies in the Caribbean islands such as Barbados and Jamaica never joined the rebellious thirteen colonies on the mainland in going to war against England. Furthermore, Britain would not end the slave trade until 1807 and slavery continued within the empire until 1833.[208]

The second event that "The 1619 Project" submits as proof that preserving slavery was a prime motivation for declaring independence is an order by the colonial governor of Virginia, Lord Dunsmore, to give freedom to any indentured servants or slaves who would take up arms against the rebellious Americans. However, Dunsmore's offer did not occur until November 15, 1775, long after the war had broken out at Lexington and Concord in Massachusetts on April 19. By this time, the Americans were already well on their way to

---

[207] Bailyn; Jerry Newcombe, "Teaching Kids That America was Always Racist," Teaching Kids That America Was Always Racist | The Stream 7 May 2021.
[208] Phillip W. Magness, *The 1619 Project: A Critique* (The American Institute for Economic Research, 2020), 39-45; Peter W. Wood, 77-98.

revolution due to a myriad of British policies enacted over the previous decade against the colonies. Furthermore, Dunsmore's offer only applied to indentured servants or slaves owned by the rebels, not those held in bondage by Americans who remained loyal to Britain. Although approximately 100,000 slaves attempted to escape during the chaos of the Revolutionary War, only about 800 to 2,000 ever joined Dunsmore. Clearly his measure was only enacted for strategic reasons *after* war had already broken out, and, like the *Somerset* case, was not a sign of some larger, long-term trend within the empire leading towards emancipation.[209]

The charge in "The 1619 Project" that a burgeoning anti-slavery movement in England threatened American slaveholders in 1776 is just not true. As Sean Wilentz explained, it was only in 1787, after the American Revolution had been fought and won, that abolitionism in Britain truly took off. Indeed, it was the anti-slavery activism taking place in the American colonies during the 1760s and 1770s that largely inspired later British efforts.[210]

The reality is that the American War for Independence from Britain had little to do with preserving slavery but much to do with limiting and eventually ending human bondage. In 1776 the Americans did far more than simply unite against their mother country and declare independence as a new nation. They created a republic based upon Christian and Enlightenment ideas regarding the inherent worth and rights of the individual. Furthermore, the words and ideas expressed in America's "mission statement" – the *Declaration of Independence* and the *Constitution* – would be acted upon immediately, leading to the abolition of slavery in the Northern states, the end of the slave trade, the prohibition of slavery in the new territories of the Northwest, and the launch of the abolitionist movement which would culminate in the Civil War (1861-1865) and ultimately leave slavery in America on the ash heap of history. Thereafter, the principles of the American Revolution would continue to drive the nation's history and shape the development of the United States to this day.

---

[209] Ibid.
[210] Sean Wilentz, "A Matter of Facts," January 22, 2020, https://www.theatlantic.com/ideas/archive/2020/01/1619-project-new-york-times-wilentz/605152/.

3 AMERICA'S MISSION STATEMENT

"The American war is over: but this is far from being the case with
the American revolution. On the contrary, nothing but the first act of
the great drama is closed. It remains yet to establish and perfect our
new forms of government; and to prepare the principles, morals, and
manners of our citizens, for these forms of government, after they
are established and brought to perfection."[1]
–Benjamin Rush, signer of the *Declaration of Independence*

On July 4, 1776, delegates from the American colonies approved
the *Declaration of Independence*. It stated the reasons for breaking from
the British Empire in terms of a broken contract or covenant. This
was an argument based upon natural law: an unwritten and
unchanging higher law that preceded any human-made statute.
Enlightenment political thought held that natural law was knowable
to anyone through their ability to reason, while Christianity
recognized a natural law which was "written in the heart" and
authored by God. In describing natural law as "the laws of nature and
of nature's God," the *Declaration* united two streams of thought,
secular and religious. Furthermore, the Founding Fathers believed
that certain principles could be derived from natural law that were
eternal truths and relevant to all people and all times.[2]

---

[1] Benjamin Rush, "Address to the People of the United States," January, 1787,
Benjamin Rush.pdf (wisc.edu).
[2] Thomas G. West, *The Political Theory of the American Founding: Natural Rights, Public
Policy, and the Moral Conditions of Freedom* (Cambridge: Cambridge University Press,

From the theory of natural law, it followed that human beings possessed equal natural rights because they all had a common Creator. Since everyone was equal in having the same rights to life, liberty, and the pursuit of happiness, that meant no one could govern another without their consent. Humanity was not naturally divided into those who rule and those who are ruled. Neither was anyone by nature a master or a slave because people owned themselves. Furthermore, all had a duty to respect the rights of others.[3]

Therefore, people could choose what kind of a government they wanted in order to protect their God-given natural rights. In effect, the citizens gave up a portion of their freedom to their rulers in exchange for this protection. However, if the rulers failed to live up to their end of the agreement, then the people had the right to change or discard their government. To put it another way, under certain circumstances the people possessed the right to revolution.

Prior to the birth of America, this was essentially a theoretical argument used to explain the origin and purpose of good government. No country had ever been created by explicitly stating these ideas, yet that is precisely what the Founding Fathers did in the preamble to the *Declaration of Independence*:

> We hold these truths to be self-evident, that all men are created equal, that they are endowed by their Creator with certain unalienable rights, that among these are life, liberty and the pursuit of happiness. That, to secure these rights, governments are instituted among men, deriving their just powers from the consent of the governed. That whenever any form of government becomes destructive of these ends, it is the right of the people to alter or to abolish it, and to institute new government, laying its foundation on such principles, and organizing its powers in such form, as to them shall seem most likely to effect their safety and happiness.[4]

2017), 1-15; Charles Kesler, Claremont McKenna College, Government 169 lecture notes, fall 2006.
[3] The President's Advisory 1776 Commission, "The 1776 Report," January, 2021, 4; West, *The Political Theory of the American Founding*, 19-42.
[4] *Declaration of Independence* in *American Heritage – A Reader*, ed. The Hillsdale College

This was followed in 1788 by the adoption of a new government based upon the United States *Constitution*. It too commenced with a preamble to explain its reason for being:

> We the people of the United States, in order to form a more perfect union, establish justice, ensure domestic tranquility, provide for the common defense, promote the general welfare, and secure the blessings of liberty to ourselves and our posterity, do ordain and establish this Constitution for the United States of America.[5]

To accomplish these ends, the new government would have to be strong enough to protect individual rights, but not so powerful as to threaten those rights. For this reason, one of the main principles underlying the *Constitution* and its structure was that the powers of the government must be limited.[6]

These two preambles comprise America's "mission statement." The first part contains the "why" and the second contains the "how" of the mission. And what is the mission? It is to create a nation that both proclaims and protects the natural individual rights of its citizens, something unprecedented in world history. Other countries had formed on the basis of a shared race, ethnicity, religion, or language, but never before had a nation declared that its citizenry would be united by a belief in an idea that everyone possessed God-given natural rights simply because they were human beings. This insistence on rights being natural – rooted in our very nature – was essential, because without it we would be at the mercy of governments, rulers, or perhaps a majority vote to determine what rights we have.[7]

However, in 1776 the United States of America was still just an experiment. As indicated by the words of Benjamin Rush which opened this chapter, a large self-governing republic was something never before attempted and which would require the founding

---

History Faculty (Hillsdale, Michigan: Hillsdale College Press, 2011), 128-131.

[5] *Constitution* in *American Heritage – A Reader*, 146-156.

[6] The President's Advisory 1776 Commission, 7, 9.

[7] Leo Strauss, *Natural Right and History* (Chicago: The University of Chicago Press, 1965), 1-8.

generation to set an example and generations thereafter to maintain through constant striving and testing. Fortunately for America, the Founding Fathers did set an example worthy of admiration, not just through their words but also through their deeds. Thereafter, whenever challenging times arose and the nation's founding principles came under attack, great Americans emerged to defend them and call the country back to its "mission statement."

The American Revolution and Slavery

The Revolutionary War encouraged and precipitated at least the partial abolition of slavery in America in several ways. First, the destabilizing effects of warfare permitted slaves and indentured servants to flee their bondage, with many ultimately serving in combat. Second, the ideological nature of the American Revolution, specifically the claim of the *Declaration of Independence* that "all men are created equal" led to thousands of slaves being freed, even in states where their owners were not compelled to do so through legislation. Finally, the influence of evangelical Christianity and its belief that all were created in the image of God and therefore shared in a basic human equality added a religious intensity to the cause of independence. The spiritual freedom which applied to everyone, black and white, became linked to earthly freedom in the minds of many.[8]

As with numerous other issues, the Continental Congress in Philadelphia representing the new nation engaged in a vigorous debate on the subject of enlisting black Americans in the war effort. As would so often be the case, the general consensus among Northern states was that black people should be able to serve, while the South disapproved. General George Washington, aware that many black men had already served and done so honorably, determined on July 9, 1775, that those on active duty could continue to do so, but restricted the enlistment of any additional black troops. However, perhaps fearing the effects of Virginia Governor Lord Dunsmore's offer to free all slaves and indentured servants owned by American rebels if they joined the British cause, Washington later petitioned Congress to renew the enlistment of black Americans into the army. On January 6, 1776, the Continental Congress changed

---

[8] Ira Berlin, *Many Thousands Gone – The First Two Centuries of Slavery in North America*, (Cambridge, Massachusetts: Belknap, 1998), 219-227, 228-255.

course and began enlisting black troops.[9]

Throughout the war, thousands of black people fought for America's freedom. In every state except for South Carolina and Georgia, both free and enslaved black Americans served in integrated army units. In the navy they served everywhere. 200 slaves enlisted in Rhode Island's First Regiment while Connecticut fielded a company comprised entirely of black Americans. Many more black men and women served in other ways throughout the conflict. Thousands of slaves gained their freedom as a result of wartime service.[10]

Perhaps the most iconic event of the war occurred on Christmas night of 1776. The first year and a half of the struggle had not gone particularly well for the Americans, who would not be formally joined by France for more than a year. Some feared that the fight against Britain was hopeless, and the enlistments of many of Commander-in-chief George Washington's men were about to expire at the end of the year. Undoubtedly, there were many who would have probably preferred to return to their families and farms rather than continue a seemingly hopeless fight against the most powerful military in the world that could result in being executed for treason.[11]

Confronted with such dire circumstances, Washington took a chance. Facing a brutal "nor'easter" wind, sleet, and snow, he led 2,400 men in a daring nighttime crossing of the icy Delaware River from Pennsylvania into New Jersey. They then marched throughout the night, reaching Trenton the next morning where they surprised and routed 1,500 Hessian mercenaries hired by the British. Combined with a subsequent American victory at Princeton in January, the spirits of Washington's army were revived and many re-enlisted.[12]

This event, which may have very well saved the cause of American independence, was famously immortalized in German

---

[9] James Oliver Horton and Lois E. Horton, *Hard Road to Freedom – The Story of African America*, vol. 1, *From African Roots Through the Civil War* (New Brunswick, New Jersey, Rutgers University Press, 2001), 53-75.

[10] James Oliver Horton and Lois E. Horton, *In Hope of Liberty – Culture, Community and Protest Among Northern Free Blacks, 1700-1860* (New York: Oxford University Press, 1997), 55-76; Berlin.

[11] Steven E. Woodworth, *The Essentials of United States History: 1500 to 1789 From Colony to Republic* (Piscataway, New Jersey: Research and Education Association, 1996), 57-70.

[12] James M. McPherson, preface to *Washington's Crossing*, by David Hackett Fischer (New York: Oxford University Press, 2004), ix-x.

immigrant Emanuel Leutze's 1851 painting *Washington Crossing the Delaware*. Leutze conceived of the painting as a means of encouraging Europeans who were engaged in numerous revolutions of their own in 1848.[13] The figure manning an oar at the front of the boat with his legs hanging over the edge may depict Oliver Cromwell, a man of biracial ancestry who was born a free man and was with Washington at the battles of Trenton, Princeton, Brandywine, Monmouth, and Yorktown.[14] At the end of the war he received a military pension and was exceedingly proud of the fact that Washington personally authored his discharge from the army.[15] Meanwhile, the figure seen manning an oar just next to Cromwell near Washington's bent knee may depict Prince Whipple, a slave who was freed after the war.[16] Leutze supported the abolition of slavery, so the inclusion of Whipple would not have been incidental.[17]

Washington Crossing the Delaware (1851) by Emanuel Leutze. Wikimedia Commons. Public domain.

---

[13] David Hackett Fischer, *Washington's Crossing* (New York: Oxford University Press, 2004), 1-6.

[14] Black Courage: African-American Soldiers in the War for Independence (stamps.org)

[15] William Cooper Nell, *The Colored Patriots of the American Revolution* (Robert F. Wallcut, 2017), 106-109.

[16] Ibid., 129-130.

[17] Fischer.

As David Hackett Fischer observed, the painting may only be a representation of the historic night, but it is undoubtedly true to the actual event in several ways. First, it conveys a genuine sense of the drama and tension worthy of the significance of the moment. Many first-hand accounts expressed fear that the American cause may have been doomed if Washington's gamble failed. Second, it depicts the revolutionary nature of the American army: a disparate group from divergent backgrounds and different parts of the country, united as free men. Furthermore, they were willingly being led by a man who knew how to inspire and motivate rather than using threats and force as one would with slaves and servants. It was this kind of ragtag crew that was matched against two of the most professional and highly organized armies in the world – that of the British and the Hessians.[18]

The painting also reflects the fact that black Americans participated in the crossing and in virtually every other battle of the war. Washington led hundreds of black troops and often recognized them as good soldiers. No other American commander led integrated units until the Korean War, over one hundred fifty years later.[19]

Independence as a new nation provided Americans with further opportunities to put their idealism into action. Accordingly, in the early decades of the new republic the founding generation ended human bondage in all of the Northern states, prohibited the expansion of slavery into new territories of the Northwest, and abolished the slave trade into the country. These were not the actions of people who looked kindly on the practice of human bondage. Thus, the claim of "The 1619 Project" that the American Revolution was fought to protect slavery or that the Founding Fathers created a nation based on slavery and the domination of one race over another is not supported by the evidence.

After decades of being thwarted by the English crown, many former colonies took advantage of their new status as states in an independent nation to abolish slavery. In one generation, a total of 8 states provided for either the immediate or gradual end of human bondage: Vermont (1777), Pennsylvania (1780), Massachusetts (1783), Connecticut (1784), Rhode Island (1784), New Hampshire (1789), New York (1799), and New Jersey (1804). Over 100,000

---

[18] Ibid.
[19] Richard Brookhiser, *What Would the Founders Do? Our Questions Their Answers* (New York: Basic Books, 2006), 163-180.

slaves were freed either by legislation or the choice of individual slave owners – even in Southern states where it was not legally required.[20]

The Founding Fathers' negative view of slavery is further evidenced by the precedent-setting enactment of the *Northwest Ordinance* in 1787. In one of the first pieces of legislation concerning territory outside of the original thirteen states, the *Articles of Confederation* Congress banned slavery in the region north of the Ohio River and west of the Appalachian Mountains.[21] The land had previously been claimed by the state of Virginia, which relinquished it to the new nation.[22] It was Virginian Thomas Jefferson, the author of the *Declaration of Independence*, who proposed that the transfer take place only if slavery was permanently banned in the region.[23] The law would be passed again by the first Congress and signed by President Washington after the United States *Constitution* replaced the *Articles*.[24] Eventually six free states were carved out of the territory.[25]

Also in 1787, the Constitutional Convention assembled in Philadelphia's Independence Hall. After several months, it passed and submitted to the states for approval a plan for a new government to replace the *Articles*. Although the United States *Constitution* did not outlaw slavery when it was ratified in 1788, this should not be viewed as condoning the practice. Far from it. Most of the founders believed that slavery was in direct conflict with the principles of the *Declaration of Independence* and the American Revolution, despite the fact that as many as thirty-five of the fifty-five original delegates to the convention may have been slaveholders at one time or another.[26] Indeed, even several Southern attendees expressed a growing realization that slavery was in conflict with the American "experiment," including George Mason of Virginia and Luther

[20] Horton and Horton, *In Hope of Liberty*; Thomas G. West, *Vindicating the Founders – Race, Sex, Class, and Justice in the Origins of America* (Lanham, Maryland: Rowman & Littlefield Publishers, Inc., 1997), xi-xv.
[21] John F. Chilton, *The Essentials of United States History: 1789 to 1841 The Developing Nation* (Piscataway, New Jersey: Research and Education Association, 1995), 59-60.
[22] Larry P. Arnn, "Orwell's 1984 and Today," *Imprimis* Vol. 49, No. 12 (December, 2020).
[23] Ibid.
[24] The President's Advisory 1776 Commission, 11.
[25] Chilton.
[26] M.E. Bradford, *Founding Fathers* (Lawrence, Kansas: University Press of Kansas, 1994), xv-xxi.

Martin of Maryland.[27] Although many of the delegates wanted to end human bondage, others in the slave-holding states of the South refused to consider its abolition, calling it a "necessary evil."[28] However, as both President Abraham Lincoln and abolitionist Frederick Douglass would later observe, neither "slave" nor "slavery" was ever mentioned in the *Constitution*. Instead "person" and "service or labor which may be due" were used. According to Lincoln, "…this mode of alluding to slaves and slavery, instead of speaking of them, was employed on purpose to exclude from the Constitution the idea that there should be property in man."[29]

Why did the Founding Fathers not abolish slavery if so many of them were opposed to it on moral grounds? According to James Madison's notes from the proceedings of the Constitutional Convention, slavery was the most heated topic among the delegates. If slavery's opponents had forced the issue, the odds were that its supporters would have left and formed a separate country with slavery firmly entrenched. No one would have been freed. Consequently, the policy of the founding generation was to limit slavery in the hope that this would lead to its ultimate abolition.[30]

The first means of restricting human bondage was to end the importation of slaves. The founders directed that twenty years after the *Constitution* was ratified, the slave trade – the importation of new slaves – could be abolished. Congress acted upon this as soon as the *Constitution* permitted in 1808. As to why the delegates did not impose an immediate ban, Madison explained, "The Southern states would not have entered into the union of America, without the temporary permission of that trade," particularly South Carolina and Georgia. He added, "Great as the evil is, a dismemberment of the union would

[27] Michael Medved, *The 10 Big Lies About America: Combating Destructive Distortions About Our Nation* (New York: Crown Forum, 2008), 46-71.
[28] Thomas G. West and Douglas A. Jeffrey, "The Rise and Fall of Constitutional Government in America" (Claremont, CA: The Claremont Institute, 2006), 1-40.
[29] Abraham Lincoln, "Address at Cooper Institute," February 27, 1860, in *Abraham Lincoln: Speeches and Writings, 1859-1865*, ed. Don E. Fehrenbacher (New York: Literary Classics of the United States, Inc., 1989), 111-130; Frederick Douglass, "What to the Slave is the Fourth of July?" in *American Heritage – A Reader*, ed. The Hillsdale College History Faculty (Hillsdale, Michigan: Hillsdale College Press, 2011), 396-413.
[30] West and Jeffrey.

be worse."[31]

The second measure limiting slavery was the three-fifths compromise. This is one of the most misunderstood provisions in the entire US *Constitution*. It was NOT an assertion that black people only equaled three-fifths of a person. The clause counted *slaves* as three-fifths for purposes of *representation*. Free black people did not fall into this category and therefore counted as one person, just like anyone else. The effect of this provision was to reduce the countable population of the slave-holding states, thereby limiting their number of representatives in Congress. The South then had less political leverage with which to protect and expand slavery. It was an *anti-slavery* measure.[32]

Admittedly, the *Constitution* also included a clause dealing with escaped slaves and provided for their re-capture. Nevertheless, even in this case, the framers were merely acknowledging slavery's existence, not endorsing it. Referring only to those "'held to service or labor in one State, under the laws thereof,'" the *Constitution* stipulated that if such a person escaped from a slave state to a non-slave state, they could not be released by the free state and had to be returned. However, again according to Madison, the original draft language referred to "'no person *legally* held to service or labor in one State, under the laws thereof,'" but the word "'legally'" was removed specifically because the founders did not want it to appear that they were claiming slavery was legal in a moral sense.[33]

Another concession to the slave states involved the treaty ratification process. A two-thirds vote in the Senate, rather than a simple majority, was required to approve agreements with foreign nations. This provision was intended to allay the fears of slave-holding interests that lands to the West might be sold off, thereby preventing the expansion of human bondage.[34]

---

[31] Ibid.; James Madison, "Speech in the Virginia Ratifying Convention on the Slave Trade Clause," June 17, 1788, in *James Madison: Writings*, ed. Jack N. Rakove (New York: Literary Classics of the United States, 1999), 391-392.
[32] Thomas Sowell, "The Real History of Slavery," in *Black Rednecks and White Liberals* (San Francisco: Encounter Books, 2005), 155; West and Jeffrey.
[33] Ryan P. Williams, "America Was Not Conceived in Racism," https://www.newsweek.com/america-was-not-conceived-racism-opinion-1518091, 15 July 2020.
[34] Woodworth, *The Essentials of United States History: 1500 to 1789 From Colony to Republic.*

To illustrate why all of these compromises over slavery were necessary to keep the new union from ripping apart, look only to the presidential election of 1860. The victory in November of that year by Abraham Lincoln, who had run on merely halting the expansion of slavery, was sufficient to cause South Carolina to secede the following month. By the spring of 1861 ten additional slave states had followed suit and the nation was in a state of civil war.

Nevertheless, as a consequence of all the antislavery measures enacted in the early period of America's independence, the free black population in the Northern states soared. Numbering only in the hundreds in the 1770s, by 1810 there were approximately 50,000 free black people in the North, nearly doubling the total of slaves in the region. The number of slaves was gradually reduced further until the Northern states became known as the free states. Individuals were freed through wartime service, by their owners, by purchasing their own freedom, via state laws mandating release, and by escape.[35]

Free black Americans founded schools, publications, and religious, political, and other social organizations. Among these were the Free African Society of Newport, Rhode Island (1780), the African Society of Philadelphia (1787), and Prince Hall's Masonic Lodge in Boston. Philadelphia also became home to several churches with black congregations including the St. Thomas African Episcopal Church led by Absalom Jones and the Mother Bethel African Methodist Episcopal Church helmed by Richard Allen.[36]

The Founding Fathers and Slavery

There was nearly universal agreement among the founding generation that slavery was both at odds with the natural rights philosophy of the American Revolution and morally wrong. The words and deeds of the leading Founding Fathers reveal their desire to eradicate human bondage as soon as possible but without destroying the nation that they had just created.

As with many men of wealth and power throughout world history, General and later President George Washington (1732-1799) owned slaves. However, later in life he clearly became conflicted about slavery, wrestled with its morality, and expressed regret for

[35] Berlin.
[36] Ibid.

having been a slaveowner.[37] In 1786 Washington wrote of slavery: "…there is not a man living who wishes more sincerely than I do, to see a plan adopted for the abolition of it…" and "…I never mean to possess another slave by purchase…"[38]

The father of our country backed up his words with deeds. In his will Washington directed that all of his slaves be freed after his wife had died. However, he did not stop there. Washington also instructed his estate to provide lifetime care to any of the former slaves of his Mount Vernon plantation who were either too elderly or too ill to live independently. For decades after his death his estate made payments for their support. Furthermore, he stipulated that children would be taught to read and write and prepared for an occupation. The section of his will concerning slavery expressed his wishes in a manner that left absolutely no doubt that he expected them to be followed to the letter:

> Upon the decease of my wife, it is my Will and desire that all the Slaves which I hold in *my own right*, shall receive their freedom…And I do hereby expressly forbid the Sale…of any Slave I may die possessed of, under any pretence whatsoever. And I do moreover most pointedly, and most solemnly enjoin it upon my Executors hereafter named, or the Survivors of them, to see that *this* clause respecting Slaves, and every part thereof be religiously fulfilled at the Epoch at which it is directed to take place; without evasion, neglect or delay…[39]

---

[37] George Washington, "Reflection on Slavery," 1788-1789, in *George Washington: Writings*, ed. John Rhodehamel (New York: Literary Classics of the United States, 1997), 701-702.

[38] George Washington, "To Robert Morris," April 12, 1786, in *The U.S. Constitution – A Reader*, ed. The Hillsdale College Politics Faculty (Hillsdale, Michigan: Hillsdale College Press, 2014), 401; George Washington, "To John Francis Mercer," September 9, 1786, in *George Washington: Writings*, ed. John Rhodehamel (New York: Literary Classics of the United States, 1997), 607-608.

[39] Sowell, "The Real History of Slavery"; George Washington, "Last Will and Testament," July 9, 1799, in *George Washington: Writings*, ed. John Rhodehamel (New York: Literary Classics of the United States, 1997), 1022-1042.

To truly understand the exceptional nature of Washington's example, it is helpful to compare his life to that of a contemporary who was also a man of great wealth and power. Antera Duke (c. 1735-c. 1809) was an African chief of the Efik people, as well as a merchant and slave trader in the region then known as Old Calabar in modern-day southeastern Nigeria. From 1785-1788 he compiled a diary detailing his life as a buyer and seller of human beings. Some of the entries from August, 1787 include the following:

> August 13, 1787
> …we heard that Captain Brighouse went away with 320 slaves.

> August 18, 1787
> …Captain Potter came ashore…after 2 o'clock I had all the captains to dinner and supper with me.

> August 25, 1787
> …at 4 o'clock in the afternoon Captain Fairweather's tender went away with 210 slaves…

While Antera Duke was doing business and dining with slave ship captains, George Washington was expressing genuine anguish over the conflict between natural rights and slavery as well as presiding over the Constitutional Convention. In fact, while Washington and the other delegates from the various states were drafting a *Constitution* which would ultimately abolish the slave trade in America, the Efik slave trade was at its height. Jealously guarding their business from local rivals including the Qua people, from 1785-1788 the Efik sold approximately 15,000 of their fellow Africans into bondage, mostly to British captains and primarily destined for sugar plantations in the West Indies or Brazil, not George Washington's young country. Antera Duke and the other Efik chiefs epitomized those whom former slave turned-abolitionist Frederick Douglass would later refer to as "the savage chiefs on the western coast of Africa, who for ages have been accustomed to selling their captives into bondage, and pocketing the ready cash for them…"[40]

---

[40] Stephen D. Behrendt, A.J.H. Latham, and David Northrup, eds. *The Diary of Antera Duke, An Eighteenth Century African Slave Trader* (New York: Oxford

Thomas Jefferson (1743-1826), the third president and primary author of the *Declaration of Independence*, was also a slaveowner. However, he understood slavery was morally incompatible with "the laws of nature and of nature's God," feared God's punishment for human bondage, and hoped for slavery's end.[41] Throughout his adult life, Jefferson's views never changed and he took steps to put slavery on the path to extinction. For example, in 1769 as a member of the Virginia colonial legislature, he supported a motion to end the requirement that slaveowners seek approval from the colonial government before freeing their slaves.[42] In his original draft of the *Declaration*, Jefferson's list of grievances against King George III included the monarch's repeated actions to thwart the efforts of the colonies to restrict or ban the importation of slaves:

> He has waged cruel war against human nature itself, violating its most sacred rights of life and liberty in the persons of a distant people who never offended him, captivating and carrying then into slavery in another hemisphere, or to incur miserable death in their transportation thither. This piratical warfare, the opprobrium of INFIDEL powers, is the warfare of the CHRISTIAN king of Great Britain. Determined to keep open a market where MEN should be bought and sold, he has prostituted his negative [veto] for suppressing every legislative attempt to prohibit or to restrain this execrable commerce.[43]

However, South Carolina and Georgia were opposed to halting the slave trade and insisted that this clause be omitted, while some in the

---

University Press, 2010), 1-9, 46-54, 207; Frederick Douglass, "African Civilization Society," February, 1859, https://teachingamericanhistory.org/document/african-civilization-society/.

[41] Thomas Jefferson, "Query XVIII: Manners," from *Notes on the State of Virginia*, in *The U.S. Constitution – A Reader*, eds. The Hillsdale College Politics Faculty (Hillsdale, Michigan: Hillsdale College Press, 2014), 403-404.

[42] Sowell, "The Real History of Slavery."

[43] Thomas Jefferson, "Draft of the Declaration of Independence," in *The U.S. Constitution – A Reader*, ed. The Hillsdale College Politics Faculty (Hillsdale, Michigan: Hillsdale College Press, 2014), 397.

North balked because of their involvement in transporting slaves.[44] Jefferson also attempted to insert a ban on the importation of slaves into the Virginia state constitution in 1776.[45] When that failed, he sought to provide for the gradual emancipation of slaves in a draft for a new state constitution in 1783.[46] The following year while serving in the Continental Congress he made a proposal which would have gone far beyond the *Northwest Ordinance* and banned slavery in all western territories, including the future cotton-growing states of Alabama and Mississippi, but it lost by one vote.[47] Decrying the failure of his proposal to pass, Jefferson wrote:

> 'Thus we see the fate of millions unborn hanging on the tongue of one man, & heaven was silent in that awful moment! But it is to be hoped it will not always be silent & that the friends to the rights of human nature will in the end prevail.'[48]

As president Jefferson signed legislation in 1807 outlawing the importation of slaves into the United States of America. In 1814 he wrote of the enslaved: "The love of justice and the love of country plead equally the cause of these people, and it is a moral reproach to us that they should have pleaded it so long in vain..."[49] In 1821 he prophesized in his autobiography, "Nothing is more certainly written in the book of fate than that these people are to be free."[50] In 1822 he expressed a desire for the United States to form an agreement with European naval powers to suppress the slave trade off of the African coast.[51] Finally, just weeks before he died, Jefferson wrote

---

[44] Thomas Jefferson, *Autobiography*, in *Thomas Jefferson: Writings*, ed. Merrill D. Peterson (New York: Literary Classics of the United States, 1984), 18.

[45] Sowell, "The Real History of Slavery."

[46] Ibid.

[47] Ibid.

[48] David Barton, *The Jefferson Lies: Exposing the Myths You've Always Believed About Thomas Jefferson* (Washington, D.C.: WND Books, 2016), 119-149.

[49] Thomas Jefferson, "To Edward Coles," August 25, 1814, in *Thomas Jefferson: Writings*, ed. Merrill D. Peterson (New York: Literary Classics of the United States, 1984), 1343-1346.

[50] Thomas Jefferson, *Autobiography*, 44.

[51] Thomas Jefferson, "To John Adams," November 1, 1822, in *The Adams-Jefferson Letters: The Complete Correspondence between Thomas Jefferson & Abigail & John Adams*, ed. Lester J. Cappon (Chapel Hill: University of North Carolina Press, 1987), 584-

that the end of slavery would remain in his prayers, whether he was "living or dying."[52]

Benjamin Franklin (1706-1790), a signer of both the *Declaration of Independence* and the *Constitution*, at one time owned slaves.[53] However, he later renounced the practice and became the President of the Pennsylvania Society for Promoting the Abolition of Slavery. In 1788 he described human bondage as:

> ...a practice...repugnant to the political principles and form of government lately adopted by citizens of the United States...[54]

The following year in a public address he proclaimed:

> ...Slavery is such an atrocious debasement of human nature, that its very extirpation, if not performed with solicitous care, may sometimes open a source of serious evils...[55]

Franklin's final public act was to sign and transmit a petition calling for Congress to "'promote mercy and justice'" and "'step to the very verge of the power vested in you for discouraging every species of traffic in the person of our fellow-men.'"[56]

John Adams (1735-1826), a signer of the *Declaration of Independence* and the second president of the United States of America, never

---

585.

[52] Thomas Jefferson, "To James Heaton," May 20, 1826, in *Thomas Jefferson: Writings*, ed. Merrill D. Peterson (New York: Literary Classics of the United States, 1984), 1516.

[53] Brookhiser.

[54] Benjamin Franklin, "To John Langdon," 1788, in *Benjamin Franklin: Writings*, ed. J.A. Leo LeMay (New York: Literary Classics of the United States, 1987), 1169-1170.

[55] Benjamin Franklin, "An Address to the Public from the Pennsylvania Society for Promoting the Abolition of Slavery, and the Relief of Free Negroes Unlawfully Held in Bondage," November 9, 1789, in *The U.S. Constitution – A Reader*, ed. The Hillsdale College Politics Faculty (Hillsdale, Michigan: Hillsdale College Press, 2014), 401.

[56] Stanley Elkins and Eric McKitrick, *The Age of Federalism: The Early American Republic, 1788-1800* (New York: Oxford University Press, 1993), 151.

owned slaves.[57] He was vehemently opposed to human bondage and hoped for it to be abolished. In 1801 he wrote:

> ...my opinion against it has always been known, and my practice has been so conformable to my sentiments that I have always employed freemen both as Domesticks and Labourers, and never in my Life did I own a slave.[58]

And in 1819 he declared:

> ...Every measure of prudence, therefore, ought to be assumed for the eventual total extirpation of slavery from the United States...I have, through my whole life, held the practice of slavery in...abhorrence...[59]

Another Founding Father, Alexander Hamilton (1755-1804), expressed his disdain for slavery in numerous ways throughout his life. As one of Washington's aides during the Revolutionary war, he helped develop a plan to free slaves in South Carolina and enlist them in the army.[60] Hamilton believed they would "make very excellent soldiers..." and stipulated that "an essential part of the plan is to give them their freedom with their muskets."[61] He was optimistic that the plan would be adopted for reasons of both "humanity and true policy."[62] Although he submitted the proposal to President of Congress John Jay, the South Carolina state legislature rejected the idea.[63] Hamilton was also one of the founders of the New-York

---

[57] Brookhiser.

[58] John Adams, "To George Churchman and Jacob Lindley," January 24, 1801, in *John Adams: Writings from the New Nation*, ed. Gordon S. Wood (New York: Literary Classics of the United States, 2016), 406-407.

[59] John Adams, "To Robert J. Evans," June 9, 1819, in *The U.S. Constitution – A Reader*, ed. The Hillsdale College Politics Faculty (Hillsdale, Michigan: Hillsdale College Press, 2014), 401.

[60] Elkins and McKitrick, 99.

[61] Alexander Hamilton, "To John Jay," March 14, 1779, in *Alexander Hamilton: Writings*, ed. Joanne B. Freeman (Literary Classics of the United States, 2001), 56-58.

[62] Ibid.

[63] Elkins and McKitrick.

Manumission Society in 1785.[64] One of the society's most notable accomplishments was the creation of an African Free School, which instructed free black children in reading and writing among other subjects.[65] In 1795 Hamilton wrote that slavery was a violation of the equal natural rights which belonged to all and said that as human beings slaves were "'capable of acquiring liberty...'"[66] Furthermore, Hamilton believed that abolishing slavery was not only the moral choice but also essential to the economic flourishing and long-term survival of the American republic. As the first Secretary of the Treasury under President Washington, he was the architect of a national plan to solidify the new nation's economic foundations and put it on the road to prosperity as a modern, industrialized country. According to biographer Ron Chernow, Hamilton's "staunch abolitionism formed an integral feature of his economic vision."[67]

The fourth president of the United States, James Madison (1751-1836), is often dubbed "the father of the Constitution" due to the outsized contributions of the diminutive Virginian to its creation. At the Constitutional Convention in 1787 he gave an impassioned speech denouncing slavery:

> ...We have seen the mere distinction of color made in the most enlightened period of time, a ground of the most oppressive dominion ever exercised by man over man...[68]

Although a Southerner and a slaveholder, Madison repeatedly acted in ways that went against his interests. In *Federalist #42* he described the constitutional measure which would eventually outlaw the slave trade as "'...a great point gained in favor of humanity...'"[69] On multiple occasions while serving in Congress, Madison sided with

---

[64] Brookhiser.

[65] Ibid.

[66] Alexander Hamilton, "Philo Camillus no. 2," August 1795, in *The U.S. Constitution – A Reader*, ed. The Hillsdale College Politics Faculty (Hillsdale, Michigan: Hillsdale College Press, 2014), 402.

[67] Ron Chernow, *Alexander Hamilton* (New York: Penguin, 2004), 6.

[68] James Madison, "Speech at the Constitutional Convention," June 6, 1787, in *The U.S. Constitution – A Reader*, ed. The Hillsdale College Politics Faculty (Hillsdale, Michigan: Hillsdale College Press, 2014), 402.

[69] Medved.

Northern states over vigorous Southern opposition to consider various antislavery petitions.[70] In 1819 he referred to slavery as "...the great evil under which the nation labors..."[71]

As Thomas Sowell has observed, people first began to question the morality of slavery in the 1700s. Thankfully, our Founding Fathers were among them. It would be extremely difficult to find a similar revolution in thinking taking place among the leadership of societies in Africa, Asia, or the Middle East during the same period.[72]

The American Revolution and Indians

Although we just assume today that taking land by force is wrong, for most of world history that was not so.[73] The right of ownership by conquest has a long history stretching back through the ages. However, as with slavery, it was in the West where some began to question this assumption. In the United States in particular, American principles dictated that property in land or anything else could only be acquired through a mutual agreement of both sides.

It was the same *Northwest Ordinance* of 1787, which permanently outlawed slavery in the territories of the American Northwest, that also demonstrated the influence of America's founding principles on Indian policy. It enshrined in law a practice which was often but not always followed of purchasing land from the tribes:

> The utmost good faith shall always be observed toward the Indians; their lands and property shall never be taken from them without their just consent, and in their property, rights, and liberty, they shall never be invaded or disturbed, unless in just and lawful wars authorized by Congress; but laws founded in justice and humanity shall from time to time be made for preventing wrongs being done to them, and for preserving peace and friendship with them.[74]

---

[70] Elkins and McKitrick, 143, 152.

[71] James Madison, "To Robert J. Evans," June 15, 1819, in *James Madison: Writings*, ed. Jack N. Rakove (New York: Literary Classics of the United States, 1999), 728-733.

[72] Thomas Sowell, "Twisted History," in The Thomas Sowell Reader (New York: Basic Books, 2011), 18-19.

[73] Ibid.

[74] *The Northwest Ordinance*, in *American Heritage – A Reader*, ed. The Hillsdale College

Consequently, any time land was unjustly taken, it was not because America was founded on the principle of theft. It was due to a *violation* of American principles.

After the ratification of the *Constitution* in 1788, the general policy of the federal government beginning in the 1790s was to recognize Indian property rights. In the view of the *Constitution*, the Indians comprised a separate nation with which the United States could make agreements to purchase land. Congress had the power to regulate commerce with the tribes and presidents could negotiate with them using the executive's treaty-making and war powers.[75]

Previous treaties made between the Continental Congress and Indians of the Northwest included those at Fort Stanwix in 1785, Fort McIntosh and Fort Finney in 1786, and Fort Hamar in 1789. However, they all failed to bring peace to the frontier. Settlers understood that until the British lived up to the *Treaty of Paris* (1783), which had ended the American War for Independence, and abandoned their frontier forts, the northwestern tribes would continue to be encouraged and provided with the means to attack Americans. This was complicated further by the fact that political leaders in the East were reluctant to spend the money that a major military expedition to the frontier would require and feared the potential threats to liberty posed by a standing army.[76]

Nevertheless, repeated Indian attacks on settlers compelled the government to respond. President Washington and Secretary of War Henry Knox approved several military campaigns in the 1790s and Congress begrudgingly created a regular 5,000-man army as well. Nevertheless, the Washington administration continued to engage in negotiations with the Indians of the Northwest until 1793. The following year US Major Anthony Wayne scored a major victory over several tribes at Fallen Timbers resulting in the *Treaty of Greenville* (1795). Although *Jay's Treaty* the same year secured a promise from the British to finally abandon their forts, this remained a chronic problem until the War of 1812. Thereafter, presidents through the administration of John Quincy Adams (1825-1829) generally

---

History Faculty (Hillsdale, Michigan: Hillsdale College Press, 2011), 137-143.
[75] Kermit L. Hall, William M. Wiecek, Paul Finkelman, eds. *American Legal History* (New York: Oxford University Press, 1991), 255-256.
[76] Elkins and McKitrick, 436-439.

defended Indian treaty rights.[77]

The arrival of Andrew Jackson to the White House brought a dramatic change to the federal government's Indian policy. In 1829 during his first annual message, the new Democratic president announced his support for removing several Indian tribes from the southeastern United States to territory west of the Mississippi River. Jackson argued that it should be done for "humanity," "national honor," and to help preserve the way of life for "the Choctaw, the Cherokee, and the Creek." Furthermore, he stated "emigration should be voluntary."[78]

However, many Americans objected when the *Indian Removal Act* (1830) was passed. As would be the case with so many other issues of the period, opinion was divided along sectional lines with the South in support while much of the North viewed it as an effort to expand slavery. The proposed law divided the people's representatives as well and only narrowly passed in both the House of Representatives and the Senate before President Jackson affixed his signature.[79]

The fight over Indian property rights led to a battle between the state of Georgia and the United States government. Georgia passed a law confiscating the lands of the Cherokee in the northern part of the state, despite the fact that the United States government had previously formed a treaty with the tribe recognizing their territorial rights. Another Georgia law made it a crime for any American to stay in Indian territory without first obtaining a license to do so and taking an oath of loyalty to the state. However, the Cherokee were supported by a group of Christian missionaries, ten of whom were arrested by the state of Georgia, beaten, and compelled to march thirty-five miles a day until they arrived at the county jail. Eventually found guilty by a jury, eight were released after swearing loyalty to the state. The two holdouts, Samuel Worcester and Elizur Butler, both received sentences of four years at hard labor.[80]

The imprisoned missionaries appealed to the Supreme Court of the United States. In *Worcester vs Georgia* (1832), Chief Justice John

---

[77] Ibid; Hall, Wiecek, and Finkelman.

[78] Andrew Jackson, "First Annual Message," in *American Heritage – A Reader*, ed. The Hillsdale College History Faculty (Hillsdale, Michigan: Hillsdale College Press, 2011), 285-294.

[79] Howard Zinn, *A People's History of the United States* (New York: Harper Perennial, 2005), 125-148.

[80] Ibid.; Hall, Wiecek, and Finkelman. 259-260.

Marshall ruled that the Georgia law confiscating Cherokee land was invalid because it violated a pre-existing agreement, based upon the *Constitution's* treaty-making powers, between the United States government and the Cherokee Nation. He also ordered Worcester and Butler to be freed. Furthermore, since the Cherokee of northern Georgia were a sovereign nation under the *Constitution* and by virtue of a US treaty, they could not be removed. American principles had been upheld by the highest court in the land.[81]

Nevertheless, in one of the boldest and most flagrant acts of defiance by a president in all of American history, Andrew Jackson chose not to uphold his duty to enforce the law. "'John Marshall has made his decision, so let him enforce it!'" declared Jackson, who then ordered the army to begin forcibly removing the Cherokee from Georgia to west of the Mississippi river. The forced march of the Indians of the Southeast during the 1830s became known as "The Trail of Tears." Other tribes compelled to leave their homes included Seminoles from Florida, Creek from Alabama, and Choctaw from Mississippi. Most were sent to the Indian Territory, which later became the state of Oklahoma. Perhaps one-fourth or more of the marchers, many of them women and children, died along the way.[82]

This was unquestionably one of the most shameful events in all of American history. However, it occurred because the President of the United States violated a Supreme Court ruling which had the force of federal law. Andrew Jackson failed to uphold his sworn duty to see that the laws were faithfully executed. It was not an example of unjust and racist American principles – it was a gross and extreme *violation* of American principles and America's "mission statement."

Once in Oklahoma, "The Five Civilized Tribes" comprised of the Cherokee, Choctaw, Chickasaw, Creek, and Seminole rebuilt their nations. They also continued to own black slaves. Furthermore, when the Civil War arrived, these tribes allied themselves with the slaveholding South.[83]

In an effort to treat tribal peoples in accordance with American principles, the US government had created the Bureau of Indian Affairs (BIA) in 1824, making it one of the oldest and later largest

---

[81] Zinn; Chilton, 39-51.
[82] Chilton.
[83] Kathleen Brush, *Racism and anti-Racism in the World: before and after 1945* (Kathleen Brush, 2020), 56.

federal agencies. By 1940, 60% of the BIA's employees were Indians, and by 1980 the US census reported that a higher percentage of Indians were working for the federal government than any other ethnic group. One of the BIA's responsibilities was to transition Indians to farming. This would ensure that they could feed themselves and not be dependent upon the government, as well as make more land available for settlement and avoid further conflict. However, many Indian men preferred their traditional roles as hunters and warriors and resisted farming because they considered it to be primarily the responsibility of women.[84]

The *Dawes Act* of 1887 was an imperfect, but genuine attempt to assimilate Indians into American society and culture. This included giving male heads-of-households 160 acres of land that they could work and acquire full title to as well as citizenship after twenty-five years. (This was the same exact amount of land offered to settlers under the *Homestead Act* of 1862.) Furthermore, children would be taught in government schools where they could learn English and civics. All Indians gained American citizenship in 1924. Nevertheless, the overall effects of the *Dawes* reforms also included an end to tribal land ownership and an erosion of traditional Indian culture.[85]

The *Indian Reorganization Act* of 1934 attempted to improve upon the *Dawes Act* by bringing back some aspects of tribal life.[86] Although the American Indian population had declined to about 243,000 by 1887, mostly due to disease, war, and alcohol, overall numbers began to steadily grow.[87] In 1970 the Indian population hit 764,000, and by 1990 it had climbed to nearly two million.[88] At least some of the growth resulted from individuals deciding to self-identify as being of Indian ancestry due to cultural trends emphasizing group identities and ethnic pride, as well as opportunities for preferential treatment in academic admissions and hiring.[89]

---

[84] Thomas Sowell, *Conquests and Cultures — An International History* (New York: Basic Books, 1998), 249-328.
[85] Thomas A. Bailey and David M. Kennedy, *The American Pageant*, vol. 2, *Since 1877*, tenth ed., (Lexington, Massachusetts: D.C. Heath and Co., 1994), 597-614; Larry Schweikart and Michael Allen, *A Patriot's History of the United States* (New York: Sentinel, 2004), 411-412.
[86] Ibid.
[87] Ibid.
[88] Sowell, Conquests and Cultures – An International History.
[89] Ibid.

The US has also addressed historic Indian property rights. The Indian Land Claims Commission operated from 1946 to 1978 for this specific purpose. Subsequent claims have been addressed through legal actions. The United States has paid several billion dollars in restitution overall. However, many tribes have benefitted far more from exclusive gaming rights at their reservation casinos. In 2017 they took in more than thirty billion dollars.[90]

Indians have been fully included in America's "mission statement" and are truly American. Many have converted to Christianity, served in all branches of the military in every major conflict from World War I to the present, and established and attended educational institutions at all levels. Numerous Indians have also served in government including Kansas Republican Charles Curtis as vice-president and Senator Ben Nighthorse Campbell, a Republican from Colorado.[91] In 2021, Deb Haaland became the first Indian presidential cabinet secretary when she was confirmed by the United States Senate as the Secretary of the Interior.[92]

The American Revolution and Class

The influence of America's revolutionary principles can also be seen in changes regarding social class. Independence ended any possibility that a hereditary nobility would arise in America. One's family background became far less consequential and upward mobility became a far greater reality than in England or much of the rest of the world. The rigid hierarchical nature of English society had never really taken root in America anyway, although large plantation owners of the South had taken on some of the appearances of an aristocracy. Nevertheless, after independence, a democratic spirit flourished and had a levelling effect. Whereas previously all were aware that they had social superiors and inferiors, many Americans grew unwilling to accept such a static system.[93]

Another development was a decline in dependency. A major reason for this was the wide availability of land. Many individuals

---

[90] Brush, 65.

[91] Bailey and Kennedy; Schweikart and Allen, 411-412.

[92] Deb Haaland confirmed, becomes first Native American Cabinet secretary (usatoday.com), March 15, 2021.

[93] Gordon Wood, *The Radicalism of the American Revolution* (New York: Vintage Books, 1993), 3-8.

who in England would have had little choice but to live and work on someone else's property could experience a life of unprecedented independence on their own freehold in America. Additionally, work, even menial labor, began to be seen as dignified and perhaps even noble as individuals aspired to improve their lives and rise in society through their own merit rather than based upon unearned privilege due to birth and family connections. This encouraged creativity and entrepreneurship amongst Americans, leading to innovation, productivity, and prosperity. Eventually society and government had to begin responding to the needs and opinions of a growing population of ordinary people who possessed both economic power and political influence.[94]

According to Gordon Wood, by the early 1800s it seemed as if there was *only* a middle class in America. In some ways, Americans could be said to have combined attributes of both the aristocracy and the working class. While many more people became educated, in part because it was considered essential to self-government in a republic, the lack of inherited wealth also made it common to work. The growing presence of commerce made many items far more readily available, helping lead to a blending of lifestyles. People even appeared to be dressing similarly. The idea of the hard-working individual American using his freedom to lift himself or herself out of poverty became a cultural ideal as well. It is no wonder that during Frenchman Alexis de Tocqueville's visit to America in the 1830s he observed that there were no peasants in the young republic, while in Europe they were seemingly everywhere.[95]

Changes in American society were reflected in government and law as well. Members of the middle class began to appear in the state legislatures. Those who were loyal to Britain, opposed to democracy, or even aspired to become part of a new American nobility had either fled to Canada or returned to England. Lawmakers abolished primogeniture and entail, property laws that kept wealth within a family by requiring that land be passed down solely to the eldest son when a father died. This practice had reflected assumptions that the eldest son would uphold his duty to care for his siblings who were

---

[94] Ibid.

[95] Ibid., 347-369; Mary Grabar, *Debunking Howard Zinn: Exposing the Fake History That Turned a Generation Against America* (Washington, D.C.: Regnery History, 2019), 241-259.

dependent upon him. However, now land could be broken up and made more widely available. This inhibited the development of an aristocracy, helping to ensure that status would be based more on wealth, which could be earned, rather than birth, which was beyond anyone's control.[96]

Unlike many failed revolutions in which people were promised that land would be *taken* from the wealthy and redistributed, in America it became possible to *acquire* property. The contention of Howard Zinn that support for the *Constitution* was strongest among property holders is correct, but it omits the fact that this was not a tiny elite – at the time of the *Constitution's* drafting more than three quarters of all American families owned property of some kind, including land, farms, debts, and certificates. This was virtually impossible in much of Europe, where land was much less plentiful and tended to remain in the same families for centuries.[97]

Societal changes also affected politics. In much of the rest of the world, the right to vote was non-existent. Even in England voting was limited to a small minority of the population who could meet the property requirement. In America, a far greater share of the population could vote, despite the existence of property requirements in some states. The wide availability of land made such requirements easier to meet, and the egalitarian nature of American society made such restrictions less acceptable. Thus, they gradually began to fall away. From 1812-1821 six new states joined the union with little to no property ownership requirements for voting. Meanwhile, from 1810-1821 six of the older states lowered their property qualifications. As regular people including farmers and workers began to enter politics, voter rolls soared. In 1824 there were approximately 355,000 voters in the presidential election. In 1828 the total climbed to 1,155,000. By 1848 the number had tripled even though the population had only doubled.[98]

Numerous states in this era did limit voting to white males.

---

[96] David Vandeventer, History 471 lecture notes, California State University, Fullerton, Fall 1994; Thomas Sowell, *The Quest for Cosmic Justice* (New York: Touchstone, 1999), 27-28.

[97] Grabar, *Debunking Howard Zinn: Exposing the Fake History That Turned a Generation Against America.*.

[98] Richard Hofstadter, *The American Political Tradition* (New York: Vintage Books, 1974), 56-85.

However, it was not the *Constitution* that mandated this. The Founding Fathers left decisions regarding voter eligibility to the individual state legislatures. Due to the spirit of 1776 and the limited-government nature of the *Constitution*, states have been empowered to freely and steadily expand the franchise throughout American history.

The American Revolution and Women

America's "mission statement" also included women. In the *Declaration of Independence* "all men are created equal" is synonymous with "all of mankind" or "all human beings" of any race or sex. Any number of such terms and phrases were used by the founding generation to describe all people. Furthermore, the *Constitution* did not prohibit women from voting any more than it kept anyone from accessing the ballot due to race, religion, ethnicity, wealth, or property. Neither the words "male" nor "female" ever appear in the document. Again, the *Constitution* gave the *states* the prerogative to determine who could vote in national elections. Indeed, some women as well as black people were already voting when the *Constitution* was ratified. There are records of women voting in New York and Massachusetts during the colonial era. In New Jersey women voted for a time in the 1790s and early 1800s. Out west, women in Wyoming were voting in 1869, long before 1920 when the *Nineteenth Amendment* began requiring all states to recognize women's suffrage.[99]

Furthermore, in America there had been marked changes in the status of women from the beginning. From colonial times the economic opportunities in America which generally improved the standard of living for men inevitably benefitted women too, since so often their fortunes were tied into those of their fathers and husbands. This reflected the role of dependency which was widespread for most people in most societies prior to modern times. Although women did not have the same property rights as men, widows often received far more than the one-third of their husband's goods to which they were legally entitled. In many places there were minimal differences in the amounts bequeathed to sons and daughters as well.[100]

Two American legal innovations benefitted women directly. The

[99] West, *Vindicating the Founders*, 71-83.
[100] Larry Schweikart, *48 Liberal Lies About American History (That You Probably Leaned in School)* (New York: Sentinel, 2008), 78-82.

first was the prenuptial agreement, which permitted women to maintain property rights within a marriage contract. Previously only single women and widows possessed such rights. Likewise, the power-of-attorney enabled women to do all the things a man could do in conducting business, including sign contracts.[101]

Marriage placed reciprocal obligations on men and women. Divorces were generally hard to come by, though less so than in Europe. Women acted as lawyers in some places where divorce was less difficult, while couples often mutually agreed to separate if a particular location made a legal dissolution nearly impossible. Rather than simply being forms of control or repression, parental involvement in selecting a mate as well as the taboo against pre-marital sex were reflective of the difficulty of getting divorced and the importance of a lasting commitment. When pregnancies outside of wedlock occurred, social pressure helped to ensure that a marriage took place and neither woman nor child were abandoned.[102]

The American Revolution elevated the importance of women. In a nation founded on the principle that government should be limited so as to promote individual liberty, self-control and the ability to self-govern became paramount virtues. Therefore, women were viewed as vital to the American experiment because of their roles as wives and mothers who raised and civilized children who would mature into good citizens of a democratic republic. Consequently, women were to be revered, not treated as property, objects, or "'beasts of burden.'"[103]

The effects of 1776 were also evident at the 1848 Seneca Falls Women's Rights Convention organized by Elizabeth Cady Stanton and Lucretia Mott. Rather than repudiating the principles of America's "mission statement," the delegates fully embraced them while asking that they be fully extended to women: "...we now demand our rights to vote *according to the declaration of the government under which we live*," [italics added] said Stanton in her convention address. Furthermore, the convention's *Declaration of Rights and Sentiments* was directly inspired by the *Declaration of Independence*.[104]

---

[101] Ibid.

[102] Ibid.

[103] Wood, *The Radicalism of the American Revolution*, 347-369.

[104] Elizabeth Cady Stanton, "Address to Woman's Rights Convention," July 19. 1848, in *American Speeches: The Revolution to the Civil War*, ed. Ted Widmer, (New York: Literary Classics of the United States, 2006), 333-353; The President's Advisory 1776 Commission, 40.

America's Continuing Fight Against Slavery

America's founding principles never ceased inspiring opposition to bigotry and slavery, even as the Revolutionary Era ended. From the earliest years of the new republic, Americans – black and white, male and female, religious and secular – continued to speak out and fight against inequality and human bondage. Civic organizations also emerged to challenge slavery, either calling for restrictions or outright abolition. Later, a second religious "Great Awakening" once again combined with America's revolutionary principles to lend additional momentum to the anti-slavery movement. The United States also joined Great Britain in waging war against the international slave trade. Finally, anti-slavery political parties formed as the nation headed towards civil war.

Pastor James Dana, in a 1790 address before the Connecticut Society for the Promotion of Freedom, asked his audience how those freed by Jesus Christ from the bondage of sin could participate in the enslavement of others? Referencing the *Declaration of Independence* and the Revolutionary War he noted:

> Our late warfare was expressly founded on such principles as these: 'All men are created equal: They are endowed by their Creator with certain unalienable rights; among these are life, liberty, and the pursuit of happiness.'

Anyone claiming to understand and believe in such principles, argued Dana, "should cheerfully unite to abolish slavery."[105]

Also invoking America's founding principles was businessman and activist James Forten. Born to free black parents in Philadelphia and educated at Quaker Anthony Benezet's African Free School, Forten later served on an American privateer ship and was captured by the British during the Revolutionary War. In 1813 he penned *Letters from a Man of Colour* to criticize a proposed law in the state senate which would have restricted the right of free black people to immigrate to Pennsylvania:

---

[105] Ellis Sandoz, ed., *Political Sermons of the American Founding Era, 1730-1805*, vol. 2, 2nd ed. (Indianapolis: Liberty Fund, 1998), 1030; James Dana, "The African Slave Trade," in *Political Sermons of the American Founding Era, 1730-1805*, ed. Ellis Sandoz, vol. 2, 2nd ed. (Indianapolis: Liberty Fund, 1998), 1031-1055.

> We hold this truth to be self-evident, that God created all men equal, and is one of the most prominent features in the Declaration of Independence, and in that glorious fabric of collected wisdom, our noble Constitution. This idea embraces the Indian and the European, the Savage and the Saint, the Peruvian and the Laplander, the white Man and the African, and whatever measures are adopted subversive of this inestimable privilege, are in direct violation of the letter and spirit of our Constitution...

In confronting an odious proposal, Forten did not denounce the country or its "mission statement." On the contrary, he appealed to America's revolutionary principles. He described the United States, with all of its faults, as "the only reasonable Republick upon earth..." He later joined the abolitionist movement against slavery as well.[106]

Founded in 1817, the American Colonization Society sought to liberate slaves and aid them in settling in West Africa. The organization attracted various members including Senator Daniel Webster of Massachusetts, Representative Henry Clay of Kentucky, future presidents John Tyler and General Andrew Jackson, and Francis Scott Key, author of "The Star-Spangled Banner." Numerous slaveholders were part of the society as well.[107]

However, the reaction of free black Americans was mixed. In New York and Philadelphia there were some black leaders willing to consider colonization. In 1820 the American Colonization Society established Liberia in West Africa to which black minister Daniel Coker led eighty-six settlers. Nevertheless, most black people rightly considered themselves *Americans*. They had helped build the country in a myriad of ways, including through service in the War for Independence and the War of 1812 – the "Second American War for Independence." Most were far more interested in remaining in America, ending slavery, and securing equal rights for all. Ultimately,

---

[106] James G. Basker, ed., *American Antislavery Writings* (New York: Literary Classics of the United States, 2012), 211; James Forten, "Letters from a Man of Colour on a Late Bill Before the Senate of Pennsylvania," in *American Antislavery Writings*, ed. James G. Basker (New York: Literary Classics of the United States, 2012), 211-215.
[107] Chilton, 59-60; Horton and Horton, *Hard Road to Freedom*, 76-103.

only a few thousand ever left the country.[108]

The colonization experiment was followed by a more radical group. The American Anti-Slavery Society (1833) was a genuine abolitionist organization, calling for the immediate release of all slaves in the United States. The founder, a Massachusetts evangelical Christian named William Lloyd Garrison, was impatient with those who counseled a gradual or more strategic course of action so as to avoid societal disruption or even war. "'The question of expedience has nothing to do with that of right,'" asserted Garrison. In 1831 he began publishing the *Liberator*, an anti-slavery newspaper, and referred to the slave as "'a man and a brother.'" In Georgia there was reportedly a $5,000 reward for anyone willing to kidnap him and bring him south.[109]

The American Anti-Slavery Society spread rapidly through the North and West. An integrated organization, in one year forty-seven local chapters sprung up in ten states. Member Gerrit Smith of New York purchased thousands of land titles near Lake Placid and in 1846 gave away 120,000 acres in 40-acre lots to 3,000 black Americans. The property, worth millions of dollars at the time, enabled the recipients to meet the state's property requirement for voting. The society also published pamphlets, sermons, and newspapers as well as presented speakers, male and female, black and white. Among the most in demand were former slaves like Frederick Douglass.[110]

A second "Great Awakening" from the 1820s to 1840s provided added momentum to the anti-slavery movement. Led by preachers like Charles Grandison Finney and Lyman Beecher, Christianity became "democratized" and salvation was said to be available to anyone who accepted Christ as their savior from sin. The belief in the eradication of sin in one's personal life helped lead to the goal of eradicating sin from society at large. This fed reform movements including ending human bondage.[111]

Opposition to slavery came from all walks of life. Thomas Weld was an abolitionist who held many of the same views as Garrison,

---

[108] Ibid.; Medved.

[109] Schweikart and Allen, 227-228; Sowell, "The Real History of Slavery."

[110] Horton and Horton, *Hard Road to Freedom*, 126-149; Mary Grabar, *Debunking the 1619 Project: Exposing the Plan to Divide America* (Washington, D.C.: Regnery History, 2021), 193-232.

[111] The Hillsdale College History Faculty, eds., *American Heritage – A Reader* (Hillsdale, Michigan: Hillsdale College Press, 2011), 259-263.

but believed in a more gradual approach. Elijah Lovejoy, the editor of an abolitionist newspaper, was eventually killed by an Illinois mob in 1837. Lewis and Arthur Tappan were abolitionist brothers; at one point there was a $50,000 bounty on Arthur's head. Meanwhile, the Grimke sisters, Sarah and Angela, were former slaveholders who inherited their father's South Carolina plantation but freed their slaves; they later moved to the North, joined the Quakers, and toured the nation as two of the first female lecturers while denouncing slavery as evil. Joining them were former slaves Sojourner Truth and Solomon Northrup, author of *Twelve Years a Slave*. His life story was later made into an Oscar-winning film.[112]

Abolitionists generally adopted one of two strategies. Moderates preferred working within the system, using moral suasion to change hearts and minds and pressure Congress to act. However, radicals, including Garrison and others, would settle for nothing less than complete abolition without delay – even if it required tearing up the *Constitution* and dissolving the union. Many in the North, even those who were anti-slavery, viewed abolitionists as too extreme in their demands and saw them as advocating lawlessness.[113]

There was also progress in the fight against international slavery. In 1808 the United States abolished the slave trade – the importation of slaves into the country. Thereafter, the Revenue Cutter Service, predecessor to the US Coast Guard, began seizing slave ships.[114] Coordinated action with Great Britain began in 1842 when Secretary of State Daniel Webster negotiated an agreement with British Foreign Secretary Lord Ashburton to patrol the African coast for slave ships and liberate the illicit human cargo.[115] In 1852 abolitionist Frederick Douglass acknowledged these US efforts:

> That trade has long since been denounced by this
> government as piracy. It has been denounced with
> burning words, from the high places of the nation, as

---

[112] Chilton; Schweikart and Allen.

[113] Chilton; Margaret H. Bacon, *The Quiet Rebels: The Story of the Quakers in America* (New York: Basic Books, Inc., 1969), 94-121.

[114] William J. Bennett and John T. E. Cribb, *The American Patriot's Almanac* (Nashville: Thomas Nelson, 2010), 309.

[115] Steven E. Woodworth, *The Essentials of United States History: 1841 to 1877 Westward Expansion and the Civil War* (Piscataway, New Jersey: Research and Education Association, 1997), 2-3.

an execrable traffic. To arrest it, to put an end to it, this nation keeps a squadron, at immense cost, on the coast of Africa.[116]

During the Civil War, President Lincoln even began permitting the British Navy to inspect American vessels suspected of illegally smuggling slaves.[117] In 1862 a slave ship carrying Africans to Cuba was intercepted by the American Navy; the ship's crew were imprisoned and the captain was hung in the United States.[118]

A final development in the continuing anti-slavery movement was the emergence in the 1840s and 1850s of anti-slavery political parties. Whether it was for moral, economic, or political reasons, all who were driven to join these organizations were united by their opposition to the spread of slavery. Many undoubtedly also objected to the encrusted, class-based nature of Southern society with the unearned status and privileges held by a few at the top. It must have seemed undemocratic, unequal, and un-American.[119]

Anti-slavery political parties sought first and foremost to halt the expansion of slavery. That meant containing human bondage within the South. Many hoped and believed that this approach would inevitably result in the death of slavery as the nation industrialized. Furthermore, a successful containment strategy provided the added benefit of ending slavery without provoking a war or the dissolution of the union.[120]

The demise of the Whig party, descendants of Alexander Hamilton's Federalists, opened the door for several anti-slavery political parties to emerge. Like the Federalists, the Whigs had supported moving the United States economy towards manufacturing, commerce, and finance, while leaving behind the more agriculturally-based vision of Thomas Jefferson's Democratic Party. The Whigs endorsed Kentucky Congressman Henry Clay's "American System" which included a national bank, protective tariffs for business, and federally-sponsored internal improvements such as

---

[116] Douglass, "What to the Slave is the Fourth of July?"
[117] Arthur Herman, *To Rule the Waves: How the British Navy Shaped the Modern World* (New York: HarperCollins Publishers, 2004), 418-423.
[118] Sowell, "Twisted History."
[119] Berlin, 358-365.
[120] Chilton.

roads, bridges, and canals to facilitate commerce – in modern parlance, "infrastructure." However, the party feared a split if it took a definitive stand one way or the other on slavery, ultimately resulting in the exodus of "conscience Whigs," those opposed to human bondage. It quickly disappeared from the American political scene.[121]

The Liberty Party, founded in 1840, was the first national anti-slavery party. It had a free-soil platform opposing the expansion of human bondage into the Western territories. Although it ran one candidate for president, it disbanded shortly thereafter.[122]

In 1848 the Free-Soil Party formed. Running with the slogan "Free Soil, Free Speech, Free Labor, and Free Men," it was comprised of several disparate groups all opposed to slavery. These included abolitionists, former Liberty Party members, and "conscience Whigs." It was also short-lived.[123]

Filling the void was another new political party, the Republicans, founded in 1854. Combining a pro-business and pro-development philosophy with opposition to the expansion of slavery, the Republicans attracted abolitionists, free-soilers, and former Whigs to its ranks. Their 1856 platform reiterated America's "mission statement" as the foundation of the party's principles and cited the example set by the Founding Fathers of restricting slavery as a justification for their efforts to do the same:

> Resolved, That the maintenance of the principles promulgated in the Declaration of Independence, and embodied in the federal constitution, is essential to the preservation of our Republican institutions, and that the federal constitution, the rights of the states, and the union of states, shall be preserved.

> Resolved, That with our republican fathers we hold it to be a self-evident truth that all men are endowed with the inalienable rights to life, liberty and the pursuit of happiness, and that the primary object and ulterior design of our Federal government were, to secure these rights to all persons within its exclusive

---

[121] The Hillsdale College History Faculty, 259-263.
[122] Chilton.
[123] Schweikart and Allen, 265.

jurisdiction; that as our republican fathers, when they had abolished slavery in all our national territory, ordained that no person should be deprived of life, liberty, or property, without due process of law, it becomes our duty to maintain this provision of the constitution against all attempts to violate it for the purpose of establishing slavery in any territory of the United States...

In 1856 the Republicans nominated John C. Fremont for president, but he was defeated by Democrat James Buchanan. However, the Republicans returned in 1860 to nominate Abraham Lincoln for the presidency and take the White House.[124]

Lincoln and the Republicans were determined to draw a distinction between constitutional principles and constitutional compromises. The provisions in the *Constitution* recognizing slavery where it existed were not endorsements of human bondage; they had been necessary to ensure ratification. These compromises did not override the principles underlying the *Declaration* and the *Constitution*. Therefore, slavery must expand no further.[125]

From a "Necessary Evil" to a "Positive Good"?

Simultaneously with these developments, one of the first great challenges to America's "mission statement" and the principles of the American Revolution emerged. As cotton developed into a profitable business and under increasing pressure from abolitionists, for the first time some Southerners began justifying slavery not as a "necessary evil" but as a "positive good." Southern political theorists went so far to claim that the Founding Fathers had been wrong. Challenging the notion that "all men are created equal," proponents of the "positive good" philosophy argued that some were by nature fit only to be slaves. Furthermore, they pushed for slavery's

---

[124] Schweikart and Allen; "Republican Party Platform of 1856," June 17, 1856, in *The U.S. Constitution – A Reader*, ed. The Hillsdale College Politics Faculty (Hillsdale, Michigan: Hillsdale College Press, 2014), 481-483.

[125] Harry V. Jaffa, *A New Birth of Freedom: Abraham Lincoln and the Coming of the Civil War* (Lanham, Maryland: Rowman and Littlefield Publishers, Inc., 2004.), 73-152, 90.

expansion into the territories of the American West.[126]

A key event leading to the rise of the South's "Cotton Kingdom" was the invention of the cotton gin in 1793. Previously, removing seeds from cotton had been an extremely slow and laborious process done by hand. However, after a teacher named Eli Whitney created a cotton engine or "gin," a box with a rotating cylinder and nails to extract cotton seeds, an individual laborer could do the work as much as fifty times faster. As Alabama, Mississippi, and Arkansas joined Georgia as prime cotton-growing states, Southern economic and cultural life were transformed. Consequently, in the years after the United States abolished the slave trade in 1808, the demand for and hence the price of slaves rose exponentially.[127]

The "positive good" school of thought was completely alien to the spirit of the American Revolution. The general consensus of the founding generation had been that slavery was a violation of natural rights. The only areas of disagreement were when and how to abolish it. Many wanted human bondage eradicated immediately, while some Southerners, particularly in Georgia and South Carolina, maintained that it was "a necessary evil." The idea that slavery might be a "positive good" developed in the South decades after the American Revolution as an attempt to justify slavery when cotton production became so profitable.[128]

The leading proponent of the "positive good" philosophy was Senator John C. Calhoun of South Carolina (1782-1850). In his speeches and writings, Calhoun defended the South, states' rights, and slavery. In no uncertain terms, he rejected the view of the American founding and the Founding Fathers that "all men are created equal." In abandoning John Locke's doctrine that men were born free and equal in a "state of nature," he instead adopted the notion of ancient Greek philosopher Aristotle that men were not born free. Instead, liberty was given to a select few who possessed intelligence and virtue. Calhoun's innovation was to apply this idea specifically to race. He argued that the "winners" of history were those who could govern themselves; those who could not were history's "losers" and destined to be governed by others. Therefore,

---

[126] West and Jeffrey.
[127] Horton and Horton, *Hard Road to Freedom*.
[128] Kesler.

slavery was not a "necessary evil," but a "positive good."[129]

Calhoun's theory bore some resemblance to the Marxist notion that history was driven by an endless struggle between various classes. In emphasizing racial groupings, Calhoun's philosophy also resembled modern identity politics. Rather than the unifying message of the *Declaration of Independence* that all human beings were created equal and shared inalienable natural rights, Calhoun referred to what he viewed as the inherent *inequality* among human beings:

> It is indeed, this inequality of condition between the front and rear ranks, in the march of progress, which gives so strong an impulse to the former to maintain their position, and to the latter to press forward into their files.

Like Marx, Calhoun viewed history as a struggle between those seeking to maintain their power and those wishing to acquire it.[130]

Calhoun openly rejected the principles of the *Declaration of Independence* and the American Revolution despite admitting that those ideas were widely-held. He referred to "the prevalent opinion that all men are born free and equal" as being "unfounded and false." Furthermore, he insisted that such a belief "rests upon the assumption of a fact, which is contrary to universal observation."[131]

Calhoun also questioned the political theory behind the *Constitution*. Madison had argued in *Federalist #10* that by establishing a republic over a large territory with many different and competing interests, it would be difficult for a single majority faction to form that could violate the rights of the minority. However, Calhoun alleged that there was a majority in the North that was tyrannizing the minority in the South where slavery was primarily located. He also claimed that separation of powers had not worked because Madison did not account for political parties, any one of which could take over all three branches of government, thereby eliminating the "checks

---

[129] Ibid.
[130] The President's Advisory 1776 Commission, 29; John C. Calhoun, "Disquisition on Government," in *American Heritage – A Reader*, ed. The Hillsdale College History Faculty (Hillsdale, Michigan: Hillsdale College Press, 2011), 373-385.
[131] Calhoun.

and balances" on one another.[132]

Fortunately, America has always been able to summon extraordinary leaders to confront threats to America's principles. One of these was an escaped slave from Maryland named Frederick Douglass. After fleeing to the North, he began publishing *The North Star*, an anti-slavery newspaper, and became one of the most popular speakers of the abolitionist movement. While some in the South were rejecting the *Declaration's* doctrine of equal natural rights and others in the North were willing to tear up the *Constitution*, Douglass fiercely defended both.[133]

Initially Douglass had agreed with William Lloyd Garrison that the United States *Constitution* protected slavery and that therefore the North should separate from the South: "With Mr. Garrison, I held it to be the first duty of the non-slaveholding states to dissolve the union with the slaveholding states; and hence my cry, like his, was, 'No union with slaveholders.'" Also like Garrison, Douglass refused to vote. However, after taking the time to truly study the nation's founding documents, Douglass came to hold a different view. He wrote that the *Constitution*:

> ...not only contained no guarantees in favor of slavery, but, on the contrary, it is, in its letter and spirit, an anti-slavery instrument, demanding the abolition of slavery as a condition of its own existence, as the supreme law of the land.

He added that "not one word can be found in the constitution" to justify a belief that it was intended "to maintain and perpetuate" slavery. Thus, instead of being an impediment to the abolition of human bondage, Douglass came to view the *Constitution* as a tool in that effort. He and Garrison eventually split over the issue.[134]

On July 5, 1852, Douglass delivered one of his most famous speeches, "What to the Slave is the Fourth of July?" He rightly condemned slavery, but of the *Declaration of Independence* he said:

---

[132] Kesler.

[133] Chilton, 59-60.

[134] Frederick Douglass, "My Bondage and My Freedom," in *Frederick Douglass: Autobiographies*, ed. Henry Louis Gates, Jr. (New York: Literary Classics of the United States, Inc., 1994), 391-393; Schweikart and Allen, 264.

The principles contained in that instrument are saving principles. Stand by those principles, be true to them on all occasions, in all places, against all foes, and at whatever the cost.

And of the signers of the *Declaration,* he noted:

The signers of the Declaration of Independence were brave men. They were great men too – great enough to give fame to a great age. It does not often happen to a nation to raise, at one time, such a number of great men…With them, nothing was 'settled' that was not right. With them, justice, liberty, and humanity were 'final;' not slavery and oppression.

Citing the example of the first president, Douglass also reminded his audience that "Washington could not die till he had broken the chains of his slaves." Finally, he vigorously defended the *Constitution* against the charge that it condoned slavery:

In *that* instrument I hold there is neither warrant, license, nor sanction of the hateful thing; but interpreted as it *ought* to be interpreted, the Constitution is a GLORIOUS LIBERTY DOCUMENT. Read its preamble, consider its purposes. Is slavery among them?…if the Constitution were intended to be by its framers and adopters a slave-holding instrument, why neither *slavery, slaveholding,* nor *slave* can anywhere by found in it…Now, take the Constitution according to its plain reading, and I defy the presentation of a single pro-slavery clause in it. On the other hand it will be found to contain principles and purposes, entirely hostile to the existence of slavery.[135]

---

[135] Douglass, "What to the Slave is the Fourth of July?"

Frederick Douglass (c. 1818-1895) by George Kendall Warren. Wikimedia Commons. Public domain.

Douglass continued defending the American founding thereafter. On March 19, 1855, he proclaimed, "'The patriots of the American Revolution clearly saw, and with all their inconsistency, they had the grace to confess, the abhorrent character of Slavery, and to hopefully predict its overthrow and complete extirpation.'" On August 2, 1858, Douglass again refuted the notion that racism and slavery were part of America's founding principles. He argued that the drafters of the Constitution "'…nowhere tell us that black men shall be Slaves and white men shall be free. They nowhere make any distinction among men in respect to rights on account of color.'"[136]

In defending America's "mission statement," Douglass demonstrated that racism and slavery were not part of America's founding principles but were in fact horrendous *violations* of those principles. If a former slave recognized this, then so should we.

Perhaps the greatest advocate for and defender of the principles of the American founding who ever lived was Abraham Lincoln. "I have never had a feeling politically that did not spring from the sentiments embodied in the Declaration of Independence," said Lincoln.[137] Throughout his public life, he counseled Americans to stay the course and adhere to their "mission statement." While some justified slavery as a "positive good," compromised with slavery by advocating "popular sovereignty" – allowing the citizens of new territories and states to decide for themselves whether or not to permit slavery – or pursued radical abolition including encouraging violence or even dissolving the union, Lincoln championed returning to the *Declaration of Independence*, the *Constitution*, natural rights, and the rule of law.[138] Like the Founding Fathers, he believed that American principles were not mere "value judgments" connected only to a particular time and place; they were objective "moral judgments" applicable to all people and all societies because they were rooted in nature and observable by reason.[139] It is not an exaggeration to say that Lincoln saved the American republic from becoming a failed experiment in self-government.

---

[136] Grabar, *Debunking the 1619 Project: Exposing the Plan to Divide America*, 193-232.

[137] Abraham Lincoln, "Speech at Independence Hall," February 22, 1861 in *American Speeches: The Revolution to the Civil War*, ed. Ted Widmer, (New York: Literary Classics of the United States, 2006), 705-706.

[138] Kesler.

[139] Jaffa, 73-152, 89.

Lincoln hated slavery. Accusations by his critics that he was only concerned with winning the Civil War or that he was a tyrant solely desirous of accumulating power for himself must be put to rest. These are not the words of a man who was ambivalent about slavery:

> I hate it because of the monstrous injustice of slavery itself. I hate it because it deprives our republican example of its just influence in the world – enables the enemies of free institutions, with plausibility, to taunt us as hypocrites – causes the real friends of freedom to doubt our sincerity, and especially because it forces so many really good men amongst ourselves into an open war with the very fundamental principles of civil liberty – criticizing the Declaration of Independence, and insisting that there is no right principle of action but *self-interest*.[140]

Not only did Lincoln hate slavery, but he also wanted to defeat slavery. The question was how? He argued that just as human bondage was a violation of natural law, radical abolition violated the rule of law. He cited two types of radical abolition: assertion, meaning to take action, violently if necessary, as was exemplified by John Brown's raid on a federal arsenal at Harper's Ferry in 1859, and withdrawal, the view of William Lloyd Garrison and others that the free states should effectively rip up the *Constitution* and dissolve the union rather than remain connected with the South. Both, Lincoln cautioned, rejected law and there could be no freedom without law.[141]

According to Harry Jaffa, Lincoln viewed slavery as a cancer on the body of the nation. Like cancer, its spread had to be stopped so that it would not kill the patient; however, if the cancer was not removed properly this would also kill the patient. Attempting to root out human bondage immediately could lead to secession, war, and the destruction of the union. The patient would "bleed to death."[142]

For Lincoln, the right way to fight and defeat slavery was to use

---

[140] "Lincoln-Douglas Debates," in *American Heritage – A Reader*, ed. The Hillsdale College History Faculty (Hillsdale, Michigan: Hillsdale College Press, 2011), 425-446.

[141] Kesler.

[142] Jaffa, 73-152, 74.

the means provided for in the United States *Constitution*: build a constitutional majority to block the expansion of slavery into the western territories. Combined with the federal government's enforcement of the ban on the importation of slaves, this would contain slavery in the South, starve it of new laborers and new lands, and ultimately result in the death of human bondage in America.[143]

In 1858 Lincoln ran as a Republican challenging incumbent Illinois Democrat Stephen A. Douglas for a seat in the United States Senate. Douglas was a leading contender for the 1860 Democratic presidential nomination, while Lincoln was a lawyer from Springfield whose prior national experience had been limited to a single congressional term in the 1840s. Several recent developments had led Lincoln to become increasingly concerned about the spread of slavery.[144]

In 1854 Congress had passed the *Kansas-Nebraska Act*, introduced and supported by Douglas. In creating the territories of Kansas and Nebraska, the law allowed for the question of slavery to be determined by the voters, a concept Douglas called "popular sovereignty." This law overturned a previous piece of legislation known as the "Missouri Compromise," which in 1820 had admitted Missouri as a slave state and Maine as a free state while also prohibiting slavery in the region where the Kansas and Nebraska territories were to be located.[145]

Those opposed to the *Kansas Nebraska Act* included anti-slavery Northerners outraged by what they viewed as a betrayal of a near-sacred promise, and Lincoln, who argued that prohibiting the expansion of slavery had been a part of the Founding Fathers' plan to eventually end human bondage in America. Citing Thomas Jefferson's proposal to ban slavery in the Northwest Territory via the *Northwest Ordinance* of 1787, Lincoln proclaimed: "Thus, with the author of the Declaration of Independence, the policy of prohibiting slavery in new territory originated." Furthermore, of the Founding Fathers as a group, Lincoln argued:

---

[143] Kesler.

[144] Woodworth, *The Essentials of United States History: 1841 to 1877 Westward Expansion and the Civil War*, 19-46.

[145] Ibid.

This same generation of men, and mostly the same individuals of the generation...who declared independence – who fought the war of the revolution through – who afterwards made the constitution under which we still live – these same men passed the ordinance of '87, declaring that slavery should never go to the north-west territory.[146]

Of perhaps even greater concern was the recent Supreme Court decision in *Dred Scott v. Sanford* (1857). Scott, a slave from Missouri, had been taken by his owner, an army surgeon, into several free territories and later was encouraged by supporters to sue for his freedom as a result. In writing the majority opinion, pro-Southern Chief Justice Roger B. Taney of Maryland read something into the *Constitution* which plainly was not there, arguing that black Americans were not citizens and therefore Scott could not even sue in court. Furthermore, the Court held that the *Constitution* protected the right to own slaves and therefore the "Missouri Compromise" was unconstitutional because it prohibited slaveowners from taking their property into certain territories of the US. While the South was exultant over the ruling, many Northerners viewed the decision as effectively sanctifying and nationalizing slavery. In this context, it seemed that human bondage could spread anywhere and everywhere.[147]

However, Lincoln argued that the decision in *Dred Scott* was wrong on both counts. First, he cited the dissenting opinion of Judge Curtis, who argued that black people:

> '...were not only included in the body of 'the people of the United States,' by whom the Constitution was ordained and established; but in at least five of the States they had the power to act, and, doubtless, did act, by their suffrages, upon the question of its adoption.'

---

[146] Ibid.; Abraham Lincoln, "Speech on the Kansas-Nebraska Act," October 16, 1854, in *Abraham Lincoln: Speeches and Writings, 1832-1858*, ed. Don E. Fehrenbacher (New York: Literary Classics of the United States, Inc., 1989), 307-348, 309, 329.
[147] Hall, Wiecek, and Finkelman, 207; Woodworth, *The Essentials of United States History: 1841 to 1877 Westward Expansion and the Civil War*.

According to Curtis, at the time that the *Constitution* was being drafted, debated, and ratified, black Americans were voting in at least five states, clearly implying that they were citizens. Second, the Court's assertion that "'the right of property in a slave is distinctly and expressly affirmed in the *Constitution*'" was characterized by Lincoln as "a mistaken statement of fact." The *Constitution* may have indirectly recognized the existence of slavery, but that was not the same thing as condoning or guaranteeing the ownership of human beings as a right.[148]

With these developments in the background, the Illinois contest between Douglas, the supporter of "popular sovereignty," and Lincoln, a steadfast opponent of slavery's expansion, took on national significance and drew national attention. Upon accepting the Republican nomination for the US Senate in Springfield on June 16, 1858, Lincoln referenced the words of Jesus Christ in Matthew 12:25, "A house divided against itself cannot stand." For Lincoln, the United States of America was facing a crisis:

> I believe this government cannot endure, permanently half *slave* and half *free*. I do not expect the Union to be *dissolved* – I do not expect the house to *fall* – but I *do* expect it will cease to be divided. It will become *all* one thing, or *all* the other. Either the *opponents* of slavery, will arrest the further spread of it, and place it where the public mind shall rest in the belief that it is in the course of ultimate extinction; or its *advocates* will push it forward, till it shall become alike lawful in all the States, *old* as well as *new* – *North* as well as *South*. Have we no *tendency* to the latter condition?

Lincoln argued that freedom and slavery could not co-exist. In light of recent events, he feared that slavery was on the march. Consequently, he urged Americans to return to their founding principles, halt slavery's expansion, and put it on the path towards

---

[148] Abraham Lincoln, "Speech on the Dred Scott Decision at Springfield, Illinois," June 26, 1857, in *Abraham Lincoln: Speeches and Writings, 1832-1858*, ed. Don E. Fehrenbacher (New York: Literary Classics of the United States, Inc., 1989), 390-403; Lincoln, "Address at Cooper Institute."

extinction or else it would consume freedom everywhere.[149]

During the subsequent 1858 campaign, Lincoln and Douglas engaged in seven epic debates which helped to clarify the issues and the stakes for the nation's future. The first candidate would speak for one hour. The second candidate would have ninety minutes to respond. The first candidate would then give a thirty-minute rejoinder.[150]

On the issue of popular sovereignty, Douglas claimed that allowing territories and states to vote on slavery would uphold democracy. Meanwhile, he attacked Lincoln as a radical extremist who not only wanted to end human bondage but also believed in racial equality and race mixing. On the other hand, Lincoln argued that popular sovereignty did not denounce slavery as immoral, and so Douglas must secretly support the institution.[151]

In a larger sense, the Lincoln-Douglas debates were also about whether the United States of America would be a democracy or a republic. In effect, Douglas's "popular sovereignty" doctrine was an endorsement of majority rule at all costs – a tyranny of the many over the few. Lincoln, on the other hand, supported America's founding as a democratic republic, based upon majority rule, but with a government limited by the rule of law which recognized the inalienable individual rights enshrined in the *Declaration of Independence* and protected by the *Constitution*.[152]

At the first debate on August 21, 1858 in Ottawa, Douglas attempted to refute Lincoln's claim that "A house divided against itself cannot stand." He insisted that the nation had developed just as the Founding Fathers had intended, with some states being slave states and others being free states, each as it saw fit. However, Lincoln argued that Douglas was wrong. The founders had meant what they said when they proclaimed "all men are created equal" in the *Declaration of Independence*. That is why they had included anti-

---

[149] William J. Bennett and John T. E. Cribb, *The American Patriot's Almanac* (Nashville: Thomas Nelson, 2010), 215; Abraham Lincoln, "House Divided" Speech, June 16, 1858, in *American Speeches: The Revolution to the Civil War*, ed. Ted Widmer, (New York: Literary Classics of the United States, 2006), 634-642; Matthew 12:25 (NKJV).
[150] The Hillsdale College History Faculty, 425-426.
[151] Woodworth, *The Essentials of United States History: 1841 to 1877 Westward Expansion and the Civil War*.
[152] Schweikart and Allen, 289.

slavery provisions within the *Constitution* and enacted anti-slavery legislation – to end the slave trade, stop slavery from spreading, and eventually end human bondage. According to Lincoln, this was in fact the real reason why slavery existed in some states and not all:

> ...when [Douglas] reminds me that I have often said to him that the institution of slavery has existed for eighty years in some states, and yet it does not exist in some others, I agree to the fact, and I account for it by looking at the position in which our fathers originally placed it – restricting it from the new territories where it had not gone, and legislating to cut off its source by the abrogation [outlawing] of the slave-trade, thus putting the seal of legislation *against its spread.* The public mind *did* rest in the belief that it [slavery] was in the course of ultimate extinction.[153]

At a subsequent debate at Galesburg on October 7, 1858, Lincoln proclaimed that all Americans had been included in the promises of the *Declaration of Independence.* Furthermore, he argued that no one, from 1776 until just a few years prior to that moment, had ever expressed anything to the contrary. Lincoln alleged that the only reason some had recently begun to rethink this was because it fit the then-current political agenda of those seeking to justify the unjustifiable practice of human bondage:

> ...I believe the entire records of the world, from the date of the Declaration of Independence up to within three years ago, may be searched in vain for one single affirmation, from one single man, that the Negro was not included in the Declaration of Independence; I think I may defy Judge Douglas to show that he ever said so, that Washington ever said so, that any President ever said so, that any member of Congress ever said so, or that any living man upon the whole earth ever said so, until the necessities of the present policy of the Democratic party, in regard to slavery, had to invent that affirmation. And I will

---

[153] "Lincoln-Douglas Debates."

remind Judge Douglas and the audience, that while Mr. Jefferson was the owner of slaves, as undoubtedly he was, in speaking upon this very subject, he used the strong language that 'he trembled for his country when he remembered that God was just;...'[154]

This was unquestionably true. While John C. Calhoun had been intellectually honest and admitted that his "positive good" justification for slavery was in direct conflict with the beliefs of the Founding Fathers, Douglas, Taney, and others were dishonestly attempting to re-write history and revise the spirit and intent of America's "mission statement" to serve their immediate interests.

At the final debate in Alton, Illinois on October 15, 1858, Lincoln argued that in the end, the real debate over slavery boiled down to right vs. wrong:

> That is the issue that will continue in this country when these poor tongues of Judge Douglas and myself shall be silent. It is the eternal struggle between these two principles – right and wrong – throughout the world. They are the two principles that have stood face to face from the beginning of time; and will ever continue to struggle. The one is the common right of humanity and the other the divine right of kings. It is the same principle in whatever shape it develops itself. It is the same spirit that says, 'You work and toil and earn bread, and I'll eat it.' No matter in what shape it comes, whether from the mouth of a king who seeks to bestride the people of his own nation and live by the fruit of their labor, or from one race of men as an apology for enslaving another race, it is the same tyrannical principle...[155]

Despite what Douglas and others may have argued in order to distract from the central issue of the immorality of slavery, Lincoln was not advocating for radical egalitarianism or calling for immediate

---

[154] Ibid.
[155] Ibid.

political and social change. He was a smart, practical statesman who understood that politics is the art of the possible. You can only accomplish that which you can persuade a majority of the people and their representatives to agree upon. He simply argued that everyone, regardless of race, was "'entitled to all the natural rights enumerated in the Declaration of Independence, the right to life, liberty, and the pursuit of happiness...'" and was equal to everyone else "'In the right to eat the bread, without leave of anybody else, which his own hand earns...'"[156]

Although Lincoln narrowly lost to Douglas in November, his passionate and eloquent defense of America's "mission statement" solidified the determination of slavery's opponents to halt its spread. Catapulted onto the national stage, in 1860 Lincoln won the Republican nomination for president and then the presidency.[157]

There has never been a chief executive who entered office under more trying circumstances than Abraham Lincoln. Having won a four-way race in November, 1860, where he had only obtained about 40% of the popular vote but a majority of the electoral college total, Lincoln witnessed the secession of South Carolina the following month. By the time he was sworn in on March 4, 1861, a total of seven states had seceded and formed the Confederate States of America (CSA).[158]

In his First Inaugural Address, Lincoln argued that the right to revolution was reserved for "a morally justifiable cause." Secession was not revolution and therefore was unconstitutional. The Union, he declared, was both "perpetual" and "unbroken."[159]

However, Lincoln was also determined to adhere to the *Constitution* and limit his actions to what was permitted by the law of the land, undoubtedly making his task of fighting slavery immensely more difficult. He was opposed to the exercise of unjust and arbitrary power, whether it was a master over a slave or a tyrant over a people. Consequently, he reiterated his campaign commitment to not

---

[156] Schweikart and Allen, 289.

[157] Woodworth, *The Essentials of United States History: 1841 to 1877 Westward Expansion and the Civil War.*

[158] Ibid.

[159] The Hillsdale College History Faculty, 473-474; Abraham Lincoln, "First Inaugural Address," March 4, 1861, in *American Heritage – A Reader*, ed. The Hillsdale College History Faculty (Hillsdale, Michigan: Hillsdale College Press, 2011), 474-481.

interfere with human bondage in the states where it already existed. He also pledged that he would not be the one to start a war:

> In your hands, my dissatisfied fellow-countrymen, and not in mine, is the momentous issue of civil war. The government will not assail you. You have no conflict without being yourselves the aggressors. You have no oath registered in heaven to destroy the government, while I shall have the most solemn one to 'preserve, protect, and defend it.'[160]

The debate between the North and the South demonstrates why, in a conflict between group rights and individual rights, the latter must prevail. Lincoln had stated that the right to revolution was only "for a morally justifiable cause." According to Confederate President Jefferson Davis, Southerners had seceded to protect states' rights. They believed that this was moral. However, as expressed by other Southerners, the states' right which they seemed most determined to protect was the right to hold slaves – a violation of *individual* rights.[161]

For example, on March 12, 1861, Confederate Vice President Alexander Stephens delivered a kind of "mission statement" for the Confederate States of America. As with Calhoun's "positive good" thesis, Stephens' "Cornerstone Speech" demonstrates that the arguments mustered in defense of racism and slavery were not based upon America's founding principles. On the contrary, they could only be supported by a direct *refutation* of those principles. While the charge that the United States of America was founded on racism and slavery is a condemnable lie – thoroughly refuted by the historical evidence – here is what an actual nation founded on racism and slavery would look like:

> The prevailing ideas entertained by him [Thomas Jefferson] and most of the leading statesmen at the time of the formation of the old constitution, were that the enslavement of the African was in violation of the laws of nature; that it was wrong in principle, socially, morally, and politically. It was an evil they

---

[160] Jaffa, 73-152, 78, 116; Lincoln, "First Inaugural Address."
[161] The Hillsdale College History Faculty, 483; Jaffa, 73-152, 87-88.

knew not well how to deal with, but the general opinion of the men of that day was that, somehow or other in the order of Providence, the institution would be evanescent and pass away...Those ideas, however, were fundamentally wrong. They rested upon the assumption of the equality of the races. This was an error...Our new government is founded on exactly the opposite idea; its foundations are laid, its corner-stone rests upon the great truth that the negro is not equal to the white man; that slavery – subordination to the superior race – is his natural and normal condition. This, our new government, is the first, in the history of the world, based upon this great physical, philosophical, and moral truth.[162]

One month later, the Civil War began. Fort Sumter, a federal installation on an island in the middle of Charleston Harbor, South Carolina, had been besieged by Confederate forces for months. When Lincoln ordered it to be resupplied, the South viewed it as an act of war and commenced fire. Over the next several weeks four more states seceded, lifting the Confederate total to eleven.[163]

At the time, slavery in America was at its height. However, certain facts surrounding human bondage in the US confound the simplistic oppressor-oppressed narrative based upon race that is advanced by so many Marxist historians. For example, approximately 9 million people resided in the South, with nearly 4 million enslaved, but the vast majority of Southerners owned no slaves. About 0.1% owned 100 or more, another 6.6% claimed 10-99, and 17.2% held 1-9. The remaining 76.1% of the population were non-slaveholders.[164]

Further complicating the situation is the fact that among those who did own slaves, a not insignificant minority were free black people. In a 2005 article in the *Journal of Southern History*, David L. Lightner and Alexander M. Ragan estimated that in 1830 there were

---

[162] Alexander Stephens, "Cornerstone Speech," March 12, 1861, in *American Heritage – A Reader*, ed. The Hillsdale College History Faculty (Hillsdale, Michigan: Hillsdale College Press, 2011), 483-493.
[163] The Hillsdale College History Faculty, 367-372; Woodworth, *The Essentials of United States History: 1841 to 1877 Westward Expansion and the Civil War*.
[164] Chilton, 71-82.

3,699 black slaveowners, about 2% of the free black population in the South. By comparison, approximately 6% of white Southerners owned slaves at the time. Although free black people sometimes purchased slaves to protect individuals, including family members, generally the race of the owner did not guarantee humane treatment for the slave. In addition, there were thousands of free and enslaved black soldiers fighting in the Confederate Army, some explicitly doing so for the purpose of maintaining their slaves. One estimate holds that 60,000 to 93,000 black people served the Confederacy in some capacity during the war.[165]

With the coming of war and the departure of the Southern representatives from Congress, the United States government had the opportunity to take greater action against slavery than at any other time since the Revolutionary Era. Emancipating slaves was not simply done as a last, desperate resort to win the war by converting slaves into Union troops. On the contrary, as early as 1861 the *Confiscation Act* declared that any property used by the Confederates for a military purpose could be seized, including slaves. In June, 1862, Congress abolished slavery in the District of Columbia and U.S. territories while also freeing the slaves of certain rebels via the *Second Confiscation Act*. The next month, President Lincoln entered into emancipation discussions with some of the loyal slave states which had not seceded, but none of these talks concerned a desperate need for black troops. Ultimately, Lincoln covertly drew up an emancipation order to free the slaves in the South, but waited for a significant Union victory to avoid the appearance of acting out of desperation. With the North's triumph at Antietam, Maryland on September 17, 1862, he had his opportunity. On September 22, 1862, President Lincoln issued the "Emancipation Proclamation," freeing all slaves in territories under Confederate control, effective January 1, 1863.[166]

Previously Lincoln had repeatedly stated that he would not touch slavery within the states where it existed because he did not believe he had the authority to do so under the *Constitution*. However,

---

[165] Grabar, *Debunking the 1619 Project: Exposing the Plan to Divide America*, 125-147; Walter Williams, "Black Confederate Soldiers," August 21, 1996, in *More Liberty Means Less Government: Our Founders Knew This Well* (Stanford: Hoover Institution Press, 1999), 38-40.
[166] Hall, Wiecek, and Finkelman, 223-225; Schweikart, 119-124.

the war had changed everything. Since the vast majority of slaves were considered the "property" of those engaging in an armed rebellion against the United States, Lincoln reasoned that he could justify seizing such "property" through his emancipation order.[167]

Some argue that since the "Emancipation Proclamation" only declared the slaves under Confederate control to be free, Lincoln had no real power to emancipate them. However, as Allen C. Guelzo has pointed out, although the enforcement of the order may not have been under Lincoln's immediate control, as President of the United States he most certainly had the authority to issue such an order. The proof of this is seen in the fact that no slave declared free under Lincoln's "Emancipation Proclamation" was ever returned to slavery after reaching Union-controlled territory.[168]

Nevertheless, Lincoln's critics still contend that "The Great Emancipator" is not truly deserving of the title. They claim that because at one time he supported voluntary foreign colonization for freed slaves, he must not have been truly committed to freedom and equality. It is true that on August 14, 1862, Lincoln met with five prominent black leaders at the White House (Edward Thomas, John F. Cook Jr., John T. Costin, Cornelius Clark, and Benjamin McCoy) to discuss just such a colonization program. Nevertheless, by this time Lincoln had already drawn up his initial emancipation order, without including colonization, and he never conditioned emancipation on the assumption that foreign colonization must follow. Neither did he ever rule out the possibility of eventual political and social equality in America after slavery had been eradicated. Furthermore, the final version of the "Emancipation Proclamation" did not include colonization either.[169]

Lincoln's support for voluntary colonization probably stemmed from a genuine concern for how the freed slaves would survive in the post-war South. He may have feared that they would be subjected to a new form of servitude and even terrorism from their defeated and undoubtedly resentful former masters. The emergence of segregation,

---

[167] James M. McPherson, "Lincoln Freed the Slaves," in *The Civil War: Opposing Viewpoints*, ed. William Dudley (San Diego: Greenhaven Press, Inc., 1995), 261-275.
[168] Allen C. Guelzo, *Lincoln's Emancipation Proclamation: The End of Slavery in America* (New York: Simon and Schuster, 2004), 1-12.
[169] Phillip W. Magness, *The 1619 Project: A Critique* (The American Institute for Economic Research, 2020), 113-124; Peter W. Wood, *1620: A Critical Response to the 1619 Project* (New York: Encounter Books, 2020), 145-164.

sharecropping, and the Ku Klux Klan after the Union Army withdrew from the South in 1877 demonstrated that his fears were well founded.[170]

Furthermore, several prominent black Americans also advocated for African colonization as one possibility for former slaves. Henry Highland Garnet founded the African Civilization Society in 1859 for the purposes of colonization and missionary work and later delivered a sermon in the House of Representatives upon the passage of the *Thirteenth Amendment* abolishing slavery.[171] Even in the twentieth century, Marcus Garvey's Universal Negro Improvement Association (UNIA) supported colonization to Liberia in Africa as one possible option for black people abroad.[172]

Lincoln was an immensely intelligent and prudent politician, and if it required supporting or appearing to support colonization to allay the fears of those who favored ending slavery but were not prepared for profound societal transformation, then he would do so. The fact that Lincoln invited a newspaper reporter to sit in on and then publicize the August, 1862 meeting where he discussed colonization with black leaders suggests that he was indeed attempting to sway undecideds to support emancipation.[173]

And Lincoln did show signs that he was truly interested in equality. First, he hinted at giving suffrage to black soldiers. Then in his final speech, he teased the prospect of extending the vote to even more black Americans. However, one member of the crowd, pro-Southern and pro-slavery John Wilkes Booth, determined at this point that he had no other choice but to assassinate the president.[174]

Admittedly, there were important military and strategic reasons

[170] Ibid.

[171] "African Civilization Society of New York," *Anti-Slavery Reporter*, 1 November 1859, https://archive.org/details/sim_anti-slavery-reporter-and-aborigines-friend_1859-11-01_7_11/page/262/mode/2up; Garnet, Henry Highland, "A memorial discourse; by Henry Highland Garnet, delivered in the hall of the House of Representatives, Washington City, D.C. on Sabbath, February 12, 1865. With an introduction by James McCune Smith, M.D.," (Philadelphia: Joseph M. Wilson), 1865, https://archive.org/details/memorialdiscourse00garn.

[172] Marcus Garvey, "Editorial," *Negro World*, 6 September 1924, https://www.international.ucla.edu/africa/mgpp/sample06.

[173] Magness; Peter W. Wood.

[174] Magness, 49; Sean Wilentz, "A Matter of Facts," January 22, 2020, https://www.theatlantic.com/ideas/archive/2020/01/1619-project-new-york-times-wilentz/605152/.

for the "Emancipation Proclamation" as well. By September, 1862 Lincoln had come to believe that he could not save the Union without freeing the slaves in areas under Confederate control. Slaves supported the Confederate war effort by maintaining agricultural production at home while soldiers were away. Furthermore, by declaring them free, Lincoln was effectively encouraging slaves to rebel against their masters, thereby opening a second battle front for the Confederacy from within. The proclamation also left little doubt that in addition to saving the Union, the conflict had become a war to end human bondage. This probably removed any possibility that Britain or France would join the struggle on behalf of the South.[175]

However, Lincoln's commitment to America's "mission statement" was real. In light of his open record of hostility not just to the expansion of slavery but to human bondage itself, it is likely that when presented with a prime opportunity to do what could be justified constitutionally and militarily to save the Union, Lincoln also acted morally. He certainly did not do so out of political expediency. Lincoln's belief that his party would be hurt by issuing the emancipation order so close to the upcoming November mid-term elections proved to be correct. Nevertheless, he described the "Emancipation Proclamation" as "an act of justice, warranted by the Constitution, upon military necessity," and called upon "the considerate judgment of mankind, and the gracious favor of Almighty God" in favor of its support. Meanwhile Frederick Douglass, who often grew frustrated by Lincoln's tendency to move at what must have seemed to him as a glacial pace, nevertheless declared: "The Star Bangled Banner is now the harbinger of liberty," and after the South and slavery had been defeated America would "higher than ever, sit as a queen among the nations of the earth."[176]

In the two years following January 1, 1863 when Lincoln's emancipation order took effect, the US Army freed millions.[177] Union

---

[175] Jaffa, 73-152, 79; Stephen T. Foster, "Emancipation Proclamation," in *Civil War Cards*, (Atlas Editions, 1991).

[176] Abraham Lincoln, "Emancipation Proclamation," September 22, 1862 in *American Legal History*, eds. Kermit L. Hall, William M. Wiecek, and Paul Finkelman (Oxford: Oxford University Press, 1991), 224; Frederick Douglass, "'The Emancipation Proclamation' is a Significant Achievement," in *The Civil War: Opposing Viewpoints*, ed. William Dudley (San Diego: Greenhaven Press, Inc., 1995), 180-186.

[177] Hall, Wiecek, and Finkelman, 223-225.

forces included 1.4 million white soldiers, 94% of whom were volunteers.[178] In the spring of 1863, Lincoln commissioned the first black regiments, including the Massachusetts 54th and 55th.[179] They were joined by thousands of male slaves either freed by the army or who fled to the Union lines, effectively freeing themselves.[180] A total of approximately 178,000 black soldiers fought for the Union army during the war.[181] Escaped slaves also served as workers, guides, and spies.[182] As it became apparent that the freed slaves were both a loss for the South and a gain for the North, ending slavery and preserving the Union became linked in the public mind.[183] One of the most popular songs of the era was Julia Ward Howe's "Battle Hymn of the Republic," with its unforgettable line encouraging Christ-like sacrifice: "'As He died to make men holy, let us die to make men free.'"[184]

Lincoln's critics who argue that he moved too slowly or that the "Emancipation Proclamation" did not go far enough overlook the fact that the President had to preserve a fragile coalition of Republicans, abolitionists, Northern Democrats, and pro-Unionists in the border slave states of Delaware, Maryland, Kentucky, and Missouri. If Lincoln had not balanced his opposition to slavery with his desire to preserve the Union, his coalition of support could have crumbled and everything – the war, the Union, and any hope of ending slavery would have been lost.[185]

On November 19, 1863, Lincoln delivered his greatest speech. The occasion was the dedication of a national cemetery to commemorate those who had fallen at Gettysburg, Pennsylvania from July 1-3, 1863. At the site of the bloodiest battle of the war, Lincoln not only honored the dead but reminded Americans of why they were fighting and what was at stake.[186]

---

[178] The Hillsdale College History Faculty, 367-372.
[179] Ibid.
[180] McPherson.
[181] The Hillsdale College History Faculty.
[182] Ira Berlin, "The Slaves Were the Primary Force Behind Their Emancipation," in *The Civil War: Opposing Viewpoints*, ed. William Dudley (San Diego: Greenhaven Press, Inc., 1995), 276-285.
[183] Ibid.
[184] Medved.
[185] McPherson.
[186] https://www.history.com/topics/american-civil-war/gettysburg-address.

Lincoln opened by referencing the founding of the nation based upon "the proposition that all men are created equal," in the *Declaration of Independence*. The conflict had come because some had rejected this principle.[187] Thus, the nation was in a state of civil war:

> Four score and seven years ago our fathers brought forth on this continent a new nation, conceived in liberty, and dedicated to the proposition that all men are created equal.
>
> Now we are engaged in a great civil war, testing whether that nation, or any nation so conceived and so dedicated, can long endure. We are met on a great battle-field of that war. We have come to dedicate a portion of that field as a final resting place for those who here gave their lives that that nation might live. It is altogether fitting and proper that we should do this.
>
> But, in a larger sense, we cannot dedicate – we cannot consecrate – we cannot hallow – this ground. The brave men, living and dead, who struggled here have consecrated it, far above our poor power to add or detract. The world will little note nor long remember what we say here, but it can never forget what they did here. It is for us the living, rather, to be dedicated here to the unfinished work which they who fought here have thus far so nobly advanced. It is rather for us to be here dedicated to the great task remaining before us – that from these honored dead we take increased devotion to that cause for which they gave the last full measure of devotion – that we here highly resolve that these dead shall not have died in vain – that this nation, under God, shall have a new birth of freedom – and that government of the people, by the people, for the people, shall not perish from the earth.[188]

---

[187] Jaffa, 73-152, 79.

[188] Abraham Lincoln, "Gettysburg Address," November 19, 1863, in *American*

Abraham Lincoln (1809-1865) by Alexander Gardner. Wikimedia Commons. Public domain.

Lincoln believed that the sacrifices of so many dead required a re-commitment to "the proposition that all men are created equal." This "new birth of freedom," would build upon and further the quest of the United States of America to be a nation based upon self-

Heritage – A Reader, ed. The Hillsdale College History Faculty (Hillsdale, Michigan: Hillsdale College Press, 2011), 499.

government and freedom and equality for all.[189]

The 1864 Presidential election was crucial in determining whether or not America would experience "a new birth of freedom." The Democratic Party platform supported engaging in negotiations with the South to restore the Union with slavery remaining. This was probably appealing to many who had grown war-weary after more than three years of intense fighting and immense death. Even some within his own party urged Lincoln to reconsider emancipation in order to facilitate peace talks. Knowing that his decision would probably lead to his defeat for re-election, Lincoln refused. On August 23, 1864, Lincoln wrote: "This morning, as for some days past, it seems exceedingly probable that this Administration will not be re-elected." Providentially, however, several Union military victories between August and November of 1864 helped carry him to victory. Lincoln's commitments to both the Union and the abolition of slavery were vindicated.[190]

In his Second Inaugural Address on March 4, 1865, Lincoln offered a message of healing and unity, despite a still ongoing and bloody struggle where more than half a million Americans had already died. Americans today would do well to heed his words:

> With malice toward none; with charity for all; with firmness in the right, as God gives us to see the right, let us strive on to finish the work we are in; to bind up the nation's wounds; to care for him who shall have borne the battle, and for his widow, and his orphan – to do all which may achieve and cherish a just, and a lasting peace, among ourselves, and with all nations.[191]

In large part because of Lincoln's leadership and commitment to America's "mission statement," the North was victorious in the Civil

---

189 Jaffa, 73-152, 79; The Hillsdale College History Faculty.

190 McPherson; Abraham Lincoln, "Memorandum on Probable Failure of Re-election," August 23, 1864, in *Abraham Lincoln: Speeches and Writings, 1859-1865*, ed. Don E. Fehrenbacher (New York: Literary Classics of the United States, Inc., 1989), 624.

191 Abraham Lincoln, "Second Inaugural Address," March 4, 1865. in *American Heritage – A Reader*, ed. The Hillsdale College History Faculty (Hillsdale, Michigan: Hillsdale College Press, 2011), 501-502.

War, the Union was preserved, and slavery was ultimately eradicated from the United States of America forever. Critics alleging that he acted too slowly, vacillated, or was insincere are probably best answered by his friend, Frederick Douglass:

> His great mission was to accomplish two things; first, to save his country from dismemberment and ruin, and second, to free his country from the great crime of slavery. To do one or the other, or both, he must have the earnest sympathy and the powerful cooperation of his loyal fellow-countrymen. Without this primary and essential condition to success, his efforts must have been vain and utterly fruitless. Had he put the abolition of slavery before the salvation of the Union, he would have inevitably driven from him a powerful class of the American people, and rendered resistance to rebellion impossible. Viewed from the genuine abolition ground, Mr. Lincoln seemed tardy, cold, dull, and indifferent: but measuring him by the sentiment of his country, a sentiment he was bound as a stateman to consult, he was swift, zealous, radical, and determined.[192]

The conclusion of the Civil War led to the passage of three constitutional amendments during the Reconstruction period of 1865-1877. These reflected the principles of the American founding and enshrined them in the nation's law of the land. The first was the *Thirteenth Amendment* (1865), abolishing all forms of slavery and involuntary servitude in the United States, its territories, and anywhere else subject to its jurisdiction. Second was the *Fourteenth Amendment* (1868) making the freed slaves full citizens both of the state in which they resided and the nation. Finally, the *Fifteenth Amendment* (1870) extended voting rights to the freed slaves.[193]

These were followed by further congressional actions. The *Civil Rights Acts* of 1866 and 1875 reinforced the Reconstruction

---

[192] Frederick Douglass, "Oration in Memory of Abraham Lincoln," April 14, 1876, in *American Speeches: Political Oratory from Abraham Lincoln to Bill Clinton*, ed. Ted Widmer (New York: Literary Classics of the United States, Inc., 2006), 74-84.
[193] West and Jeffrey.

amendments. The Bureau of Refugees, Freedmen, and Abandoned Lands, created in 1865 and also known as the "Freedmen's Bureau," did some important work towards integrating former slaves into society. It represented the very first federal welfare program and combined government and private charitable efforts to provide food, shelter, education and legal protection. Its greatest success was in establishing schools and teaching people to read.[194]

Separate But Equal?

Although legally the rights of American citizenship had been extended to the former slaves, in many parts of the country those liberties continued to be denied. The right to vote and in some cases the right to one's property had not become a reality for many black Americans. Furthermore, segregation – the separation of people by race – was enforced by law in the Southern states.[195]

It was the 1896 Supreme Court decision in *Plessy vs. Ferguson* that established the doctrine of "separate but equal" – essentially enshrining legal segregation. The lone dissenter in the 8-1 decision upholding a Louisiana state law separating train car passengers by race was Justice John Marshall Harlan, a former slaveowner. His dissent was replete with references to the United States *Constitution* and the principles of equality before the law and civil rights for all:

> ...in view of the Constitution, in the eye of the law, there is in this country no superior, dominant, ruling class of citizens. There is no caste here. Our Constitution is color-blind, and neither knows nor tolerates classes among citizens. In respect of civil rights, all citizens are equal before the law. The humblest is the peer of the most powerful. The law regards man as man, and takes no account of his surroundings or of his color when his civil rights as guaranteed by the supreme law of the land are involved.[196]

---

[194] Hall, Wiecek, and Finkelman, 235-236.
[195] Ibid.
[196] Bennett and Cribb, 177; *Plessy v. Ferguson*, 163 U.S. 537 (1896) in *American Legal History*, eds. Kermit L. Hall, William M. Wiecek, and Paul Finkelman (Oxford: Oxford University Press, 1991), 250-255.

Harlan's dissent unequivocally declared segregation to be a breach of America's "mission statement." The law of the land did not permit separating people into groups and treating them unequally. His words inspired civil rights advocates in the twentieth century, and President John F. Kennedy referenced them directly in his 1963 "Address on Civil Rights," which directly led to the 1964 *Civil Rights Act* and the desegregation of public facilities and accommodations.[197]

Besides being un-American, segregation made poor economic sense. The fact that Southern state and local governments had to impose segregation under punishment of law suggests that there were some Southerners, both black and white, who wanted to hire, do business, or otherwise associate with one another. It would make sense if private businesses and farmers, left to their own, wished to compete for the best employees and customers regardless of race. Unless the government imposed segregation on all businesses, any individual company engaging in discrimination would put itself at a distinct disadvantage.[198]

Many private bus and trolley companies resisted governmental attempts to impose segregation. Operators of these companies understood that they could lose customers and profits if they offended their black passengers by requiring them to sit in the back of the vehicle or even stand if the only available seats were in the "whites only" section. These private companies fought in the legislatures and the courts. After losing such battles repeatedly, many companies simply ignored segregation laws and black and white passengers sat wherever they pleased for many years. It was only when governments threatened operators and employees of municipal transit companies with prosecution that laws mandating segregation began to be enforced.[199]

Railroad companies similarly resisted governmental efforts to impose segregation on their businesses. Carrying white and black passengers in separate train cars required purchasing additional

---

[197] Bennett and Cribb; John F. Kennedy, "Address to the Nation on Civil Rights," June 11, 1963, in *American Speeches: Political Oratory from Abraham Lincoln to Bill Clinton*, ed. Ted Widmer (New York: Literary Classics of the United States, Inc., 2006), 548-553.

[198] Dinesh D'Souza, *America: Imagine a World Without Her* (Washington, D.C.: Regnery Publishing, 2014), 137-151.

[199] Thomas Sowell, *Discrimination and Disparities* (New York: Basic Books, 2018), 38-40.

coaches and added to fuel costs to move heavier trains. Whatever the racial views of the various railroad management personnel, they had to resist segregation laws for their own economic interests. In fact, in the *Plessy* case the railroads had cooperated with Homer Plessy to bring a test case before the courts.[200]

Several of the earliest examples of American principles triumphing over discrimination and segregation in the twentieth century occurred in the federal courts. In *Guinn v. United States* (1915) the US Supreme Court ruled that Oklahoma's "grandfather clause," which effectively prohibited someone from voting if their grandfather had been a slave, was unconstitutional. Then in 1944 the Court held in *Smith v. Alright* that prohibiting black voters from participating in a party primary election was also unconstitutional.[201]

Further advances occurred during the presidency of Democrat Harry S. Truman. Immediately after the end of World War II Truman ordered the creation of a civil rights commission, which in 1947 issued "To Secure These Rights" – a report calling for an end to segregation. The following year Truman acted when he banned racial discrimination in federal government hiring and desegregated the United States military.[202]

Under President Dwight D. Eisenhower, a Republican, progress continued. Public services in Washington, D.C., naval yards, and veterans' hospitals were all desegregated. Most notably, in 1954 the United States Supreme Court ended the "separate but equal" doctrine from *Plessy v. Ferguson* as it applied to public schools. In *Brown v. Board of Education*, a 9-0 majority not only stated that "separate but equal" was unconstitutional but also declared that "separate educational facilities are *inherently* unequal." Eventually this decision helped lead to the desegregation of other public facilities.[203]

In the 1950s another great American, Reverend Martin Luther King, Jr., emerged to once again call America back to its "mission statement." The Atlanta pastor employed the Christian gospel, non-

---

[200] Ibid.

[201] Hall, Wiecek, and Finkelman, 446-447.

[202] Gary Land, *The Essentials of United States History: America Since 1941: Emergence as a World Power* (Piscataway, New Jersey: Research and Education Association, 2000), 24-29.

[203] Ibid, 30-35; *Brown v. Board of Education of Topeka, Kansas*, 347 U.S. 483 (1954) in *American Legal History*, eds. Kermit L. Hall, William M. Wiecek, and Paul Finkelman (Oxford: Oxford University Press, 1991), 510-516.

violence, and the principles of the American founding to advocate for equal civil rights for all. Regarding the right to protest, King said:

> And certainly, certainly, this is the glory of America, with all of its faults. This is the glory of our democracy. If we were incarcerated behind the iron curtains of a Communistic nation we couldn't do this. If we were dropped in the dungeon of a totalitarian regime we couldn't do this. But the great glory of American democracy is the right to protest for right.[204]

King maintained a generally positive and optimistic view of America and Americans. He knew that most were not hateful, and he believed that civil rights activists could "'wear you down by our capacity to suffer, and in winning our freedom we will so appeal to your heart and conscience that we will win you in the process.'"[205]

He first came to prominence after helping to organize a bus boycott to protest a Montgomery, Alabama city ordinance segregating passengers by race. It is important to note that this was a local government policy, not the rule of the bus company itself. Again, treating customers poorly is not a smart business practice.[206]

Like the American founders, King made a natural law argument to resist unjust government actions. Consider his "Letter from the Birmingham City Jail," of April 16, 1963. In answering critics who claimed his tactics of direct-action including sit-ins and marches amounted to law-breaking, King argued that any human law which violated the higher, pre-existing moral law was "'no law at all.'" This echoed the argument of the *Declaration of Independence* that according to "the laws of nature and of nature's God" the people had inherent rights and could abolish a government that failed to secure those rights. Likewise, King argued that it was just to resist a government's unjust law:

---

[204] Martin Luther King, Jr., "Speech to the Montgomery Improvement Association," December 5, 1955, in *American Speeches: Political Oratory from Abraham Lincoln to Bill Clinton*, ed. Ted Widmer (New York: Literary Classics of the United States, Inc., 2006), 516-519.
[205] Schweikart and Allen, 662-664.
[206] Ibid.

> There are *just* laws and there are *unjust* laws. I would
> be the first to advocate obeying just laws. One has
> not only a legal but moral responsibility to obey just
> laws. Conversely, one has a moral responsibility to
> dis-obey unjust laws.

The question was, how did you determine which was which?
According to King:

> A just law is a manmade code that squares with the
> moral law or the law of God. An unjust law is a code
> that is out of harmony with the moral law. To put it
> in the terms of Saint Thomas Aquinas, an unjust law
> is a human law that is not rooted in eternal and
> natural law. Any law that uplifts human personality is
> just. Any law that degrades human personality is
> unjust.

Segregation laws, argued King, were unjust because "segregation
distorts the soul and damages the personality." Furthermore, it gave
the one doing the segregating "a false sense of superiority" and it
gave the segregated "a false sense of inferiority." Finally, in arguably
the most stirring part of the letter, King directly tied the movement
for civil rights to the spirit of the American founding:

> One day the South will know that when these
> disinherited children of God sat down at lunch
> counters they were in reality standing up for the best
> in the America dream and the most sacred values in
> our Judeo-Christian heritage, and thus carrying our
> whole nation back to great wells of democracy which
> were dug deep by the founding fathers in the
> formulation of the Constitution and the Declaration
> of Independence.[207]

---

[207] Martin Luther King, Jr., "Letter from the Birmingham City Jail," April 16, 1963,
in *American Heritage – A Reader*, ed. The Hillsdale College History Faculty (Hillsdale,
Michigan: Hillsdale College Press, 2011), 835-849.

In his "I Have A Dream" speech of August 28, 1963 as part of the March on Washington, King again referenced America's "mission statement." Although he was aware that more radical and revolutionary groups were willing to divide people into opposing racial identity blocs to fight discrimination, King bravely refused. As his biographer David Garrow has stated, "MLK would have most certainly rejected ANY identity-based classification of human beings," such as critical race theory (CRT).[208]

Rather than denouncing America or its creed, he described the *Declaration of Independence* and the *Constitution* as a "promissory note to which every American was to fall heir." He stirred the consciences of Americans by challenging them to live more fully in accordance with their principles:

> In a sense we've come to our nation's capital to cash a check. When the architects of our republic wrote the magnificent words of the Constitution and the Declaration of Independence, they were signing a promissory note to which every American was to fall heir. This note was a promise that all men, yes, black men as well as white men, would be guaranteed the 'unalienable Rights of Life, Liberty, and the pursuit of Happiness.' It is obvious today that America has defaulted on this promissory note insofar as her citizens of color are concerned. Instead of honoring this sacred obligation, America has given the Negro people a bad check, a check which has come back marked 'insufficient funds.'
>
> But we refuse to believe that the bank of justice is bankrupt. We refuse to believe that there are insufficient funds in the great vault of opportunity of this nation. And so we've come to cash this check, a check that will give us upon demand the riches of freedom and the security of justice.[209]

---

[208] The President's Advisory 1776 Commission, 30; Paul Kengor, "Teach MLK, Not CRT," December 3, 2021, https://spectator.org/mlk-not-crt/.

[209] Martin Luther King, Jr., "Address to the March on Washington," August 28, 1963, in *American Speeches: Political Oratory from Abraham Lincoln to Bill Clinton*, ed. Ted

Martin Luther King, Jr. (1929-1968). Wikimedia Commons. Public domain.

King's words undoubtedly spurred Americans to action. However, their consciences were also awakened by television broadcasts into homes across the nation showing peaceful black and white civil rights marchers in the South being attacked and beaten. Most Americans recognized that segregation, the denial of civil rights, and violence against people peacefully exercising their right to protest were blatant and despicable violations of America's "mission statement." This generated great nationwide support in Congress to pass legislation in 1964 banning segregation in public facilities and accommodations. The following year the passage of a voting rights

Widmer (New York: Literary Classics of the United States, Inc., 2006), 556-560.

act sought to ensure that all Americans could make their voices heard at the ballot box. Finally, a 1968 law prohibited discrimination in housing.[210]

Progress or Progressivism?

Another great challenge to America's "mission statement" arose in the late 1800s. Progressivism, an ideology seemingly driven by the desire to reform society and improve people's lives, in many cases resulted in empowering government at the expense of individual rights. This was a direct inversion of the intent of the founders.

Momentous changes had come to American society in the years following the Civil War. Industrialization led to the rise of powerful, wealthy corporations that many feared were a threat to both personal freedom and economic independence. Likewise, the domination of large cities by a single political party, whose control was so total that they were often referred to as "political machines," seemed to threaten democracy itself. Industrialization also lured a new wave of immigrants from Europe to work in factories, introducing a variety of foreign languages, cultures, and religions. How would the country absorb and assimilate these new arrivals as they filled the large cities of the East and Midwest? Could the American experiment in self-government survive as the country transitioned from a predominantly agrarian society comprised of independent small farmers into an increasingly urban one made up of wage earners who were dependent on businesses for their survival?[211]

Progressives argued that modern life had become too complicated for the philosophy of the American founding to address society's problems. Rather than the Founding Fathers' vision of a nation built upon equal individual rights as described in the *Declaration of Independence* and secured by a limited government based upon the *Constitution*, perhaps a more sophisticated and complex system was now called for to meet the needs of the times. Members of the more educated elite began to criticize the natural rights philosophy of the American founding because it did not guarantee equal outcomes, particularly in terms of wealth. For progressives it was not enough to acknowledge that all human beings should be

---

[210] Harry Jeffrey, History 476 lecture notes, California State University, Fullerton, Summer, 1997; West and Jeffrey.
[211] Richard Hofstadter, *The Age of Reform* (New York: Vintage Books, 1955), 3-22.

treated equally. They had to be equal. This was a fundamental change. Rather than power belonging to the people who then delegated it to their leaders, progressivism held that it was the duty of the government to empower the people.[212]

Just as progressivism redefined equality, it also changed the meanings of rights and duties. Previously, the natural rights of life, liberty, and the pursuit of happiness were those which all individuals possessed at birth. Government simply acknowledged and protected them. For every right, there was a corresponding duty to respect that right, meaning that it could not be taken away without a just cause. However, under progressivism rights because a claim on someone else's property, which the government had a duty to redistribute to make society fairer. Instead of rights being natural, belonging to individuals, and existing prior to the creation of governments, rights became connected to economic benefits (such as housing, education, and health care) and were awarded by the government to groups who were deemed to be worthy.[213]

Perhaps not surprisingly then, progressives increasingly came to view the *Constitution* as an obstacle to their plans because by design it limited the government's ability to act beyond certain boundaries. This led reformers to favor a "living constitution" that could be adapted to meet their goals. In practice this meant changing the way each of the three branches of the federal government carried out its duties. For example, instead of the judicial branch interpreting whether a law was valid under the *Constitution*, judges would rule in such a manner as to create a new law if they believed it met some greater purpose. Meanwhile, as the elected leader of the executive branch, the president would no longer have the exclusive authority to enforce laws because a massive bureaucracy comprised of "experts" below the chief executive would wield much of the power. Likewise, the legislative branch would not write, debate, and vote on legislation but rather delegate its responsibility to agencies which created regulations that had the force of law.[214]

Cumulatively these changes took power away from the people's elected representatives, who could be held accountable at the ballot box, and put control into the hands of unelected officials and

---

[212] West and Jeffrey.
[213] Ibid.
[214] Ibid.

bureaucrats. Among these were various "experts" supposedly better equipped to address the increasingly complex problems of modernity. However, despite their training as professional administrators, doctors, lawyers, economists, or social workers, none of them had been elected. Such an evolution in the way government functioned could even be seen as a denial of the people's right to give their consent to actions affecting their lives.[215]

Furthermore, in replacing the founders' *Constitution* with a "living constitution," the national government massively expanded. It evolved from handling matters of a national concern to increasingly overtaking the duties which might have been better left to state and local governments because of their greater proximity to the people.[216]

Progressivism was not limited to one party. Probably the first truly prominent national progressive was President Theodore Roosevelt, a Republican. After serving in the White House from 1901-1909, Roosevelt criticized his successor, William Howard Taft, for having taken the party back to its more traditional, conservative, and pro-business roots. In "The New Nationalism," an address delivered on August 31, 1910, Roosevelt pushed for greater government involvement in the political economy of the nation.[217]

The speech revealed the typical frustrations felt by progressives over the delegation of powers to the state and local governments as well as the system of checks and balances amongst the three branches of the federal government. Like other progressives desirous of making reforms to which they were passionately committed, Roosevelt objected to these constitutional limitations:

> The American people are right in demanding that
> New Nationalism, without which we cannot hope to
> deal with new problems. The New Nationalism puts
> the national need before sectional or personal
> advantage. It is impatient of the utter confusion that
> results from local legislatures attempting to treat
> national issues as local issues. It is still more impatient
> of the impotence which springs from over-division of

---

[215] Robert H. Wiebe, *The Search for Order 1877-1920, The Making of America* (New York: Hill and Wang, 1967), 164-195.
[216] West and Jeffrey.
[217] The Hillsdale College History Faculty, 605.

governmental powers, the impotence which makes it
possible for local selfishness or for legal cunning,
hired by wealthy special interests, to bring national
activities to a deadlock.[218]

President Woodrow Wilson (1913-1921), a Democrat, was
another important early progressive. However, Wilson much more
explicitly argued that American society had outgrown the individual
liberty and limited government vision of the Founding Fathers. He
believed that major changes to America's system of governance were
imperative because the old ideas about dividing powers between the
federal government and the states as well as checks and balances at
the national level hindered the ability of politicians to address
modern society's most difficult problems.[219]

In Wilson's 1913 speech, "The New Freedom," he argued that
just as times changed, so did human nature and therefore what was
best for people. What may have worked for one generation did not
necessarily apply to another. Like many progressives, Wilson was
influenced by Charles Darwin and his belief that only the fittest
creatures survived. He applied this notion to his view of the
Constitution as a living organism and claimed that it too needed to
change or else it would perish. Wilson held that society was not a
fixed machine based upon Newton's laws of mechanics; it was a
living organism subject to Darwin's principles of evolution. He even
went so far as to say that Americans needed to move beyond the
Declaration of Independence, the nation's founding document and the
ultimate expression of its ideals:

> The old political formulas do not fit the present
> problems; they read now like documents taken out of
> a forgotten age…We used to say that the ideal of
> government was for every man to be left alone and
> not interfered with, except when he interfered with
> somebody else; and that the best government was the
> government that did as little governing as possible.

---

[218] Theodore Roosevelt, "The New Nationalism," August 31, 1910, in *American
Heritage – A Reader*, ed. The Hillsdale College History Faculty (Hillsdale, Michigan:
Hillsdale College Press, 2011), 605-618.
[219] The Hillsdale College History Faculty, 619.

That was the idea that obtained in Jefferson's time. But we are coming now to realize that life is so complicated that we are not dealing with the old conditions, and that the law has to step in and create new conditions under which we may live, the conditions which will make it tolerable for us to live...Living political constitutions must be Darwinian in structure and practice. Society is a living organism and must obey the laws of life, not of mechanics; it must develop. All that progressives ask or desire is permission...to interpret the Constitution according to the Darwinian principle; all they ask is recognition of the fact that a nation is a living thing and not a machine. Some citizens of this country have never got beyond the Declaration of Independence, signed in Philadelphia, July 4th, 1776...The Declaration of Independence did not mention the questions of our day.[220]

One of the most significant results of the Progressive Era was the ratification of the *Sixteenth Amendment* in 1913. Not only did it give Congress the power to institute taxes on any source of income, but it imposed no limit on the amount. Previously the legislative branch had held the power to levy taxes, but these were usually excise taxes on individual items or tariffs on imported goods. In those cases, the consumer retained a choice as to what and how much was purchased and therefore how much in taxes was paid. Now, a government originally designed to *protect* property had been transformed into one claiming a preemptive right to *take* property.

One of the first Americans to challenge progressivism and reassert and reinvigorate a commitment to the spirit of 1776 was President Calvin Coolidge, a Republican from New England who served in the White House from 1923-1929. Coolidge, a true believer in America's "mission statement," extolled both the natural rights philosophy of the *Declaration of Independence* as well as the limited government design of the *Constitution*. To commemorate the 150th

---

[220] Woodrow Wilson, "The New Freedom," in *American Heritage – A Reader*, ed. The Hillsdale College History Faculty (Hillsdale, Michigan: Hillsdale College Press, 2011), 620-627.

anniversary of the birth of America, on July 5, 1926, he delivered an address on "The Inspiration of the Declaration." He described its origins as religious, spiritual, moral, and therefore unchanging and eternal. He argued that retreating from them would not be a mark of "progress." On the contrary, he labelled such thinking as "backward" and "reactionary":

> It is often asserted that the world has made a great deal of progress since 1776, that we have had new thoughts and new experiences which have given us a great advance over the people of that day, and that we may therefore very well discard their conclusions for something more modern. But that reasoning cannot be applied to this great charter. If all men are created equal, that is final. If they are endowed with inalienable rights, that is final. If governments derive their just powers from the consent of the governed, that is final. No advance, no progress can be made beyond these propositions. If anyone wishes to deny their truth or their soundness, the only direction in which he can proceed historically is not forward, but backward toward the time when there was no equality, no rights of the individual, no rule of the people. Those who wish to proceed in that direction can not lay claim to progress. They are reactionary. Their ideas are not more modern, but more ancient, than those of the Revolutionary fathers.

Coolidge's commitment to limited government was real – he was the last president to have budget surpluses every year.[221]

Progressivism continued to challenge America's "mission statement" throughout the twentieth century. Democratic President Franklin D. Roosevelt's (1933-1945) "New Deal" was a prime example. It featured a vastly expanded role for the federal government in order to address the economic challenges resulting

---

[221] The Hillsdale College History Faculty, 631-634; Calvin Coolidge, "The Inspiration of the Declaration," July 5, 1926, in *American Heritage – A Reader*, ed. The Hillsdale College History Faculty (Hillsdale, Michigan: Hillsdale College Press, 2011), 667-675.

from the Great Depression. It is sometimes described as a series of experiments, with those that worked being kept and those that did not being discarded. Many of its varied programs duplicated others; sometimes they contradicted them.[222]

Like earlier progressives, supporters of the New Deal viewed the *Constitution* as an obstacle to their plans. How could it not be? The document was *designed* to limit government intrusion into personal freedom, not just to protect the rights of individual citizens from other citizens or foreign invaders. The ideas of President Roosevelt and others in his administration, many of which had been influenced by Italian fascism and Soviet socialism, were bound to conflict with America's "mission statement."[223]

Supporters of various versions of European-style collectivism were legion in Franklin Roosevelt's administration. Economic advisor Rexford Guy Tugwell referred to Mussolini's fascist system in Italy as "'the cleanest, neatest most efficiently operating piece of social machinery I've ever seen. It makes me envious.'" Meanwhile economic advisor Lauchlin Currie, Harry Dexter White in the Treasury Department, Lee Pressman of the Agricultural Adjustment Administration and the Works Progress Administration, and Alger Hiss in the State Department all had ties to the American Communist Party or its masters in Soviet Russia.[224]

The New Deal was not simply a series of practical attempts to pull the nation out of the depression. On September 23, 1932 while on the campaign trail, Roosevelt delivered his "Commonwealth Club Address" where he divided individual rights into two categories: civil and property. While civil rights such as free speech and voting were described as "'preferred,'" the right to one's property was judged to be more negotiable, leaving open the possibility of redistribution in order to achieve "'equal outcomes.'" Like other progressives, Roosevelt believed that the *Declaration of Independence* and *Constitution* had become outdated. Their principles of individual rights and limited government were seen as complicating his efforts to assist

---

[222] William Turner, *The Essentials of United States History 1912 to 1941: World War I, the Depression, and the New Deal* (Piscataway, New Jersey: Research and Education Association, 1995), 77-97.

[223] Amity Shlaes, *The Forgotten Man: A New History of the Great Depression* (New York: Harper Perennial, 2008), 1-14.

[224] Jonah Goldberg, *Liberal Fascism: The Secret History of the American Left, from Mussolini to the Politics of Change* (New York: Broadway Books, 2009), 1-24; Shlaes.

those that he believed had been left behind by capitalism:

> The Declaration of Independence discusses the problem of government in terms of a contract. Government is a relation of give and take – a contract, perforce, if we would follow the thinking out of which it grew. Under such a contract rulers were accorded power, and the people consented to that power on consideration that they be accorded certain rights. The task of statesmanship has always been the redefinition of these rights in terms of a changing and growing social order. New conditions impose new requirements upon government and those who conduct government.[225]

Not only did Roosevelt misstate the origins of contractual government, but he also undermined the very concept of a contract itself. First, he described government as essentially a deal by which leaders were given power and the people were given rights. However, both parts of America's "mission statement" – the *Declaration of Independence* and the *Constitution* – held that individual rights were natural and inalienable. Therefore, the purpose of government was to recognize and secure those already existing rights, not "accord" or distribute them here and there as rulers saw fit. Furthermore, the type of contract Roosevelt described was really no contract at all – any agreement where one side, in this case the ruler, can alter the terms if he finds them inconvenient provides no security to the other party, in this case the people. And yet, that was precisely what Roosevelt was suggesting with his contention that a stateman's job was to "redefine" rights. Where in his formulation was the right of the governed to give their consent? Why was there no mention of the democratic process of amending the *Constitution* when a sizeable majority of Americans agreed that a given reform was necessary?

On the other hand, didn't Franklin Roosevelt and the New Deal "save capitalism?" Wasn't it Roosevelt's various policies and

---

[225] The Hillsdale College History Faculty, 717-718; Franklin D. Roosevelt, "Commonwealth Club Address," September 23, 1932, in *American Heritage – A Reader*, ed. The Hillsdale College History Faculty (Hillsdale, Michigan: Hillsdale College Press, 2011), 718-728.

programs which, though perhaps imperfect, nevertheless ended the Great Depression or at least prevented it from becoming even worse? According to Thomas Sowell, a case can be made that the seemingly endless series of experiments by the Roosevelt administration created uncertainty in the marketplace and thereby may have *prolonged* the Great Depression. America had usually recovered from previous depressions in less time naturally and without massive government tinkering. Furthermore, while Roosevelt's various jobs programs may have provided some with temporary relief, what ultimately ended the problem of chronic unemployment during the 1930s was the demands of fighting the Second World War (1939-1945).[226]

The New Deal most certainly did, however, bequeath an era where a "liberal consensus" emerged. In order to address an economic crisis of the moment, the Great Depression of the 1930s, the Roosevelt administrations from 1933-1945 abandoned the American tradition of limited government. The idea that the state should play a large and active role in the economy to guarantee prosperity and "economic equality" became something largely taken for granted, with little regard for the costs.[227]

In the years following World War II, progressivism continued to challenge the founders' limited-government vision. In the 1960s, Democratic President Lyndon B. Johnson went so far as to redefine equality. No longer would it be sufficient for the government to treat all citizens equally. Now it had to *make* everyone equal:

> Thus it is not enough just to open the gates of opportunity. All our citizens must have the ability to walk through those gates. This is the next and the more profound stage of the battle for civil rights. We seek not just freedom but opportunity. We seek not just legal equity but human ability, not just equality as a right and a theory but equality as a fact and equality as a result.[228]

---

[226] Sowell, *The Quest for Cosmic Justice*, 132-133.

[227] Iwan W. Morgan, *Beyond the Liberal Consensus: A Political History of the United States Since 1965* (New York: St. Martin's Press, 1994), 8-11.

[228] The Hillsdale College Politics Faculty, eds., *The U.S. Constitution – A Reader* (Hillsdale, Michigan: Hillsdale College Press, 2014), 765; Lyndon B. Johnson, "Commencement Address at Howard University," June 4, 1965, in *The U.S. Constitution – A Reader*, eds. The Hillsdale College Politics Faculty (Hillsdale,

The belief that the state should not just *recognize* equality but actually seek to *create* equality was behind such well-intentioned federal government welfare programs as Aid to Families with Dependent Children (AFDC). Originally created as part of Franklin Roosevelt's New Deal, it was greatly expanded under Johnson's "War on Poverty," part of his "Great Society" domestic agenda. Previously the program had exclusively benefitted widows who had lost the family's primary earner, but in the 1960s any family without a husband or father in the home became eligible. If a man joined the household, then the family could lose its aid.[229]

The Johnson administration oversaw the largest welfare increase in American history, at least up to that time. Indeed, public assistance doled out by various government programs from 1965-1970 represented the greatest voluntary transfer of wealth in the history of the world. The number of AFDC recipients alone nearly doubled in less than a decade, increasing from 7.8 million in 1965 to 14.4 million in 1974. Nevertheless, households headed by women remained poor during the 1960s.[230]

One of the key reasons why the Great Society failed to substantially alleviate poverty was that the expansion of AFDC contributed to the breakdown of the family in America. As early as the 1870s, just after the end of slavery but still in the midst of deep racism, discrimination, and segregation, perhaps as many at 80% of black children lived in two-parent families.[231] According to United States Census statistics, from 1890-1940 overall marriage rates were relatively high with the percentage among black Americans slightly exceeding that of white Americans.[232] Additionally, from 1940-1960 the black poverty rate fell by about 40%.[233]

However, commencing in the mid-1960s, women who had been effectively incentivized to have children out-of-wedlock married less and gave birth to more fatherless children to obtain greater benefits from the government. The poor in general and black Americans in

Michigan: Hillsdale College Press, 2014), 765-772.
[229] Schweikart and Allen, 687-689.
[230] Morgan, 41-51; Schweikart and Allen, 686.
[231] Walter Williams, "We Are Not Bright," February 8, 1995, in *More Liberty Means Less Government: Our Founders Knew This Well*, 40-42.
[232] Walter Williams, "Race Hustlers," December 14, 1997, in *More Liberty Means Less Government: Our Founders Knew This Well*, 23-25.
[233] Sowell, *Discrimination and Disparities*, 112.

particular were most affected. Whereas in 1950 78% of black families and 88% of white families had a mother and father in the home, by 1979 two-parent black families had fallen to just 59% of the total while similarly situated white families had decreased to 85%. Cultural changes including the sexual revolution added to the increase of fatherless children throughout society, with black families being hardest hit and reaching a 70% illegitimacy rate or higher by the 1980s. Besides the attendant effects, including rises in crime among impoverished and fatherless boys, perhaps the saddest result is that the poverty rate remained virtually unchanged.[234]

In the midst of the tumultuous 1960s, another champion of America's founding philosophy emerged to counter progressivism as a threat to individual freedom and prosperity. Ronald Reagan, a former actor, president of the Screen Actors Guild, and Democrat, made his political debut with a televised speech on October 27, 1964 in support of the Republican nominee for president, Senator Barry Goldwater of Arizona. The speech, "A Time for Choosing," not only marked his formal transition into politics, but also encapsulated his political philosophy and that of a growing movement to return to the nation's founding principles as expressed in its "mission statement." By this time, progressivism had taken such a hold on American life that simply articulating the nation's founding ideals on individual liberty and limited government was labeled "conservative," rather than what it actually was – quintessentially American:

> It's time we asked ourselves if we still know the freedoms intended for us by the Founding Fathers. James Madison said, 'We base all our experiments on the capacity of mankind for self-government.' This idea that government was beholden to the people, that it had no other source of power except the sovereign people, is still the newest, most unique idea in all the long history of man's relation to man. For almost two centuries we have proved man's capacity for self-government, but today we are told we must choose between a left and right or, as others suggest, a third alternative, a kind of safe middle ground. I suggest to you there is no left or right, only an up or

[234] Morgan.

187

down. Up to the maximum of individual freedom consistent with law and order, or down to the ant heap of totalitarianism;

...the full power of centralized government was the very thing the Founding Fathers sought to minimize. They knew you don't control things; you can't control the economy without controlling *people*. So we have come for a time for choosing. Either we accept the responsibility for our own destiny, or we abandon the American Revolution and confess that an intellectual elite in a far-distant capital can plan our lives for us better than we can plan them ourselves.[235]

Although Goldwater suffered a landslide defeat in the general election against President Johnson, Reagan's performance had provided him with a nationwide platform. It also helped to re-introduce America's founding principles of individual rights and limited government as a viable alternative to progressivism and the liberal welfare state. In 1966 he upset incumbent Edmund G. Brown, Sr. to become the governor of California.

With his actor's good looks and ability to forcefully – yet clearly and warmly – articulate American principles, Reagan was the epitome of the right man arriving at the right time. Ever since the New Deal, the dominant political philosophy in America had been progressivism or liberalism, which held that the role of government was to identify a problem, design a solution, and then allocate funds to implement a policy or program. This represented a radical transition from the founding philosophy where government existed to secure individual rights to a vision in which the state guaranteed entitlements to various groups. As increased taxation and expanded government continued throughout the era of Johnson's "Great Society," a backlash arose due to rising crime, racial unrest including violent riots, anti-war demonstrations, and attacks on traditional culture and societal morays. Indeed, it could be argued that a cultural civil war began in the 1960s between progressives on the left and

---

[235] Ronald Reagan, "A Time for Choosing," October 27, 1964, in *The U.S. Constitution – A Reader*, ed. The Hillsdale College Politics Faculty (Hillsdale, Michigan: Hillsdale College Press, 2014), 773-783.

conservatives on the right. While progressives on the one hand believed in absolute personal autonomy and freedom over private concerns (particularly involving sexuality) they were also adamant about demanding government action in the form of entitlements and welfare benefits while pushing for greater regulations of business. Meanwhile, conservatives adhered to religion, morality, and tradition, while expressing a populist distaste for the liberal elites running government, media, entertainment, academia, and even filtering into the mainline churches.[236]

After serving two terms as governor of California, Reagan attempted to unseat incumbent President Gerald R. Ford for the 1976 Republican nomination. Although narrowly failing, Reagan was far from finished. By the late 1970s confidence in government had plummeted due to the resignation of President Richard Nixon in the wake of the Watergate scandal, America's loss of South Vietnam and numerous other nations to communism, and a generally flaccid economy with both high unemployment and high interest rates. The pervasive mood in the country seemed to be that America's time as an economic, military, and global leader was passing away.[237]

Reagan refused to accept this fate for America. When he defeated incumbent Democrat Jimmy Carter for the presidency in 1980, it signaled the end of the New Deal Era. In his "First Inaugural Address" on January 20, 1981, he re-asserted the founding principles of individual rights and limited government as well as declared that government was not the solution to America's problems; in many ways, it was the problem:

> In this present crisis, government is not the solution to our problem; government is the problem. From time to time we've been tempted to believe that society has become too complex to be managed by self-rule, that government by an elite group is superior to government for, by, and of the people. Well, if no one among us is capable of governing himself, then who among us has the capacity to govern someone else?

---

[236] Jeffrey; The Hillsdale College History Faculty, 741-746.
[237] Ibid.

...We are a nation that has a government – not the other way around. And this makes us special among the nations of the Earth. Our government has no power except that granted it by the people. It is time to check and reverse the growth of government, which shows signs of having grown beyond the consent of the governed.

...If we look to the answer as to why for so many years we achieved so much, prospered as no other people on Earth, it was because here in this land we unleashed the energy and individual genius of man to a greater extent than has ever been done before. Freedom and the dignity of the individual have been more available and assured here than in any other place on Earth. The price for this freedom at times has been high, but we have never been unwilling to pay that price.[238]

A pivotal concept underlying Reagan's domestic agenda was devolution, returning to state and local governments greater control over those affairs that were most relevant to the everyday lives of the people. The intent was to help restore the balance between the government and the citizen. State and local governments were often less expensive and more efficient and had greater accountability because they were closer to the communities that they served. Devolution would also enable the private sector, including businesses, charities, and civic organizations, to play a more prominent role in American life.[239]

One of the most effective ways to accomplish devolution was to slow the rate of growth in federal government spending. Reagan sought to accomplish this in his 1981 federal budget by focusing on numerous domestic programs, but without affecting those benefitting the elderly and leaving the social safety net in place for the truly

---

[238] Jeffrey; Ronald Reagan, "First Inaugural Address," January 20, 1981, in *American Heritage – A Reader*, ed. The Hillsdale College History Faculty (Hillsdale, Michigan: Hillsdale College Press, 2011), 871-876.
[239] Jeffrey.

needy.[240] Despite claims that Reagan sacrificed the poor in order to engage in a massive military buildup, social spending always remained higher than defense spending.[241]

Scaling back the size and scope of the federal government against an entrenched bureaucracy, interest groups, and the opposition party in control of the House of Representatives during the entire eight years of his presidency proved to be one of Reagan's greatest challenges and arguably his biggest failure. However, he did reintroduce the founding principle of limited government back into American political life as a viable alternative to the inexorable growth of the state ushered in by a century of progressivism.

Reagan's greatest success domestically was in reducing taxation. The *Economic Recovery Tax Act* (ERTA) passed in 1981 phased in a 25% tax cut over three years to everyone, with the highest individual rate lowered from 70% to 50%.[242] Business taxes were cut as well to encourage investment, including allowing for deductions resulting from depreciation of tools, equipment, and vehicles.[243] ERTA also included individual retirement accounts (IRAs) enabling individuals to plan for their futures by investing earned income of up to $2,000 annually with taxes on both principle and interest deferred.[244] The $162 billion tax cut was the largest in American history at the time.[245]

ERTA was followed by the *Tax Reform Act* (TARA) of 1986. In signing this piece of legislation, Reagan effectively declared that taxation would no longer be used to redistribute wealth and re-engineer society. The top tax rate was lowered further from 50% to 28%, and the tax code overall was simplified to just two brackets, 28% and 15%. Business tax rates were reduced from 46% to 34%, but many tax credits, deductions, shelters, and loopholes utilized by business were removed. Accusations that Reagan favored business and the wealthy over working and poor families are directly rebutted by TARA. In general, this second tax law represented an attempt to move taxation away from individuals and towards businesses. Six million poor families were completely removed from the tax rolls

---

[240] Ibid.
[241] Schweikart and Allen, 748-750.
[242] Schweikart and Allen., 748-749; Land, 77-86.
[243] Land, 77-86.
[244] Ibid.
[245] Jeffrey.

altogether.[246]

Criticisms that Reagan's tax cuts reduced revenue to the federal government, triggered annual budget deficits, and grew the overall national debt are demonstrably false. While it is true that the deficit (the amount that the government spends in excess of what it takes in during a given year) increased from $59 billion in 1980 to $195 billion in 1983, by 1985 it had fallen to $179 billion. Furthermore, at the same time that the deficit was growing, so was the overall economy. Consequently, revenue to the federal treasury nearly doubled during the 1980s, increasing from $517 billion in 1981 to just under $1 trillion by 1989. Thus, as a percentage of gross domestic product (GDP), from 1981-1989 the deficit remained virtually unchanged at around 2.5%.[247]

Budget deficits and an increased national debt are better explained by rising domestic spending, not tax reductions which grew the economy, increased revenue to the federal treasury, and allowed citizens to keep more of their income. In fact, every budget that Reagan submitted to Congress during his two terms in office was rejected in favor of higher spending, with the lone exception of 1984 – a presidential election year.[248] Thus, despite Reagan's efforts, federal government spending increased by about 40% during his eight years in office.[249]

To elaborate, although defense spending rose under Reagan from about 22% of the US budget in 1980 to around 27% by 1989, this represented approximately just 1% of the Gross National Product (GNP). Furthermore, increased military spending arguably contributed to ultimate victory over Soviet communism and the end of the forty-year Cold War. Meanwhile, social spending for such domestic programs as housing, housing assistance, health care, Social Security, and agricultural programs also rose.[250]

On balance, Reagan's economic record was a clear success. Inflation, unemployment, and interest rates all fell dramatically in the

---

[246] Land; Jeffrey.

[247] Land.; Schweikart and Allen, 750-751, 760; Chairman of the Council of Economic Advisors, *Economic Report of the President*, available at https://www.govinfo.gov/app/collection/erp/2019.

[248] Norman B. Ture, "To Cut and To Please," *National Review*, 31 August 1992, 35-39.

[249] Schweikart and Allen, 748-750.

[250] Schweikart, 233-238.

1980s. From a high of 12% in 1979, inflation plummeted to 2.2% by 1986. Meanwhile, unemployment declined from 10.2% in 1983 to 5.3% in 1989 and interest rates were halved from 21.5% in 1980 to 10.5% in 1983. Although trade deficits increased as other countries sent products into the open American market, it is estimated that 14 million new jobs were created as US manufacturing rebounded from its 1970s decline. Perhaps most significantly, the United States became the global leader in the new high-tech industry. Although the rate of wage growth did slow somewhat, overall per capita income increased 14% for whites and 18% for blacks from 1982-1988. When contrasted with the meager 2.4% and 1% increases in the same categories from 1977-1982, the benefits of Reagan's policies for all become even more evident.[251]

Ronald Reagan by Michael Evans. Wikimedia Commons. Public domain.

---

[251] Land, Schweikart and Allen, 750-751,760.

CONCLUSION: FOUNDED ON FREEDOM

"...the preservation of the sacred fire of liberty, and the destiny of the republican model of government, are justly considered as *deeply*, perhaps as *finally* staked, on the experiment entrusted to the hands of the American people."[1]
–George Washington

"Freedom is a fragile thing and it's never more than one generation away from extinction. It is not ours by way of inheritance; it must be fought for and defended constantly by each generation, for it comes only once to a people. And those in world history who have known freedom and then lost it have never known it again."[2]
–Ronald Reagan

The establishment of the United States of America is one of the greatest events in the history of human freedom. For the first time in world history, a nation was explicitly founded on the principle that governments exist to protect our inherent individual rights. In eventually spanning the North American continent, the United States has provided more security, opportunity, and prosperity to more

---

[1] George Washington, "First Inaugural Address," April 30, 1789, in American Heritage – A Reader, ed. The Hillsdale College History Faculty (Hillsdale, Michigan: Hillsdale College Press, 2011), 199-202.
[2] Ronald Reagan, "January 5, 1967: Inaugural Address (Public Ceremony)", January 5, 1967: Inaugural Address (Public Ceremony) | Ronald Reagan (reaganlibrary.gov), 12 June 2021.

people than any other country that has ever existed. What we have here is unique. It is precious. We must protect and preserve it.

Throughout American history the principles of the American Revolution have permeated people's hearts and minds, reshaping and reforming them as water does to hardened stone. Therefore, today we must once again return to America's mission statement: the founding principles embodied in the preambles to the *Declaration of Independence* and the United States *Constitution*. The argument that America has had and still has flaws does not justify abandoning our foundational ideas. On the contrary, history provides ample evidence of how those principles were put to work to indeed form a more perfect union. Simply because we have not attained perfection – an impossible goal – does not justify discarding the American experiment.

Freedom is Rare. Slavery is Not.

It is important for Americans to be aware of and acknowledge the role that slavery played in their country's history. However, it is equally essential for Americans to not become so narrowly focused on American involvement in what was an ancient and global practice that they ignore or disregard the entire history and scope of human bondage. What is at stake is not only failing to put America's role in that execrable commerce in perspective, but also missing how the principles of the American Revolution were put to the service of ending slavery, both at home and abroad.

Comparisons with other nations are instructive. For example, in the Western Hemisphere, Puerto Rico (1873), Cuba (1886), and Brazil (1888) all ended slavery later than did the United States. In many nations of the Middle East slavery was not officially abolished until well into the 1900s. Iran outlawed human bondage in its 1906 constitution. Most independent Muslim nations only ended chattel slavery in the period between the World Wars. Yemen and Saudi Arabia outlawed slavery in 1962, while Mauritania did not act until 1980. Nevertheless, human bondage continues to exist extra-legally in parts of the Middle East.[3]

---

[3] Rodney Stark, *The Victory of Reason – How Christianity Led to Freedom, Capitalism, and Western Success* (New York: Random House, 2005), 220; Bernard Lewis, *Race and Slavery in the Middle East: An Historical Inquiry* (New York: Oxford University Press, 1990), 78-84.

Slavery is still practiced unofficially in Africa as well. In 2018 the Global Slavery Index estimated that 9.2 million Africans live in some form of servitude against their will.[4] Ghana, Benin, Nigeria,[5] Libya, and Sudan are among the worst offenders. Christian Solidarity International (Christian Solidarity International - USA (csi-usa.org)), a Non-Governmental Organization (NGO) currently active around the world, purchases the freedom of Christians and animists from South Sudan who have been captured in slave raids emanating from the Muslim north.[6]

Both the African slave trade in Africa and the Islamic slave trade in Africa and the Middle East lasted longer and involved far more human beings than did the Trans-Atlantic slave trade to the Americas. Literally millions of Africans have been enslaved by fellow Africans for thousands of years. In the Muslim world, an estimated 17 million Africans were brought to North Africa and the Middle East as slaves over the course of a millennium. The presence of black slaves in the Muslim world was so ubiquitous for so long that to this day the Arabic word for slave, abd, is also used to describe a black man.

However, it is worth noting that today there is not a large population of black people in the Middle East. Generally speaking, black slaves in the Muslim world were less likely to form families, had lower reproduction rates, suffered higher mortality rates, and experienced greater vulnerability to diseases than did slaves in the Americas. This was particularly true in the case of the United States, which was perhaps the only country in the world where the slave population grew naturally, even after the slave trade was abolished in 1808.[7]

---

[4] Mary Grabar, *Debunking Howard Zinn: Exposing the Fake History That Turned a Generation Against America* (Washington, D.C.: Regnery History, 2019), 89-112.

[5] Thomas Sowell, *Conquests and Cultures – An International History* (New York: Basic Books, 1998), 99-173.

[6] Michael Medved, *The 10 Big Lies About America: Combating Destructive Distortions About Our Nation* (New York: Crown Forum, 2008), 46-71.

[7] Sowell, *Conquests and Cultures*; Grabar, *Debunking Howard Zinn: Exposing the Fake History That Turned a Generation Against America*.

Industrial Revolution or "King Cotton"?

Just as the American experience with slavery needs to be understood in its proper context, slavery's role in the development of the Industrial Revolution and the American economy also requires perspective. Roughly encompassing the years 1760-1830, the Industrial Revolution transitioned many Western economies away from relying primarily on land and agriculture to depending more upon manufacturing and commerce. Beginning in Great Britain, industrialization later spread to the rest of Europe and then the United States. However, it was not until after 1800 that American cotton cultivated by slaves became a significant British import.[8]

The Industrial Revolution in the Northern United States was based on many factors. Certainly, one of these was the rise of textile mills where Southern cotton produced by slave labor was spun into cloth fibers and clothing.[9] Nevertheless, the textile industry was also facilitated by the invention of Elias Howe's and later Isaac Singer's mechanical sewing machines.[10] Such mechanization then spread to other sectors of the economy including agriculture, where the absence of slave labor necessitated and encouraged the invention of mechanical reapers and threshers as Northern farm production expanded into the fertile lands of the Midwest.[11] Another example of mechanization, with direct implications for the outcome of the Civil War, was the production of firearms, where the North outpaced the South by approximately 32:1.[12] The steam engine and coke blast furnace also contributed to the overall modernization of the region.[13] Most importantly, the development and expansion of railroads from about 3,000 miles of track in 1840 to approximately 30,000 by 1860 connected the North with the West and created a national market for

---

[8] Corey Iacono, "No, Slavery Did Not Make America Rich," Foundation for Economic Education, https://fee.org/articles/no-slavery-did-not-make-america-rich/?fbclid=IwAR0HU3hQjSLTNLdLAG4Fe moxhOEGBMxelBGr6-3OcWsa7zRVkLeThRRKE, 28 September 2019.
[9] Ibid.
[10] Steven E. Woodworth, *The Essentials of United States History: 1841 to 1877 Westward Expansion and the Civil War* (Piscataway, New Jersey: Research and Education Association, 1997), 18-42.
[11] Ibid.
[12] Larry Schweikart and Michael Allen, *A Patriot's History of the United States* (New York: Sentinel, 2004), 308.
[13] Iacono.

goods leading to the rise of big business.[14] It also aided the transport of men and materials during the Civil War and undoubtedly contributed to the North's victory.[15]

Meanwhile in the South, cotton reigned. Some large plantation owners as well as others involved in the cotton industry became extremely wealthy as a result. Cotton also fed textile mills in Britain and France and steadily increased as a percentage of total US exports in the years prior to the Civil War. By 1820 it represented about one-third of all American exports, rising to more than 50% in 1840 and reaching nearly 60% by 1860.[16]

On the other hand, the South became a player in the world cotton market relatively late, long after the Industrial Revolution had taken off in Europe. Additionally, even at its height cotton exports never amounted to more than approximately 5% of the total American economy as defined by gross domestic product (GDP).[17]

More important, however, is what the South lost by having an economy dependent on slavery. Before the Civil War, most Southern investment was in slaves, thereby diverting resources away from developing the necessary infrastructure to build a modern economy. Consequently, the South fell far behind the North in constructing railroads, building schools, and developing a banking, finance, and business sector. Reliance on slavery and agriculture delayed other aspects of modernization as well, including establishing factories and enticing immigrants to work in them. All of these factors left the South with a pronounced economic, industrial, and numerical disadvantage in its eventual war with the North.[18]

One could argue that before the Civil War and the eradication of slavery, the American South was frozen in time. Rather than small family farms and cities bustling with immigrants, commerce, and industry as became commonplace in the North, the South resembled a feudalistic society from the Middle Ages with a hierarchical social structure and static economic system. A few wealthy planters at the

---

[14] Woodworth, *The Essentials of United States History: 1841 to 1877 Westward Expansion and the Civil War.*
[15] Ibid., 46-66.
[16] Iacono; James Oliver Horton and Lois E. Horton, *Hard Road to Freedom – The Story of African America*, vol. 1, *From African Roots Through the Civil War* (New Brunswick, New Jersey, Rutgers University Press, 2001), 126-149.
[17] Iacono.
[18] Ibid.

top held the lion's share of economic and political power while presiding as "Lords of the manor" over slaves working plantations who resembled latter-day peasants and serfs. In fact, in 1861 the South possessed perhaps less than 10% of America's skilled labor and capital. As Wilfred Reilly has observed, "medieval-style plantation agriculture built upon the backs of abused people who cannot read is not a very effective way to utilize land and make money."[19]

The Southern plantation and slave-based economy neither maximized productivity from its workers nor created a good marketplace for Northern manufactured goods. Although it did generate wealth and consequent spending power for a relative few, the demand for the most expensive and luxurious products was limited to the plantation owners, who then spent the minimum to sustain their slaves. Until the United States rid itself of slavery, the ability to generate sufficient market demand to sustain a burgeoning industrial economy was extremely limited. Slaves with no money did not make good customers.[20]

And what about all the people in between? Most Southerners owned no slaves. They were mostly poor small farmers just trying to grind out a living. When North Carolinian Hinton Rowan Helper published *The Impeding Crisis of the South* (1859), arguing that slavery had actually been economically harmful to the region, it hit on one of the greatest fears of the slaveholding planter aristocracy – small farmers might realize that slavery only benefitted a very powerful few at the top while keeping the standard of living for most well behind that of the North. The fact that the book was banned in the South, while Republicans in the North distributed an abridged version as campaign propaganda, demonstrated the potential threat of Helper's argument.[21]

In some ways, the notions in Howard Zinn's *A People's History of the United States* and the *New York Times'* "The 1619 Project" that the United States was built upon slave labor or owes its modern-day

---

[19] Wilfred Reilly, "Why Woke History Is Not the Answer," Why Woke History Is Not the Answer - American Greatness (amgreatness.com), 7 January 2021.
[20] David S. Landes, *The Wealth and Poverty of Nations: Why Some Are So Rich and Some So Poor* (New York: W.W. Norton & Co., 1998), 294.
[21] Woodworth, *The Essentials of United States History: 1841 to 1877 Westward Expansion and the Civil War*, 19-46.

wealth and prosperity to slavery is similar to the pre-Civil War South's "King Cotton" myth. According to Phillip W. Magness, during the 1850s, political economist David Christy argued that Southern cotton produced by slave labor was a much greater part of both the American and world economies than was conventionally believed. One of the chief promoters of the theory was James Henry Hammond, a slavery-supporting politician. The idea that "cotton was king" was used by the South to threaten the North as well as Europe if either ever attempted to interfere with slavery. Hammond and other Southern politicians claimed that if the South seceded from the Union or stopped producing cotton altogether "'we could bring the whole world to our feet.'"[22]

It was entirely nonsense. During the Civil War, the Union used its navy to effectively strangle the South by controlling its ports and blocking all traffic in or out, while simultaneously ramping up its industrial war machine to utterly destroy the Confederacy. Meanwhile, no European nations were so dependent upon Southern cotton that they felt compelled to intervene on the South's behalf. When the Southern crop became unavailable, European textile mills found Egypt and India to be reliable suppliers of raw cotton.[23]

Whatever slavery contributed to the American economy, the Civil War which ended human bondage exacted great costs from the United States in blood and treasure. Besides the billions of dollars that the federal government had to borrow to wage the conflict, 620,000 Americans died. Of these, about 360,000 Union soldiers were killed fighting for the North, about one for every nine slaves eventually freed.[24]

Nevertheless, the defeat of the Confederacy and the eradication of slavery enabled the country to truly begin directing its efforts towards industrialization and modernization. Almost as soon as the South seceded, projects which had either been pushed to the side by the slavery issue or blocked outright by the agrarian South were permitted to go forth as Republicans in Congress passed and

---

[22] Phillip W. Magness, "The 1619 Project Resurrects King-Cotton Ideology of the Old South," American Institute for Economic Research, https://www.aier.org/article/the-1619-project-resurrects-king-cotton-ideology-of-the-old-south/, 11 September 2019.

[23] Ibid.

[24] Reilly, "Woke History is Not the Answer."

President Lincoln signed various pro-business and pro-development legislation. The transcontinental telegraph system was completed in 1861. The same year, passage of the *Morrill Tariff* protected American Northern manufacturing against less expensive foreign goods, but also raised prices for consumers.[25] Disagreement between the North and South as to a fitting location for a national railroad was put to rest with the passage of the *Transcontinental Railroad Act* (1862).[26] Southerners may have feared that a railroad connecting East and West and running through the northern part of the country could have opened new territories to small farms rather than slave plantations.[27] Finally, the *Homestead Act* of 1862 granted up to 160 acres of land to small farmers who were willing to work and develop it for five years, paying only a nominal fee of about $30.[28] Once again, Southern obstruction probably had been driven by concerns that such legislation would preclude the development of plantations and hinder the expansion of slavery into new territories.[29]

The emergence of the United States of America as the world's leading economic power only became possible *after* the scourge of human bondage had been wiped away from the land. In 1860 on the eve of the Civil War, the US was the fourth largest manufacturing country in the world; by 1894 it was first.[30] From 1870-1900 the US Patent Office granted 400,000 patents, more than ten times the number issued in the first eighty years of the country's existence.[31] Railroads, capital investment, mining of natural resources like iron, oil, and coal, communications advances including the telegraph and telephone, and the emergence of new industries like steel, oil, and electricity also contributed to America's incredible post-war growth.[32] At the end of the war in 1865, the gross domestic product of the

---

[25] Howard Zinn, *A People's History of the United States* (New York: Harper Perennial, 2005), 238.

[26] Salvatore Prisco III, *The Essentials of United States History: 1877-1912 – Industrialism, Foreign Expansion and the Progressive Era* (Piscataway, New Jersey: Research and Education Association, 1995), 3.

[27] Ibid.

[28] Thomas A. Bailey and David M. Kennedy, *The American Pageant*, vol. 2, *Since 1877,* tenth ed., (Lexington, Massachusetts: D.C. Heath and Co., 1994), 597-614.

[29] Ibid.

[30] Prisco.

[31] Schweikart and Allen, 429-435.

[32] Prisco.

United States was about 15 billion dollars; by 2020 it had risen to well over 15 trillion dollars, more than a 10,000% increase.[33] This economic expansion was clearly not driven by slavery, but by a free enterprise system encouraging innovation and inviting millions of legal immigrants from across the globe who were seeking economic opportunity.[34]

Generally speaking, the more slaves a nation or region had, the poorer it was. Although individual slaveowners may have become extremely wealthy, that did not equate to entire societies becoming wealthy. Cuba and especially Brazil had far more slaves than did the United States, and yet they have always remained much poorer than America. Similarly, the region most associated with slavery in the US, the South, continually trailed the rest of the country in terms of economic development until recent times. Outside of the Western Hemisphere, North Africa and the Middle East took far more slaves, both from sub-Saharan Africa and from Eastern and Southern Europe, for a much longer period of time than did America, but remained largely impoverished until the discovery of oil.[35]

America Today

There is much which can and should be celebrated in the United States of America today. It is true that for far too long freedom as fully-integrated citizens in American society was often blocked for former slaves and their descendants due to prejudice, discrimination, and segregation. However, beginning with court decisions including *Brown vs. Board of Education* in 1954 and legislation such as the *Civil Rights Acts of 1964, 1965, and 1968*, segregation was officially outlawed in the United States of America. These efforts have been largely successful in moving America towards more fully living out its "mission statement."[36]

Consider wealth. A look at the top ten income-earning groups in America as of 2019 includes Indians, Taiwanese, Filipinos, Indonesians, Persians, Lebanese Arabs, and South Africans (both

---

[33] Riley, "Woke History is Not the Answer."

[34] Ibid.

[35] Thomas Sowell, "The Real History of Slavery," in *Black Rednecks and White Liberals* (San Francisco: Encounter Books, 2005), 157-169

[36] Wilfred Reilly, The Good News They Won't Tell You About Race in America - Wilfred Reilly, Commentary Magazine, April, 2021.

black and white). Indian-Americans, for example, earn a median household income of $127,000, nearly twice that of white households.[37]

Although there is an income gap between American white households and black households ($65,902 to $43,862), this shrinks dramatically when other factors besides race are considered. For example, earnings usually increase with age, and the difference in median age between white Americans (58) and black Americans (27) explains some of the gap. Aptitude, test scores, region where one resides, and years of education are other important variables. When one looks at black and white Americans with similarities across these categories, the income differential almost disappears. Similar gaps in income among other ethnic groups including Hispanic-Americans as well as between men and women also nearly evaporate when looking at a broad variety of factors.[38]

Consider also immigration. People vote with their feet. There must be something exceptional about the United States of America to have drawn so many from around the world for so many years. For example, black immigrants to the United States far outnumber black emigrants from America to Africa.[39] Likewise, the total number of black immigrants from the Caribbean, Latin America, and Africa vastly exceeds the number of those who were brought unwillingly centuries ago as slaves.[40] Many from Nigeria, Ghana, Guyana, and the West Indies in particular have thrived. Nigerians are perhaps the most well-educated group in the entire country and along with other African immigrants from Ghana and Guyana earn significantly more than the typical white household.[41] Meanwhile various West Indian groups earn about the same as whites.[42]

Those who today promote cultural Marxism, critical race theory, and "The 1619 Project" are merely the latest in a long line of deniers of the truths of America's "mission statement" and founding principles. Instead of adhering to the belief that "all men are created equal," they resemble Calhoun, Taney, and Stephens in holding that

[37] Ibid.
[38] Ibid.
[39] Thomas Sowell, *The Quest for Cosmic Justice* (New York: Touchstone, 1999), 32.
[40] Medved.
[41] Reilly, The Good News They Won't Tell You About Race in America - Wilfred Reilly, Commentary Magazine.
[42] Ibid.

history is simply made up of competing groups of "winners" and "losers" or "oppressors" and "oppressed." Similar to those who claimed that "cotton was king," these modern-day Marxists charge that slavery built America's power, influence, and wealth, while ignoring or minimizing the roles of free enterprise, economic opportunity, perseverance, and hard work. And just as the progressives of the past, the totalitarians of the present believe that modern life has become too complicated for individuals to govern themselves. They argue that a constitutionally-limited government with separate branches of power that check and balance one another is insufficient to deal with issues surrounding "social justice" including racism, sexism, economic inequality, and property redistribution. Instead, they propose an ever-expanding unelected bureaucracy as the solution to society's ills. They believe that new agencies, such as a "Department of Antiracism," combining all the powers of government – executive, legislative, and judicial – in the hands of elites with the proper education and expertise would be far more efficient in addressing our problems. Never mind that this kind of conglomeration of power was labelled "'the very definition of tyranny'" by the Founding Fathers.[43]

Those who rail against America's "mission statement" are also ambitious. They are not satisfied to be leaders of society – they seek to be revolutionaries. Rather than merely stewarding the nation created by the Founding Fathers, these radicals wish to transform it into something new which they can call their own creation. In 1838 Abraham Lincoln warned that such people had existed throughout history, and America would not be immune:

> It is to deny, what the history of the world tells us is true, to suppose that men of ambition and talents will not continue to spring up amongst us. And, when they do, they will as naturally seek the gratification of their ruling passion, as others have *so* done before them. The question then, is, can that gratification be found in supporting and maintaining an edifice

---

[43] Coleman Hughes, "How to be an Anti-Intellectual," October 27, 2019, "How To Be An Antiracist" is Wrong on its Facts and in its Assumptions. (city-journal.org); Charles R. Kesler, *Crisis of the Two Constitutions: The Rise, Decline, & Recovery of American Greatness* (New York: Encounter Books, 2021), ix-xviii.

[structure] that has been erected by others? Most certainly it cannot.

Lincoln argued that if our nation was ever destroyed, it would not be by external forces but by those from within who were opposed to American principles and institutions and desired to tear them down because they thought they knew better than the founders.[44]

Any human endeavor will always be imperfect. That is why the Founding Fathers crafted the *Declaration of Independence* based upon an ideal, "all men are created equal," and a *Constitution*, "to form a *more* perfect union," as well as included a democratic process to amend it. But when those who claim to be reformers or agents of improvement and progress speak of "fundamental transformation" and "systemic inequities," they are revealing that they desire something far different than "a more perfect union." They are calling for a kind of revolution. Efforts to achieve "social justice," in whatever form they may take, inevitably result in people of ambition acquiring and wielding greater control over our lives, our freedom, and our property, and thereby perpetrating acts of injustice against individuals. As Alexis de Tocqueville wrote in the 1830s:

> 'It may easily be seen that almost all the able and ambitious members of a democratic community will labor unceasingly to extend the powers of government, because they all hope at some time or other to wield those powers themselves.'[45]

So, what is to be done? How shall we preserve America's "mission statement"? We must believe in it, take pride in it, teach it, defend it, and never apologize for it. It begins with us. As British author, political commentator, and self-proclaimed admirer of America Douglas Murray has stated, "We can't wait for the cavalry to come and save us. We are the cavalry…"[46]

---

[44] Abraham Lincoln, "Address to the Young Men's Lyceum of Springfield, Illinois: The Perpetuation of Our Political Institutions," January 27, 1838, in *Abraham Lincoln: Speeches and Writings, 1832-1858*, ed. Don E. Fehrenbacher (New York: Literary Classics of the United States, Inc., 1989), 28-36; Sowell, *The Quest for Cosmic Justice*, 147-149.

[45] Sowell, *The Quest for Cosmic Justice*, 151.

[46] "Speak the Truth, 3 April 2021, Speak the Truth – Live Not by Lies.

As they signed the *Declaration of Independence*, the Founding Fathers knew that from that moment forward they would be nothing more than traitors in the eyes of Britain. If the revolution failed to secure American independence, they were likely to die at the end of a hangman's noose. Nevertheless, each and every one of them swore:

> ...for the support of this Declaration, with a firm reliance on the protection of divine Providence, we mutually pledge to each other our Lives, our Fortunes and our sacred Honor.[47]

How can we do any less?

---

[47] *Declaration of Independence* in *American Heritage – A Reader*, ed. The Hillsdale College History Faculty (Hillsdale, Michigan: Hillsdale College Press, 2011), 128-131.

BIBLIOGRAPHY

Adams, John. "To George Churchman and Jacob Lindley," January 24, 1801. In *John Adams: Writings from the New Nation*, ed. Gordon S. Wood, 406-407. New York: Literary Classics of the United States, 2016.

Adams, John. "To Robert J. Evans," June 9, 1819. In *The U.S. Constitution – A Reader*, ed. The Hillsdale College Politics Faculty, 401. Hillsdale, Michigan: Hillsdale College Press, 2014.

"African Civilization Society of New York." *Anti-Slavery Reporter*. 1 November 1859. https://archive.org/details/sim_anti-slavery-reporter-and-aborigines-friend_1859-11-01_7_11/page/262/mode/2up.

Allison, Robert J. "Benjamin Franklin and Slavery in America." *The Age of Benjamin Franklin*. Chantilly, Virginia: The Teaching Company/The Great Courses, 2018. CD.

Allison, Robert J. "Georgia – Dreams and Realities." *Before 1776: Life in the American Colonies*. Chantilly, Virginia: The Teaching Company/The Great Courses, 2009. CD.

Allison, Robert J. "The Great Awakening." *Before 1776: Life in the American Colonies*. Chantilly, Virginia: The Teaching Company/The Great Courses, 2009. CD.

Allison, Robert J. "Pontiac's Revolt Against the British." *Before 1776: Life in the American Colonies*. Chantilly, Virginia: The Teaching Company/The Great Courses, 2009. CD.

Arnn, Larry P. "Orwell's 1984 and Today." *Imprimis* Vol. 49, No. 12. (December, 2020).

Bacon, Margaret H. *The Quiet Rebels: The Story of the Quakers in America*. New York: Basic Books, Inc., 1969.

Bailey, Thomas A. and David M. Kennedy. *The American Pageant*. Vol. 2. *Since 1877*. Tenth ed. Lexington, Massachusetts: D.C. Heath and Co., 1994.

Bailyn, Bernard. *The Ideological Origins of the American Revolution.* Cambridge, Massachusetts: The Belknap Press of Harvard University Press, 1992.

Bakken, Gordon Morris. History 393 Lecture Notes. California State University, Fullerton. Spring 1992.

Baldwin, Ebeneezer. "An Appendix, Stating the Heavy Grievances the Colonies Labour under from Several Late Acts of the British Parliament, and Shewing What We Have Just Reason to Expect the Consequences of These Measures Will Be." In *The American Revolution: Writings from the Pamphlet Debate 1773-1776*, ed. Gordon S. Wood, 343-378. New York: Literary Classics of the United States, Inc., 2015.

Barton, David. *The Jefferson Lies: Exposing the Myths You've Always Believed About Thomas* Jefferson. Washington, D.C.: WND Books, 2016.

Basker, James G., ed. *American Antislavery Writings.* New York: Literary Classics of the United States, 2012.

Behrendt, Stephen D., A.J.H. Latham, and David Northrup, eds. *The Diary of Antera Duke, An Eighteenth Century African Slave Trader.* New York: Oxford University Press, 2010.

Benezet, Anthony. "Observations on the Inslaving, Importing and Purchasing of Negroes." In *American Antislavery Writings*, ed. James G. Basker, 28-33. New York: Literary Classics of the United States, 2012.

Bennett, William J. and John T. E. Cribb. *The American Patriot's Almanac.* Nashville: Thomas Nelson, 2010.

Berlin, Ira. *Many Thousands Gone – The First Two Centuries of Slavery in North America.* Cambridge, Massachusetts: Belknap, 1998.

Berlin, Ira. "The Slaves Were the Primary Force Behind Their Emancipation." In *The Civil War: Opposing Viewpoints*, ed. William Dudley, 276-285. San Diego: Greenhaven Press, Inc., 1995.

Black Courage: African-American Soldiers in the War for Independence (stamps.org).

Bradford, M.E. *Founding Fathers.* Lawrence, Kansas: University Press of Kansas, 1994.

Bradford, William. *Of Plymouth Plantation.* San Antonio: Vision Forum, 2008.

Brookhiser, Richard. *What Would the Founders Do? Our Questions Their Answers.* New York: Basic Books, 2006.

Brown v. Board of Education of Topeka, Kansas, 347 U.S. 483 (1954). In *American Legal History,* eds. Kermit L. Hall, William M. Wiecek, and Paul Finkelman, 510-513. Oxford: Oxford University Press, 1991.

Brush, Kathleen. *Racism and anti-Racism in the World: before and after 1945.* Kathleen Brush, 2020.

Calhoun, John C. "Disquisition on Government." In *American Heritage – A Reader,* eds. The Hillsdale College History Faculty, 373-385. Hillsdale, Michigan: Hillsdale College Press, 2011.

Chairman of the Council of Economic Advisors. *Economic Report of the President.* https://www.govinfo.gov/app/collection/erp/2019.

Chernow, Ron. *Alexander Hamilton.* New York: Penguin, 2004.

Chilton, John F. *The Essentials of United States History: 1789 to 1841 The Developing Nation.* Piscataway, New Jersey: Research and Education Association, 1995.

Constitution. In *American Heritage – A Reader,* eds. The Hillsdale College History Faculty, 146-156. Hillsdale, Michigan: Hillsdale College Press, 2011.

Coolidge, Calvin. "The Inspiration of the Declaration." In *American Heritage – A Reader,* eds. The Hillsdale College History Faculty, 667-675. Hillsdale, Michigan: Hillsdale College Press, 2011.

Crabbs, Jack. History 466A Lecture Notes. California State University, Fullerton. Fall 1993.

Crocker, H.W. *Don't Tread on Me: A 400-Year History of America at War, from Indian Fighting to Terrorist Hunting.* New York: Crown Forum, 2006.

Dana, James. "The African Slave Trade." In *Political Sermons of the American Founding Era, 1730-1805*, ed. Ellis Sandoz, 1031-1055. Vol. 2. 2nd ed. Indianapolis: Liberty Fund, 1998.

Deb Haaland confirmed, becomes first Native American Cabinet secretary (usatoday.com). March 15, 2021.

Declaration of Independence. In *American Heritage – A Reader*, eds. The Hillsdale College History Faculty, 128-131. Hillsdale, Michigan: Hillsdale College Press, 2011.

Diamond, Jared. *Guns, Germs, and Steel: The Fates of Human Societies.* New York: W.W. Norton & Co., 1999.

Dickinson, John. "Letters From a Farmer in Pennsylvania." In *Colonies to Nation, 1763-1789: A Documentary History of the American Revolution*, ed. Jack P. Greene, 122-133. New York: W.W. Norton & Company, 1975.

Douglass, Frederick. "African Civilization Society." February, 1859. https://teachingamericanhistory.org/document/african-civilization-society/.

Douglass, Frederick. "'The Emancipation Proclamation' is a Significant Achievement." In *The Civil War: Opposing Viewpoints*, ed. William Dudley, 180-186. San Diego: Greenhaven Press, Inc., 1995.

Douglass, Frederick. "My Bondage and My Freedom." In *Frederick Douglass: Autobiographies*, ed. Henry Louis Gates, Jr., 392-393. New York: Literary Classics of the United States, Inc., 1994.

Douglass, Frederick. "Oration in Memory of Abraham Lincoln," April 14, 1876. In *American Speeches: Political Oratory from Abraham Lincoln to Bill Clinton*, ed. Ted Widmer, 74-84. New York: Literary Classics of the United States, Inc., 2006), 74-84.

Douglass, Frederick. "What to the Slave is the Fourth of July?", June 5, 1852. In *American Heritage – A Reader*, ed. The Hillsdale College History Faculty, 396-413. Hillsdale, Michigan: Hillsdale College Press, 2011.

D'Souza, Dinesh. *America: Imagine a World Without Her.* Washington, D.C.: Regnery Publishing, 2014.

Dunn, Mary Maples and Richard S. "The Founding, 1681-1701." In *Philadelphia: A 300-Year History,* ed. Russell F. Weigley, 1-32. New York: W.W. Norton & Company, 1982.

Edwards, Jonathan. "A Faithful Narrative of the Surprising Work of God in the Conversion of Many Hundred Souls in Northampton, and the Neighbouring Towns and Villages of the County of Hampshire in the Province of the Massachusetts-Bay in New-England." In *Jonathan Edwards: Writings From the Great Awakening,* ed. Philip F. Gura, 1-83. New York: Literary Classics of the United States, 2013.

Elder, Larry. "Slavery: What They Didn't Teach in My High School." Townhall.com, 12 July 2018.

Elkins, Stanley and Eric McKitrick. *The Age of Federalism: The Early American Republic, 1788-1800.* New York: Oxford University Press, 1993.

Exodus. NKJV.

Fairbank, John K., Edwin O. Reischauer, and Albert M. Craig. *East Asia – Tradition and Transformation.* Boston: Houghton Mifflin Company, 1989.

Farrow, Anne. "Chapter Seven: The Last Slaves." September 29, 2002. Chapter Seven: The Last Slaves - Hartford Courant.

Feldman, George Franklin. *Cannibalism, Headhunting and Human Sacrifice in North America: A History Forgotten.* Chambersburg, Pennsylvania: Alan C. Hood & Co., Inc., 2008.

Ferguson, Niall. *Civilization: The West and the Rest.* New York: Penguin Books, 2011.

Fischer, David Hackett. *Washington's Crossing.* New York: Oxford University Press, 2004.

Flores, Dan. *The Natural West – Environmental History in the Great Plains and Rocky Mountains.* Norman: University of Oklahoma Press, 2001.

Flynn-Paul, Jeff. "The Myth of the 'Stolen Country.'" 23 September 2020. https://spectator.us/myth-stolen-country-america-new-world/.

Forten, James. "Letters from a Man of Colour on a Late Bill Before the Senate of Pennsylvania." In *American Antislavery Writings*, ed. James G. Basker, 211-215. New York: Literary Classics of the United States, 2012.

Foster, Stephen T. "Emancipation Proclamation." In *Civil War Cards*. Atlas Editions, 1991.

Franklin, Benjamin. "An Address to the Public from the Pennsylvania Society for Promoting the Abolition of Slavery, and the Relief of Free Negroes Unlawfully Held in Bondage," November 9, 1789. In *The U.S. Constitution – A Reader*, eds. The Hillsdale College Politics Faculty, 401. Hillsdale, Michigan: Hillsdale College Press, 2014.

Franklin, Benjamin. "To John Langdon," 1788. In *Benjamin Franklin: Writings*, ed. J.A. Leo LeMay, 1169-1170. New York: Literary Classics of the United States, 1987.

Galatians. NKJV.

Garnet, Henry Highland. "A memorial discourse; by Henry Highland Garnet, delivered in the hall of the House of Representatives, Washington City, D.C. on Sabbath, February 12, 1865. With an introduction by James McCune Smith, M.D." Philadelphia: Joseph M. Wilson, 1865. https://archive.org/details/memorialdiscourse00garn.

Garvey, Marcus. "Editorial." *Negro World*. 6 September 1924. https://www.international.ucla.edu/africa/mgpp/sample06.

"Gettysburg Address." https://www.history.com/topics/american-civil-war/gettysburg-address.

Goldberg, Jonah. *Liberal Fascism: The Secret History of the American Left, from Mussolini to the Politics of Change.* New York: Broadway Books, 2009.

Grabar, Mary. *Debunking Howard Zinn: Exposing the Fake History That Turned a Generation Against America.* Washington, D.C.: Regnery History, 2019.

Grabar, Mary. *Debunking the 1619 Project: Exposing the Plan to Divide America.* Washington, D.C.: Regnery History, 2021.

Guasco, Michael. "The Misguided Focus on 1619 as the Beginning of Slavery in the U.S. Damages Our Understanding of American History." 13 September 2017. The Misguided Focus on 1619 as the Beginning of Slavery in the U.S. Damages Our Understanding of American History | History | Smithsonian Magazine.

Guelzo, Allen C. *Lincoln's Emancipation Proclamation: The End of Slavery in America.* New York: Simon and Schuster, 2004.

Hall, Kermit L., William M. Wiecek, Paul Finkelman, eds. *American Legal History.* New York: Oxford University Press, 1991.

Hamilton, Alexander. "To John Jay," March 14, 1779. In *Alexander Hamilton: Writings,* ed. Joanne B. Freeman, 56-58. Literary Classics of the United States, 2001.

Hamilton, Alexander. "Philo Camillus no. 2," August 1795. In *The U.S. Constitution – A Reader,* eds. The Hillsdale College Politics Faculty, 402. Hillsdale, Michigan: Hillsdale College Press, 2014.

Hannah-Jones, Nikole. Introduction to "The 1619 Project." *New York Times Magazine.* 18 August 2019. 14-26.

Heimert, Alan. Introduction to *The Great Awakening,* eds. Alan Heimert and Perry Miller. Indianapolis: Bobbs-Merrill Educational Publishing, 1967.

Herman, Arthur. *To Rule the Waves: How the British Navy Shaped the Modern World.* New York: HarperCollins Publishers, 2004.

Hillsdale College History Faculty, The, eds. *American Heritage – A Reader.* Hillsdale, Michigan: Hillsdale College Press, 2011.

Hillsdale College Politics Faculty, The, eds. *The U.S. Constitution – A Reader.* Hillsdale, Michigan: Hillsdale College Press, 2014.

Hinderaker, John. "Slavery? We Were a Footnote." 29 November 2019. https://www.powerlineblog.com/archives/2019/11/slavery-we-were-a-footnote.php?utm_source=facebook&utm_medium=sw&utm_campaign=sw&fbclid=IwAR0MTGEL1bHDCZ2Xoaz_j5vxqlPgSdK4Lg-eswwdzd5gZcd13tJufOYBJII.

History Channel, The. *Desperate Crossing: The Untold Story of The Mayflower*. A & E Television Networks, 2006. DVD.

Hobbes, Thomas. *Leviathan*, ed. Richard Tuck. Cambridge, UK: Cambridge University Press, 1996.

Hofstadter, Richard. *The Age of Reform*. New York: Vintage Books, 1955.

Hofstadter, Richard. *The American Political Tradition*. New York: Vintage Books, 1974.

Hopkins, Samuel. "A Dialogue Concerning the Slavery of the Africans." In *American Antislavery Writings*, ed. James G. Basker, 69-74. New York: Literary Classics of the United States, 2012.

Hopkins, Stephen. "The Rights of the Colonies Examined." In *The American Revolution: Writings from the Pamphlet Debate 1764-1772*, ed. Gordon S. Wood, 121-142. New York: Literary Classics of the United States, Inc., 2015.

Horn, James, ed. *Captain John Smith: Writings with other Narratives of Roanoke, Jamestown, and the First English Settlement in America*. New York: Literary Classics of the United States, Inc., 2007.

Horton, James Oliver and Lois E. Horton. *Hard Road to Freedom – The Story of African America*. Vol. 1, *From African Roots Through the Civil War*. New Brunswick, New Jersey, Rutgers University Press, 2001.

Horton, James Oliver and Lois E. Horton. *In Hope of Liberty – Culture, Community and Protest Among Northern Free Blacks, 1700-1860*. New York: Oxford University Press, 1997.

Hughes, Coleman, "How to be an Anti-Intellectual." 27 October 2019. "How To Be An Antiracist" is Wrong on its Facts and in its Assumptions. (city-journal.org).

Iacono, Corey. "No, Slavery Did Not Make America Rich." Foundation for Economic Education. 28 September 2019. https://fee.org/articles/no-slavery-did-not-make-america-rich/?fbclid=IwAR0HU3hQjSLTNLdLAG4Fe_moxhOEGBMxelBGr6-3OcWsa7zRVkLeThRRKE.

Isenberg, Andrew C. *The Destruction of the Bison*. New York: Cambridge University Press, 2000.

Jackson, Andrew. "First Annual Message," December 8, 1829. In *American Heritage – A Reader*, eds. The Hillsdale College History Faculty, 285-294. Hillsdale, Michigan: Hillsdale College Press, 2011.

Jaffa, Harry V. *A New Birth of Freedom: Abraham Lincoln and the Coming of the Civil War*. Lanham, Maryland: Rowman and Littlefield Publishers, Inc., 2004.

Jefferson, Thomas. *Autobiography*. In *Thomas Jefferson: Writings*, ed. Merrill D. Peterson, 1-101. New York: Literary Classics of the United States, 1984.

Jefferson, Thomas. "Draft of the Declaration of Independence." In *The U.S. Constitution – A Reader*, eds. The Hillsdale College Politics Faculty, 397. Hillsdale, Michigan: Hillsdale College Press, 2014.

Jefferson, Thomas. "To Edward Coles," August 25, 1814. In *Thomas Jefferson: Writings*, ed. Merrill D. Peterson, 1343-1346. New York: Literary Classics of the United States, 1984.

Jefferson, Thomas. "To James Heaton," May 20, 1826. In *Thomas Jefferson: Writings*, ed. Merrill D. Peterson, 1516. New York: Literary Classics of the United States, 1984.

Jefferson, Thomas. "To John Adams," November 1, 1822. In *The Adams-Jefferson Letters: The Complete Correspondence between Thomas Jefferson & Abigail & John Adams*, ed. Lester J. Cappon, 584-585. Chapel Hill: University of North Carolina Press, 1987.

Jefferson, Thomas. "Query XVIII: Manners," from *Notes on the State of Virginia*. In *The U.S. Constitution – A Reader*, eds. The Hillsdale College Politics Faculty, 403-404. Hillsdale, Michigan: Hillsdale College Press, 2014.

Jefferson, Thomas. "A Summary View of the Rights of British America." In *Tracts of the American Revolution*, ed. Merrill Jensen, 256-276. Indianapolis: Hackett Publishing Company, Inc., 2003.

Jeffrey, Harry. History 476 Lecture Notes. California State University, Fullerton. Summer, 1997.

Jensen, Merrill, ed. *Tracts of the American Revolution*. Indianapolis: Hackett Publishing Company, Inc., 2003.

Johnson, Lyndon B. "Commencement Address at Howard University," June 4, 1965. In *The U.S. Constitution – A Reader*, eds. The Hillsdale College Politics Faculty, 765-772. Hillsdale, Michigan: Hillsdale College Press, 2014.

Jordan, Don and Michael Walsh. *White Cargo – The Forgotten History of Britain's White Slaves in America*. New York: New York University Press, 2008.

Kengor, Paul. "Teach MLK, Not CRT." 3 December 2021. https://spectator.org/mlk-not-crt/.

Kennedy, John F. "Address to the Nation on Civil Rights," June 11, 1963. In *American Speeches: Political Oratory from Abraham Lincoln to Bill Clinton*, ed. Ted Widmer, 548-553. New York: Literary Classics of the United States, Inc., 2006.

Kesler, Charles. Government 169 Lecture Notes. Claremont McKenna College. Fall 2006.

Kesler, Charles R. *Crisis of the Two Constitutions: The Rise, Decline, & Recovery of American Greatness*. New York: Encounter Books, 2021.

King, Martin Luther, Jr. "Address to the March on Washington," August 28, 1963. In *American Speeches: Political Oratory from Abraham Lincoln to Bill Clinton*, ed. Ted Widmer, 556-560. New York: Literary Classics of the United States, Inc., 2006.

King, Martin Luther, Jr. "Letter from the Birmingham City Jail," April 16, 1963. In *American Heritage – A Reader*, eds. The Hillsdale College History Faculty, 835-849. Hillsdale, Michigan: Hillsdale College Press, 2011.

King, Martin Luther, Jr., "Speech to the Montgomery Improvement Association," December 5, 1955. In *American Speeches: Political Oratory from Abraham Lincoln to Bill Clinton*, ed. Ted Widmer, 516-519. New York: Literary Classics of the United States, Inc., 2006.

Krech, Shepard III. *The Ecological Indian – Myth and History*. New York: W.W. Norton & Company, 1999.

Land, Gary. *The Essentials of United States History: America Since 1941 Emergence as a World Power*. Piscataway, New Jersey: Research and Education Association, 2000.

Landes, David S. *The Wealth and Poverty of Nations: Why Some Are So Rich and Some So Poor*. New York: W.W. Norton & Co., 1998.

Laws of Virginia. In *American Heritage – A Reader*, eds. The Hillsdale College History Faculty, 9-12. Hillsdale, Michigan: Hillsdale College Press, 2011.

Lay, Benjamin. "All Slave-Keepers that Keep the Innocent in Bondage." In *American Antislavery Writings*, ed. James G. Basker, 23-24. New York: Literary Classics of the United States, 2012.

Lewis, Bernard. *Race and Slavery in the Middle East: An Historical Inquiry*. New York: Oxford University Press, 1990.

Lincoln, Abraham. "Address at Cooper Institute," February 27, 1860. In *Abraham Lincoln: Speeches and Writings, 1859-1865*, ed. Don E. Fehrenbacher, 111-130. New York: Literary Classics of the United States, Inc., 1989.

Lincoln, Abraham. "Address to the Young Men's Lyceum of Springfield, Illinois: The Perpetuation of Our Political Institutions," January 27, 1838, in *Abraham Lincoln: Speeches and Writings, 1832-1858*, ed. Don E. Fehrenbacher, 28-36. New York: Literary Classics of the United States, Inc., 1989.

Lincoln, Abraham. "Emancipation Proclamation," September 22, 1862. In *American Legal History*, eds. Kermit L. Hall, William M. Wiecek, and Paul Finkelman, 224. Oxford: Oxford University Press, 1991.

Lincoln, Abraham. "First Inaugural Address," March 4, 1861. In *American Heritage – A Reader*, eds. The Hillsdale College History Faculty, 474-481. Hillsdale, Michigan: Hillsdale College Press, 2011.

Lincoln, Abraham. "Gettysburg Address," November 19, 1863. In *American Heritage – A Reader*, eds. The Hillsdale College History Faculty, 499. Hillsdale, Michigan: Hillsdale College Press, 2011.

Lincoln, Abraham. "House Divided" Speech, June 16, 1858. In *American Speeches: The Revolution to the Civil War*, ed. Ted Widmer, 634-642. New York: Literary Classics of the United States, 2006.

Lincoln, Abraham. "Memorandum on Probable Failure of Re-election," August 23, 1864. In *Abraham Lincoln: Speeches and Writings, 1859-1865*, ed. Don E. Fehrenbacher, 624. New York: Literary Classics of the United States, Inc., 1989.

Lincoln, Abraham. "Second Inaugural Address," March 4, 1865. In *American Heritage – A Reader*, eds. The Hillsdale College History Faculty, 501-502. Hillsdale, Michigan: Hillsdale College Press, 2011.

Lincoln, Abraham. "Speech on the Dred Scott Decision at Springfield, Illinois," June 26, 1857. In *Abraham Lincoln: Speeches and Writings, 1832-1858*, ed. Don E. Fehrenbacher, 390-403. New York: Literary Classics of the United States, Inc., 1989.

Lincoln, Abraham. "Speech at Independence Hall," February 22, 1861. In *American Speeches: The Revolution to the Civil War*, ed. Ted Widmer, 705-706. New York: Literary Classics of the United States, 2006.

Lincoln, Abraham. "Speech on the Kansas-Nebraska Act," October 16, 1854. In *Abraham Lincoln: Speeches and Writings, 1832-1858*, ed. Don E. Fehrenbacher, 307-348. New York: Literary Classics of the United States, Inc., 1989.

"Lincoln-Douglas Debates." In *American Heritage – A Reader*, eds. The Hillsdale College History Faculty, 425-446. Hillsdale, Michigan: Hillsdale College Press, 2011.

Locke, John. *The Second Treatise of Government.* In *Two Treatises of Government*, ed. Peter Laslett. Cambridge: Cambridge University Press, 1988.

Madison, James. "To Robert J. Evans," June 15, 1819. In *James Madison: Writings*, ed. Jack N. Rakove, 728-733. New York: Literary Classics of the United States, 1999.

Madison, James. "Speech at the Constitutional Convention," June 6, 1787. In *The U.S. Constitution – A Reader*, eds. The Hillsdale College Politics Faculty, 402. Hillsdale, Michigan: Hillsdale College Press, 2014.

Madison, James. "Speech in the Virginia Ratifying Convention on the Slave Trade Clause," June 17, 1788. In *James Madison: Writings*, ed. Jack N. Rakove, 391-392. New York: Literary Classics of the United States, 1999.

Magness, Phillip W. *The 1619 Project: A Critique.* The American Institute for Economic Research, 2020.

Magness, Phillip W. "The 1619 Project Resurrects King-Cotton Ideology of the Old South." American Institute for Economic Research. 11 September 2019. https://www.aier.org/article/the-1619-project-resurrects-king-cotton-ideology-of-the-old-south/.

Marx, Karl and Friedrich Engels. *The Communist Manifesto*, ed. Joseph Katz. New York: Simon & Schuster, Inc., 1964.

"Massachusetts Body of Liberties." In *Puritan Political Ideas 1558-1794*, ed. Edmund S. Morgan, 177-203. Indianapolis: Hackett Publishing Company, Inc., 2003.

Matthew. NKJV.

"Mayflower Compact," November 11, 1620. In *American Heritage – A Reader*, eds. The Hillsdale College History Faculty, 13-14. Hillsdale, Michigan: Hillsdale College Press, 2011.

Mayhew, Jonathan. "The Snare Broken." In *Political Sermons of the American Founding Era, 1730-1805*, ed. Ellis Sandoz, 233-264. Vol. 1. 2nd ed. Indianapolis: Liberty Fund, 1998.

McPherson, James M. "Lincoln Freed the Slaves." In *The Civil War: Opposing Viewpoints*, ed. William Dudley, 261-275. San Diego: Greenhaven Press, Inc., 1995.

McPherson, James M. Preface to *Washington's Crossing*, by David Hackett Fischer. New York: Oxford University Press, 2004.

Medved, Michael. *The 10 Big Lies About America: Combating Destructive Distortions About Our Nation*. New York: Crown Forum, 2008.

Miller, John J. "Buffaloed." *National Review*, 9 October 2000, 28.

Morgan, Edmund S. *American Slavery, American Freedom*. New York: W.W. Norton & Company, 1975.

Morgan, Edmund S., ed. *Puritan Political Ideas 1558-1794*. Indianapolis: Hackett Publishing Company, Inc., 2003.

Morgan, Iwan W. *Beyond the Liberal Consensus: A Political History of the United States Since 1965*. New York: St. Martin's Press, 1994.

Murray, Charles. *American Exceptionalism – An Experiment in History*. Washington, D.C.: American Enterprise Institute, 2013.

Nash, Gary B. *Quakers and Politics: Pennsylvania, 1681-1726*. Princeton, New Jersey: Princeton University Press, 1968.

Nell, William Cooper. *The Colored Patriots of the American Revolution*. Robert F. Wallcut, 2017.

Newcombe, Jerry. "Teaching Kids That America Was Always Racist." 7 May 2021. Teaching Kids That America Was Always Racist | The Stream.

Northwest Ordinance. In *American Heritage – A Reader*, eds. The Hillsdale College History Faculty, 137-243. Hillsdale, Michigan: Hillsdale College Press, 2011.

Otis, James. "The Rights of the British Colonies Asserted and Proved." In *The American Revolution: Writings from the Pamphlet Debate 1764-1772*, ed. Gordon S. Wood, 41-119. New York: Literary Classics of the United States, Inc., 2015.

Paine, Thomas. "The American Crisis, Number I," December 19, 1776. In *Thomas Paine – Collected Writings*, ed. Eric Foner, 91-99. New York: Literary Classics of the United States, Inc., 1995.

Parkman, Francis. "The Conspiracy of Pontiac and the Indian War after the Conquest of Canada." In *The Oregon Trail/The Conspiracy of Pontiac*, ed. William R. Taylor, 343-918. New York: Literary Classics of the United States, Inc., 1991.

Parkman, Francis. "The Jesuits in North America in the Seventeenth Century." In *France and England In North America, Vol. I*, ed. David Levin, 331-712. New York: Literary Classics of the United States, Inc., 1983.

Parkman, Francis. "La Salle and the Discovery of the Great West." In *France and England In North America, Vol. I*, ed. David Levin, 713-1054. New York: Literary Classics of the United States, Inc., 1983.

Parkman, Francis. "Montcalm and Wolfe." In *France and England In North America, Vol. II*, ed. David Levin, 829-1479. New York: Literary Classics of the United States, Inc., 1983.

Philbrick, Nathaniel. *Mayflower: A Story of Courage, Community, and War*. New York: Viking, 2006.

Pipes, Richard. *Property and Freedom: The Story of How Through the Centuries Private Ownership Has Promoted Liberty and the Rule of Law*. New York: Alfred A. Knopf, 2000.

Plessy v. Ferguson, 163 U.S. 537 (1896). In *American Legal History*, eds. Kermit L. Hall, William M. Wiecek, and Paul Finkelman, 250-255. Oxford: Oxford University Press, 1991.

"Pocahontas." Pocahontas | St George's Church Gravesend (stgeorgesgravesend.org). 7 March 2021.

Prager, Dennis. *The Rational Bible: Exodus – God, Slavery and Freedom.* Edited by Joseph Telushkin. Washington, D.C.: Regnery Faith, 2018.

President's Advisory 1776 Commission, The. "The 1776 Report." January, 2021 https://trumpwhitehouse.archives.gov/wp-content/uploads/2021/01/The-Presidents-Advisory-1776-Commission-Final-Report.pdf.

Prisco, Salvatore, III. *The Essentials of United States History: 1877-1912 – Industrialism, Foreign Expansion and the Progressive Era.* Piscataway, New Jersey: Research and Education Association, 1995.

Reagan, Ronald. "First Inaugural Address," January 20, 1981. In *American Heritage – A Reader*, eds. The Hillsdale College History Faculty, 871-876. Hillsdale, Michigan: Hillsdale College Press, 2011.

Reagan, Ronald. "January 5, 1967: Inaugural Address (Public Ceremony)." January 5, 1967: Inaugural Address (Public Ceremony) | Ronald Reagan (reaganlibrary.gov).

Reagan, Ronald. "A Time for Choosing," October 27, 1964. In The *U.S. Constitution – A Reader*, eds. The Hillsdale College Politics Faculty, 773-783. Hillsdale, Michigan: Hillsdale College Press, 2014.

Reilly, Wilfred. "The Good News They Won't Tell You About Race in America." April, 2021. The Good News They Won't Tell You About Race in America - Wilfred Reilly, Commentary Magazine.

Reilly, Wilfred. "Why Woke History Is Not the Answer." 7 January 7 2021. Why Woke History Is Not the Answer - American Greatness (amgreatness.com).

"Republican Party Platform of 1856," June 17, 1856. In *The U.S. Constitution – A Reader*, eds. The Hillsdale College Politics Faculty, 481-483. Hillsdale, Michigan: Hillsdale College Press, 2014.

"Resolution of Germantown Mennonites." In *American Antislavery Writings*, ed. James G. Basker, 1-3. New York: Literary Classics of the United States, 2012.

Roberts, J. M. *The Penguin History of the World*. New York: Penguin Books, 1992.

Robertson, Gordon. *Pocahontas: Dove of Peace*. The Christian Broadcasting Network, 2016. DVD.

Romans. NKJV.

Roosevelt, Franklin D. "Commonwealth Club Address," September 23, 1932. In *American Heritage – A Reader*, ed. The Hillsdale College History Faculty, 718-728. Hillsdale, Michigan: Hillsdale College Press, 2011.

Roosevelt, Theodore. "The New Nationalism," August 31, 1910. In *American Heritage – A Reader*, eds. The Hillsdale College History Faculty, 605-618. Hillsdale, Michigan: Hillsdale College Press, 2011.

Rufo, Christopher. "Critical Race Theory Briefing Book." Critical Race Theory Briefing Book (christopherrufo.com).

Rush, Benjamin. "Address to the People of the United States," January, 1787. Benjamin Rush.pdf (wisc.edu).

Sandoz, Ellis, ed. *Political Sermons of the American Founding Era, 1730-1805*, Vol. 1. 2nd ed. Indianapolis: Liberty Fund, 1998.

Sandoz, Ellis, ed. *Political Sermons of the American Founding Era, 1730-1805*, Vol. 2. 2nd ed. Indianapolis: Liberty Fund, 1998.

Schweikart, Larry. *48 Liberal Lies About American History (That You Probably Learned in School)*. New York: Sentinel, 2008.

Schweikart, Larry and Michael Allen. *A Patriot's History of the United States – From Columbus's Great Discovery to the War on Terror*. New York: Sentinel, 2004.

Segal, Ronald. *Islam's Black Slaves: The Other Black Diaspora*. New York: Farrar, Straus and Giroux, 2001.

Sewall, Samuel. "The Selling of Joseph: A Memorial." In *American Antislavery Writings*, ed. James G. Basker, 9-14. New York: Literary Classics of the United States, Inc., 2012.

Shlaes, Amity. *The Forgotten Man: A New History of the Great Depression*. New York: Harper Perennial, 2008.

Smith, John. "A True Relation." In *Captain John Smith: Writings with other Narratives of Roanoke, Jamestown, and the First English Settlement in America*, ed. James Horn, 1-36. New York: Literary Classics of the United States, Inc., 2007.

Smith, Lacey Baldwin. *This Realm of England 1399 to 1688*. Boston: D.C. Heath and Company, 1966.

Sowell, Thomas. *Conquests and Cultures – An International History*. New York: Basic Books, 1998.

Sowell, Thomas. *Discrimination and Disparities*. New York: Basic Books, 2018.

Sowell, Thomas. *Ethnic America – A History*. New York: Basic Books, Inc., 1981.

Sowell, Thomas. *The Quest for Cosmic Justice*. New York: Touchstone, 1999.

Sowell, Thomas. "The Real History of Slavery." In *Black Rednecks and White Liberals*. San Francisco: Encounter Books, 2005.

Sowell, Thomas. "Twisted History." In The Thomas Sowell Reader. New York: Basic Books, 2011.

"Speak the Truth," April 3, 2021. Speak the Truth – Live Not by Lies.

Stanton, Elizabeth Cady. "Address to Woman's Rights Convention," July 19, 1848. In *American Speeches: The Revolution to the Civil War*, ed. Ted Widmer, 333-353. New York: Literary Classics of the United States, 2006.

Stark, Rodney. *The Victory of Reason – How Christianity Led to Freedom, Capitalism, and Western Success.* New York: Random House, 2005.

Stephens, Alexander. "Cornerstone Speech," March 12, 1861. In *American Heritage – A Reader*, eds. The Hillsdale College History Faculty, 483-493. Hillsdale, Michigan: Hillsdale College Press, 2011.

Straus, Leo. *Natural Right and History.* Chicago: The University of Chicago Press, 1965.

Taylor, Colin. *The American Indian.* London: Salamander Books Ltd., 2004.

Thomas, Hugh. *The Slave Trade – The Story of the Atlantic Slave Trade: 1440-1870.* New York: Simon & Schuster Paperbacks, 1997.

Ture, Norman B. "To Cut and To Please." *National Review.* 31 August 1992, 35-39.

Turner, William. *The Essentials of United States History: 1912 to 1941 World War I, the Depression, and the New Deal.* Piscataway, New Jersey: Research and Education Association, 1995.

Van Deventer, David. History 471 Lecture Notes. California State University Fullerton. Fall 1994.

Vaughn, Alden T. *New England Frontier – Puritans and Indians, 1620-1675.* Norman: University of Oklahoma Press, 1995.

Wallbuilders. "America's Exceptional History of Anti-Slavery." America's Exceptional History of Anti-Slavery - WallBuilders. 6 April 2020.

Waltz, Kenneth N. *Theory of International Politics.* New York: McGraw-Hill, Inc., 1979.

Washington, George. "First Inaugural Address," April 30, 1789. In *American Heritage – A Reader*, eds. The Hillsdale College History Faculty, 199-202. Hillsdale, Michigan: Hillsdale College Press, 2011.

Washington, George. "To John Francis Mercer," September 9, 1786. In *George Washington: Writings*, ed. John Rhodehamel, 607-608. New York: Literary Classics of the United States, 1997.

Washington, George. "Last Will and Testament," July 9, 1799. In *George Washington: Writings*, ed. John Rhodehamel, 1022-1042. New York: Literary Classics of the United States, 1997.

Washington, George. "To Phyllis Wheatley," February 28th, 1776. In *George Washington: Writings*, ed. John Rhodehamel, 216. New York: Literary Classics of the United States, 1997.

Washington, George. "Reflection on Slavery," c. 1788-1789. In *George Washington: Writings*, ed. John Rhodehamel, 701-702. New York: Literary Classics of the United States, 1997.

Washington, George. "To Robert Morris," April 12, 1786. In *The U.S. Constitution – A Reader*, ed. The Hillsdale College Politics Faculty, 401. Hillsdale, Michigan: Hillsdale College Press, 2014.

West, Thomas G. *The Political Theory of the American Founding: Natural Rights, Public Policy, and the Moral Conditions of Freedom*. Cambridge: Cambridge University Press, 2017.

West, Thomas G. *Vindicating the Founders – Race, Sex, Class, and Justice in the Origins of America*. Lanham, Maryland: Rowman & Littlefield Publishers, Inc., 1997.

West, Thomas G. and Douglas A. Jeffrey. "The Rise and Fall of Constitutional Government in America." Claremont, CA: The Claremont Institute, 2006.

Wheatley, Phillis. "To the Right Honourable William, Earl of Dartmouth, His Majesty's Principal Secretary of State for North America, & c." In *American Antislavery Writings*, ed. James G. Basker, 54-55. New York: Literary Classics of the United States, 2012.

Whitaker, Alexander. *Good Newes from Virginia*. United Kingdom: Dodo Press.

Wiebe, Robert H. *The Search for Order 1877-1920: The Making of America.* New York: Hill and Wang, 1967.

Wilentz, Sean. "A Matter of Facts." 22 January 2020. https://www.theatlantic.com/ideas/archive/2020/01/1619-project-new-york-times-wilentz/605152/.

Williams, Ryan P. "America Was Not Conceived in Racism." 15 July 2020. https://www.newsweek.com/america-was-not-conceived-racism-opinion-1518091. 15 July 2020.

Williams, Walter. "Black Confederate Soldiers," August 21, 1996. In *More Liberty Means Less Government: Our Founders Knew This Well.* Stanford: Hoover Institution Press, 1999.

Williams, Walter. "Race Hustlers," December 14, 1997. In *More Liberty Means Less Government: Our Founders Knew This Well.* Stanford: Hoover Institution Press, 1999.

Williams, Walter. "We Are Not Bright," February 8, 1995. In *More Liberty Means Less Government: Our Founders Knew This Well.* Stanford: Hoover Institution Press, 1999.

Wilson, Woodrow. "The New Freedom," in *American Heritage – A Reader,* eds. The Hillsdale College History Faculty, 620-627. Hillsdale, Michigan: Hillsdale College Press, 2011.

Winchester, Elhanan. "The Reigning Abominations, Especially the Slave Trade, Considered as Causes of Lamentation." In *American Antislavery Writings,* ed. James G. Basker, 57-60. New York: Literary Classics of the United States, 2012.

Winslow, Edward. *Good Newes from New England: A True Relation of Things Very Remarkable at the Plantation of Plimoth in New England.* Bedford, Massachusetts: Applewood Books.

Winslow, Edward. "A Letter sent from New England to a Friend in these parts, setting forth a brief and true declaration of the worth of that plantation; as also certain useful directions for such as intend a voyage into those parts." In *Mourt's Relation: A Journal of the Pilgrims at Plymouth*, ed. Dwight B. Heath, 81-87. Bedford, Massachusetts: Applewood Books, 1963.

Winthrop, John. "A Model of Christian Charity." In *American Heritage – A Reader*, eds. The Hillsdale College History Faculty, 16-28. Hillsdale, Michigan: Hillsdale College Press, 2011.

Wood, Gordon S., ed. *The American Revolution: Writings from the Pamphlet Debate 1764-1772*. New York: Literary Classics of the United States, Inc., 2015.

Wood, Gordon S., ed. *The American Revolution: Writings from the Pamphlet Debate 1773-1776*. New York: Literary Classics of the United States, Inc., 2015.

Wood, Gordon. *The Creation of the American Republic 1776-1787*. New York: W.W. Norton & Co., Inc., 1993.

Wood, Gordon. *The Radicalism of the American Revolution*. New York: Vintage Books, 1993.

Wood, Peter W. *1620: A Critical Response to the 1619 Project*. New York: Encounter Books, 2020.

Woodworth, Steven E. *The Essentials of United States History: 1500 to 1789 From Colony to Republic*. Piscataway, New Jersey: Research and Education Foundation, 1996.

Woodworth, Steven E. *The Essentials of United States History: 1841 to 1877 Westward Expansion and the Civil War*. Piscataway, New Jersey: Research and Education Association, 1997.

Zinn, Howard. *A People's History of the United States*. New York: Harper Perennial, 2005.

INDEX

commerce, 42, 66, 102, 107, 123, 129, 134, 142, 195, 197, 198

commodity, 15, 38

common law, 78, 83, 108

Commonwealth Club Address, 183, 184, 223

communism, 189

communities, 9, 27, 37, 94, 190

Confederacy, 46, 52, 161, 164, 200

Confederate Army, 161

Confederate States of America (CSA), 158

Confederates, 161

Confiscation Act, 161

Congo, 72

Congress, 118

Connecticut, 40, 103, 107, 114, 116, 138

conservative, 179, 187, 190

constitution, 29, 46, 124, 143, 144, 147, 153, 159, 178, 179, 195

Constitution, 2, 3, 46, 109, 112, 117, 118, 119, 121, 122, 123, 125, 126, 127, 129, 131, 135, 136, 139, 141, 144, 146, 147, 148, 150, 151, 152, 153, 154, 155, 156, 158, 161, 164, 170, 174, 175, 177, 178, 179, 180, 181, 183, 184, 185, 188, 195, 205, 207, 209, 212, 213,215, 216, 219, 222, 226

Constitutional Convention, 117, 118, 122, 127, 219

Continental Congress, 104, 107, 113, 124, 129

continents, 7, 20

Cook, John F., Jr., 162

Cooke, Samuel, 103

Coolidge, Calvin, 181, 182, 209

corn, 15, 22, 30, 33

"Cornerstone Speech," 159, 160, 225

Costin, John T., 162

cotton, 74, 124, 144, 145, 197, 198, 200, 204, 219

cotton gin, 145

Cotton Kingdom, 145

covenant, 29, 35, 36, 47, 97, 102, 110

covenantal ideology, 102

cowrie shells, 72

Creek, 9, 10, 27, 130, 131

Crete, 61, 74

crime, 59, 77, 91, 104, 130, 169, 187, 188

Crimea, 70

critical race theory, 4, 175, 203

Cromwell, Oliver, 115

Crow Creek Sioux Reservation, 9

Cuba, 71, 142, 195, 202

cultural Marxism, 203

Currie, Lauchlin, 183

Curtis, Charles, 133

Curtis, Judge, 153

Cypress, 60, 74

Dahomey, 72

Dalits, 62

Dana, James, 138, 210

Danbury, 103

Darwin, Charles, 180

Davis, Jefferson, 159

Dawes Act of 1887, 132

de Soto, Hernando, 19

Declaration of Independence, 1, 2, 55, 76, 96, 99, 102, 105, 107, 108, 109, 110, 111, 113, 117, 123, 125, 136, 137, 138, 139, 143, 146, 147, 148, 150, 151, 152, 155, 156, 158, 166, 173, 174, 175, 177, 180, 181, 183, 184, 195, 205, 206, 210, 215

Declaration of Rights and Sentiments, 137

deer, 13, 33, 34, 47, 49

defense spending, 191, 192

deism, 96

Delaware, 42, 43, 45, 46, 51, 91, 107,
114, 115, 165
Delaware Indians, 43, 46
Delaware River, 42, 43, 114
Delaware Valley, 42, 91
Democratic party, 142, 168
democratic process, 184, 205
Democrats, 165
dependency, 95, 133, 136
development, 7, 8, 15, 23, 47, 58, 59,
66, 74, 75, 78, 84, 93, 109, 133,
135, 142, 143, 197, 201, 202
devolution, 190
devsirme, 63
Dickinson, John, 98, 99, 210
Discovery, 21
discrimination, 171, 172, 177, 186,
202
disease, 8, 9, 13, 18, 19, 22, 27, 31,
41, 53, 54, 56, 63, 72, 79, 81, 85,
132, 196
District of Columbia, 161
divine law, 57
Douglas, Stephen, 151, 152, 154,
155, 156, 157, 158, 219
Douglass, Frederick, 118, 122, 123,
140, 141, 142, 147, 148, 149, 150,
164, 169, 210
Dred Scott v. Sanford (1857), 153
drought, 13
Dunsmore, Lord, 108, 109, 113
Dutch, 7, 39, 42, 61, 65, 73, 74, 78
Dutch West Indies Company, 41
duty, 5, 92, 93, 111, 113, 131, 134,
144, 147, 178

Earl of Dartmouth, 99, 100, 226
East Africa, 65, 66
Eastern Europe, 70
Eastern Woodlands, 12, 56, 62
economic, 4, 20, 45, 47, 75, 82, 85,
87, 88, 108, 127, 134, 136, 142,

145, 171, 172, 177, 178, 182, 183,
185, 189, 192, 198, 201, 202, 204
Economic Recovery Tax Act (ERTA),
191
economy, 85, 142, 179, 185, 188,
189, 192, 197, 198, 199, 200
education, 170, 178, 203, 204
Edwards, Jonathan, 94, 211
Efik, 122
Egypt, 7, 63, 69, 95, 96, 200
Egyptians, 3, 59, 63, 69
Eisenhower, Dwight D., 172
Eliot, John, 37, 38
Elmina, 72, 73, 74
"Emancipation Proclamation," 161,
162, 164, 165, 210, 212, 213, 218
empires, 3, 16, 59
English, 3, 7, 8, 12, 14, 15, 19, 21,
22, 23, 24, 25, 26, 27, 29, 30, 31,
32, 33, 38, 39, 40, 41, 42, 44, 45,
46, 50, 51, 52, 53, 54, 57, 62, 65,
73, 77, 78, 86, 87, 91, 93, 102,
108, 116, 132, 133, 214, 224
Enlightenment, The, 47, 96, 97, 109,
110
enslavement, 4, 14, 41, 47, 58, 61, 62,
64, 80, 103, 138, 159
equality, 3, 4, 25, 42, 91, 92, 94, 95,
113, 155, 160, 162, 168, 170, 178,
182, 185, 186
Es Siout, 69
Ethiopian, 63
ethnic group, 57, 132
ethnicity, 5, 56, 112, 136
Europe, 1, 7, 8, 16, 18, 19, 20, 27, 39,
50, 55, 56, 58, 60, 61, 62, 64, 70,
74, 75, 77, 97, 134, 135, 137, 177,
197, 198, 200, 202
European settlements, 13
Europeans, 8, 9, 12, 18, 19, 20, 26,
31, 38, 43, 50, 55, 62, 63, 64, 65,

49, 50, 51, 55, 61, 65, 74, 80
French and Indian War, 46, 49, 50,
    51, 55
fundamental transformation, 205

Galesburg, 156
Gambia, 79
Garnet, Henry Highland, 163, 212
Garrison, William Lloyd, 140, 141,
    147, 151
Garrow, David, 175
Garvey, Marcus, 163, 212
gender, 5
gender identity, 5
genocide, 4, 6, 18, 20, 27, 40, 41, 56
George III, 96, 108, 123
Georgia, 27, 45, 69, 78, 80, 95, 114,
    118, 123, 130, 131, 140, 145, 207
Georgia Trustees, 80
German Lutherans, 94
Germans, 60
Germantown, 91, 223
Gettysburg, 165
"Gettysburg Address," 166, 212, 218
Ghana, 64, 65, 196, 203
Ghanaians, 64
glass, 98
Global Slavery Index, 196
Glorious Revolution, 97
God, 3, 5, 16, 25, 29, 33, 35, 36, 42,
    47, 58, 61, 91, 92, 94, 95, 97, 102,
    103, 104, 110, 111, 112, 113, 123,
    139, 157, 164, 166, 168, 173, 174,
    211, 222
Godspeed, 21
Goldwater, Barry, 187, 188
Gookin, Daniel, 41
government, 1, 2, 8, 16, 28, 29, 43,
    45, 46, 57, 59, 62, 63, 67, 73, 87,
    97, 102, 110, 111, 112, 117, 123,
    125, 129, 130, 131, 132, 133, 134,

136, 137, 141, 143, 146, 150, 152,
154, 155, 159, 160, 161, 166, 170,
171, 172, 173, 177, 178, 179, 180,
181, 182, 183, 184,185, 186, 187,
188, 189, 190, 191, 192, 194, 200,
204, 205
grandfather clause, 172
Gravesend, 25, 26, 222
Great Awakening, 93, 94, 95, 99,
    138, 140, 207, 211, 213
Great Depression, 183, 185, 224
Great Emancipator, 162
Great Plains, 11, 12, 13, 211
Great Society, 186, 188
Great Temple in Mexico, 16
Greece, 7, 60, 62, 74
Greeks, 3
Grenville, George, 55
Grimke, Sarah and Angela, 141
Gross Domestic Product (GDP),
    192, 198
Gross National Product (GNP), 192
group identity, 5
Guelzo, Allen C., 162, 213
Guinn v. United States, 172
Gulf of Guinea, 74
guns, 15, 23, 39, 64, 65, 72, 82
Guyana, 203

Haaland, Deb, 133, 210
Hall, Prince, 34, 117, 120, 129, 130,
    150, 153, 161, 164, 170, 172, 209,
    213, 218, 221
Hamilton, Alexander, 126, 127, 142,
    209, 213
Hammond, James Henry, 200
Hammurabi, 59
Han Dynasty, 61
Hapsburgs, 16
Harlan, John Marshall, 170, 171
Harper's Ferry, 151

Mason, George, 117

Massachusett, 37, 38

Massachusetts, 28, 33, 34, 35, 39, 40, 56, 72, 90, 91, 92, 94, 98, 99, 103, 107, 108, 113, 116, 132, 136, 139, 140, 165, 201, 207, 208, 211, 219, 227, 228

Massachusetts 54th and 55th, 165

Massachusetts Bay Colony, 35

"Massachusetts Body of Liberties," 90, 91, 219

massacres, 9, 14

Massasoit, 31, 32, 33, 34, 39, 40

master, 82, 83, 95, 111, 158

Mayans, 17

Mayflower Compact, 29, 97, 220

Mayhew, Jonathan, 98, 220

McCoy, Benjamin, 162

measles, 18

Mecca, 64, 71

mechanical reapers, 197

mechanization, 197

Medina, 71

Mediterranean, 20, 60, 74, 75

Mediterranean Sea, 20, 74

Mesoamerica, 16

Mesopotamia, 7

Mesopotamians, 3

Metacomet, 40

Methodism, 80

Mexico, 16, 20, 62

Middle Ages, 56, 60, 66, 198

Middle colonies, 55, 90, 96, 99

Middle East, 7, 16, 18, 60, 64, 66, 67, 74, 128, 195, 196, 202, 217

Middle Passage, 67, 71

Midwest, 177, 197

military buildup, 191

military spending, 192

militia, 43, 55

mission statement, 2, 4, 110, 112,

113, 131, 133, 136, 137, 139, 143, 144, 150, 157, 158, 159, 164, 168, 171, 172, 175, 176, 177, 181, 182, 183, 184, 187, 195, 202, 203, 204, 205

Mississippi, 18, 19, 49, 50, 52, 124, 130, 131, 145

Mississippi Valley settlement, 18

Missouri, 152, 153, 165

Missouri Compromise, 152, 153

"Model of Christian Charity," 35, 36, 228

modernization, 197, 198, 200

Mohawk, 47, 48

Mohawks, 46, 48

Mohegans, 39, 40

Mongol Empire, 16

Mongols, 3, 20, 70

Monmouth, 115

Montgomery, 173, 217

Moravian, 55

Morocco, 71

Morrill Tariff, 201

Mosaic code, 91

Mott, Lucretia, 137

Mount Vernon, 121

Muhammad, 58, 62, 66

Murray, Douglas, 205

Muslim, 56, 58, 60, 62, 63, 64, 67, 71, 72, 75, 195, 196

Mussolini, Benito, 183, 212

Mystic River, 40

Namontack, 22

Nantucket, 105

Narragansett, 31, 39, 40

nation, 1, 4, 5, 6, 12, 16, 18, 26, 52, 57, 59, 64, 100, 107, 109, 112, 113, 116, 117, 120, 127, 128, 129, 131, 137, 138, 141, 142, 147, 148, 151, 155, 157, 159, 166, 167, 168,

Spanish, 7, 12, 15, 19, 20, 26, 65, 73, 78, 80, 84

Springfield, 3, 152, 154, 205, 218

Squanto, 31, 33

St. Lawrence River, 47

Stamp Act, 98, 105

Stanton, Elizabeth Cady, 137, 224

Star-Spangled Banner, 139

state and local governments, 171, 179, 190

state legislatures, 134, 136

state of nature, 4, 7, 8, 15, 16, 26, 40, 46, 145

steam engine, 197

Stephens, Alexander, 159, 160, 203, 225

subarctic region, 21

sub-Saharan, 18, 63, 64, 75, 202

sub-Saharan Africa, 18, 202

Sudan, 196

Sudanese, 63

Supreme Court, 130, 131, 153, 170, 172

Susan Constant, 21

Swahili, 66

Swann, Alfred J., 69

Sweden, 21, 42

systemic inequities, 205

Taft, Wiliam Howard, 179

Taiwanese, 202

Taney, Roger B., 153, 157, 203

Tanzania, 66

Tappan, Lewis and Arthur, 141

tariffs, 64, 142, 181

Tatars, 70

Tax Reform Act (TARA), 191

taxation, 98, 188, 191

tea, 98

tenant farmers, 77

Tennessee, 49

territories, 109, 116, 124, 143, 145, 150, 152, 153, 155, 156, 161, 169, 201

textile mills, 197, 198, 200

textiles, 77

Thanksgiving, 33, 34

Thirteenth Amendment, 163, 169

Thomas, Edward, 162

three-fifths compromise, 119

threshers, 197

Thugs, 62

"Time for Choosing," 187, 188, 222

Tippu Tip, 69, 70

"to form a more perfect union," 2, 112, 205

"To Secure These Rights," 172

tobacco, 24, 74, 77, 78, 80, 81, 82, 83, 84, 87

Tocqueville, Alexis de, 134, 205

Townshend Acts, 98

trade deficits, 193

Trail of Tears, 131

Trans-Atlantic and Intra-American Slave Trade Database, 75

Trans-Atlantic slave trade, 67, 71, 72, 75, 76, 196

Transcontinental Railroad Act, 201

Treaty of Greenville (1795), 129

Treaty of Paris (1763), 50

Treaty of Paris (1783), 129

Trenton, 114, 115

tribe, 9, 22, 26, 27, 31, 39, 40, 47, 130

tribes, 3, 4, 11, 12, 13, 14, 18, 19, 23, 26, 38, 39, 40, 41, 43, 46, 47, 49, 51, 56, 58, 60, 65, 71, 72, 128, 129, 130, 131, 133

Tripoli, 63

Truman, Harry S., 172

Truth, Sojourner, 141

trypanosomiasis, 63

tsetse fly, 63
tuberculosis, 13
Tugwell, Rexford Guy, 183
Turks, 3, 62, 67, 70
Tuscarora, 27
Tuscaroras, 46
Tutsis, 65
Two Treatises of Government, 7, 219
Tyler, John, 139
typhus, 18
tyranny, 102, 103, 155, 204

Ukraine, 70
Ulster, 45
unalienable rights, 2, 4, 111, 138
unemployment, 185, 189, 192
unfree labor, 76, 77, 80, 83, 84, 85, 88
Union, 46, 154, 158, 161, 162, 163, 164, 165, 168, 169, 200
Union Army, 163
Union soldiers, 200
United States, 1, 2, 3, 4, 5, 6, 15, 20, 21, 22, 23, 42, 48, 49, 51, 55, 58, 62, 63, 69, 71, 73, 75, 76, 77, 91, 92, 93, 94, 98, 99, 100, 103, 104, 105, 109, 110, 111, 112, 114, 117, 118, 119, 121, 124, 125, 126, 127, 128, 129, 130, 131, 132, 133, 137, 138, 139, 140, 141, 142, 144, 145, 147, 150, 152, 153, 154, 155, 158, 159, 160, 161, 162, 167, 168, 169, 170, 171, 172, 173, 176, 183, 185, 186, 193, 194, 195, 196, 197, 198, 199, 200, 201, 202, 203, 205, 207, 208, 209, 210, 211, 212, 213, 214, 215, 216, 217, 218, 219, 220, 221, 222, 223, 224, 225, 226, 227, 228
United States Census, 186
United States of America, 2, 4, 5, 6, 21, 42, 55, 75, 77, 112, 124, 125,

154, 155, 159, 167, 169, 194, 201, 202, 203
Universal Negro Improvement Association (UNIA), 163
untouchables, 62
Upper Congo, 69
Upper Egypt, 69
upward mobility, 133
US Army, 164
US Patent Office, 201
Utah, 10

Vermont, 116
Vikings, 3
Virginia, 19, 21, 22, 23, 24, 25, 26, 27, 28, 42, 51, 54, 77, 78, 80, 81, 82, 83, 85, 86, 87, 88, 90, 93, 94, 102, 104, 105, 107, 108, 113, 117, 119, 123, 124, 207, 216, 217, 219, 226
Virginia Company of London, 21, 26, 28, 78

Wahunsonacock, 22, 26
Wales, 56
Wampanoag, 31, 32, 33, 38, 39, 40, 41
Wang Mang, 61
war, 4, 5, 8, 11, 14, 16, 24, 26, 27, 32, 39, 41, 46, 51, 55, 56, 59, 60, 62, 63, 64, 108, 110, 113, 114, 115, 116, 120, 123, 126, 129, 132, 138, 140, 142, 151, 153, 159, 160, 161, 162, 164, 165, 166, 168, 188, 198, 200, 201, 212
War for Independence, 109, 115, 129, 139, 208
War of 1812, 129, 139
War on Poverty, 186
warriors, 11, 32, 49, 52, 62, 132
Washington, D.C., 1, 13, 16, 58, 60,

Made in United States
North Haven, CT
21 February 2023

32980863R00143